ecpr PRESS

policy making in multilevel systems

federalism, decentralisation, and performance in the OECD countries

Jan Biela, Annika Hennl, and André Kaiser

ecpr PRESS

First published by the ECPR Press in 2013

The ECPR Press is the publishing imprint of the European Consortium for Political Research (ECPR), a scholarly association, which supports and encourages the training, research and cross-national co-operation of political scientists in institutions throughout Europe and beyond.

ECPR Press
University of Essex
Wivenhoe Park
Colchester
CO4 3SQ
UK

Typeset by AnVi
Printed and bound by Lightning Source

British Library Cataloguing in Publication Data
A catalogue record for this book is available from the British Library

ISBN: 978-1-907301-33-9

www.ecpr.eu/ecprpress

The Personalisation of Politics: A Study of Parliamentary Democracies
(ISBN: 9781907301032) Lauri Karvonen

The Politics of Income Taxation: A Comparative Analysis
(ISBN: 9780954796686) Steffen Ganghof

The Return of the State of War: A Theoretical Analysis of Operation Iraqi Freedom (ISBN: 9780955248856) Dario Battistella

Urban Foreign Policy and Domestic Dilemmas: Insights from Swiss and EU City-regions (ISBN: 9781907301070) Nico van der Heiden

Widen the Market, Narrow the Competition: Banker Interests and the Making of a European Capital Market (ISBN: 9781907301087) Daniel Mügge

You may also be interested in the Essays series

Hans Kelsen and the Case for Democracy (ISBN: 9781907301247) Sandrine Baume

Is Democracy a Lost Cause? (ISBN: 9781907301384) Alfio Mastropaolo

Just Democracy (ISBN: 9781907301148) Philippe Van Parijs

Maestri of Political Science (ISBN: 9781907301193) Donatella Campus, Gianfranco Pasquino, Martin Bull

Masters of Political Science (ISBN: 9780955820335) Donatella Campus, Gianfranco Pasquino

Please visit www.ecpr.eu/ecprpress for up-to-date information about new publications.

| contents

| list of tables and figures

| the authors

JAN BIELA is a Doctoral Student and Researcher at the University of Lausanne, Switzerland, Department of Political Science. He participated in the research project 'Federalism and Decentralisation as Dimensions of State Activity' at the University of Cologne. Currently, he works on the democratic legitimacy and accountability of regulatory agencies. His research interests include issues of delegation, regulatory governance, participatory democracy, and comparative federalism.

ANNIKA HENNL is a Researcher in Political Science, Department of Political Science at the Goethe University Frankfurt. Before that she participated in the research project 'Federalism and Decentralisation as Dimensions of State Activity' at the University of Cologne. Next to comparative federalism, her research interests include political representation, electoral systems, and political parties. She has recently published in *Comparative Political Studies, Electoral Studies, Politische Vierteljahresschrift*, and *Zeitschrift für Politikwissenschaft*.

ANDRÉ KAISER is Professor of Comparative Politics at the University of Cologne and Faculty in the International Max Planck Research School 'The Social and Political Constitution of the Economy', the Cologne Graduate School in Management, Economics and Social Sciences and the Cologne Research Training Group 'Social Order and Life Chances in Cross-National Comparison'. He was Principal Investigator of the research project 'Federalism and Decentralisation as Dimensions of State Activity'. His recent publications include *Mehrheitsdemokratie und Institutionenreform* (2002), *Demokratietheorie und Demokratieentwicklung* (2004), *New Labour und die Modernisierung Großbritanniens* (2006) and articles, among others, in *American Journal of Political Science, Electoral Studies, European Journal of Political Theory, European Union Politics, Journal of Legislative Studies, Journal of Theoretical Politics, Party Politics, Political Studies, Politische Vierteljahresschrift, Regional and Federal Studies, West European Politics*, and *Zeitschrift für Politikwissenschaft*. His research focuses on the relevance of institutions for political action.

| acknowledgements

This book is based on a research project carried out at the University of Cologne's Department of Political Science between 2005 and 2008. We are grateful to the generous funding made available by the German Research Foundation.[1] We were fortunate to have been supported by a highly motivated group of young researchers. In particular, we thank Niels Ehlert for his comprehensive contributions, especially with regard to conceptual and methodological problems to be solved in the early stages, Gregor Zons, Thorsten Kemper, Sibylle Seubert, and David Allmann for able research support. Anne Gelling, Jill Summer and Jaclyn Verghis skillfully smoothed several English-language versions. We are also grateful for constructive comments by colleagues at several stages of the project. In particular we thank an anonymous referee for very helpful suggestions on an earlier draft; Wolfgang C. Müller, Adrian Vatter, Christoffer Green-Pedersen, and Dietmar Braun for initial information on our cases; a large number of country and policy area experts (see references) who contributed their time and knowledge to our endeavour; the participants at seminars at the University of Lüneburg, University of Bamberg, and the Australian National University, at the workshop on 'Exploring New Avenues of Comparative Federalism Research' at the ECPR Joint Sessions in Helsinki, and at the panel 'Beyond Decentralisation: Conceptualising and Measuring the Interlocked State' at the ECPR General Conference in Potsdam, for their comments on earlier drafts, especially Jan Erk and Wilfried Swenden; and finally the 'monastery's' staff at the Chair of Comparative Politics, Jörn Fischer, Daniela Jäger, Ingo Rohlfing, Jan Sauermann, and Saskia Ruth for moral support and helpful advice.

---

1   The German Research Foundation's project numbers are KA 1741/2–1 and KA 1741/2–2.

| abbreviations

Common

CG   Central government

EAGGL   European Agricultural Guidance and Guarantee Fund

EMU   European Economic and Monetary Union

ERDF   European Regional Development Fund

ESF   European Social Fund

EU   European Union

GDP   Gross Domestic Product

LEADER   European Union Community Initiative for Rural Development

LG   Local government

MP   Member of Parliament

NSRF   National Strategic Reference Framework

OECD   Organisation for Economic Co-operation and Development

PPP   Public Private Partnership

PR   Proportional representation

RDP   Regional Development Plan

RG   Regional government

SME   Small and Medium-Sized Enterprises

Switzerland

AG NRP   *Arbeitsgruppe Neue Regionalpolitik*, Working Group New Regional Policy

ARE   *Bundesamt für Raumentwicklung*, Federal Office of Spatial Development

ASTRA   *Bundesamt für Strassen*, Federal Roads Office

BADAC   *Banque de données sur les structures des administrations cantonales*, Database on the structure of the cantonal administrations

BAV   *Bundesamt für Verkehr*, Federal Office of Transport

BGB   *Bundesgesetz über die Gewährung von Bürgschaften und Zinskostenbeiträgen in Berggebieten*, Federal Act on the provision of guarantees and interest subsidies in mountain areas

BV   *Bundesverfassung der Schweizerischen Eidgenossenschaft*, Swiss Constitution

BWE   *Bundesbeschluss zugunsten wirtschaftlich bedrohter Regionen (wirtschaftlicher Erneuerungsgebiete)*, Federal Decree for economically threatened regions (economic development areas)

EFV   *Eidgenössische Finanzverwaltung*, Federal Finance Administration

EVD   *Eidgenössisches Volksdepartement*, Federal Department of Economic Affairs

FDK   *Konferenz der kantonalen Finanzdirektorinnen und Finanzdirektoren*, Conference of Cantonal Finance Directors

FinöV   *Gesamtschau zu Bau und Finanzierung von Infrastrukturvorhaben des öffent-lichen Verkehrs*, Funds for the Financing of Public Transport

HKG   *Bundesgesetz über die Förderung des Hotel- und Kurortkredits*, Federal Act on the Promotion of the hotel and resort credit

IHG   *Bundesgesetz über Investitionshilfe im Berggebiet*, Federal Act on Investment Aid in Mountain Areas

KoSeReG   *Konferenz der Sekretäre der Schweizerischen Bergregionen*, Conference of Executive Directors of Mountainous Regions

KÖV   *Konferenz der öffentlichen Verkehrsdirektoren*, Cantonal Conference of Directors of Public Transport

NEAT   *Neue Eisenbahn-Alpentransversale*, New Railway Link through the Alps

NFA   *Neugestaltung des Finanzausgleichs und der Aufgabenteilung zwischen Bund und Kantonen*, New Financial Equalisation System

NHT   *Neue Haupttransversale*, New Main Transversal

NRP   *Neue Regionalpolitik*, New Regional Policy

NWRK   *Nordwestschweizer Regierungskonferenz*, Conference of North-Western Cantonal Governments

RKGK   *Regierungskonferenz der Gebirgskantone*, Conference of Mountainous Cantonal Governments

SAB   *Schweizerische Arbeitsgemeinschaft für die Berggebiete*, Swiss Consortium for Mountainous Regions

SBB   *Schweizerische Bundesbahnen*, Swiss Federal Railways

SECO   *Staatssekretariat für Wirtschaft*, State Secretariat for Economic Affairs

SFR   *Schweizer Franken*, Swiss Francs (currency)

SVP   *Schweizerische Volkspartei*, Swiss People's Party

UVEK   *Eidgenössisches Departement für Umwelt, Verkehr, Energie und Kommunikation*, Department of the Environment, Transport, Energy and Communications

ZEB   *Zukünftige Entwicklung der Bahninfrastruktur*, Future Development of Railway Infrastructure

Austria

ASFINAG *Autobahnen- und Schnellstraßen-Finanzierungs-Aktiengesellschaft*, Motor- and Expressway-Financing Corporation

AWSG *Austria Wirtschaftsservice GmbH*, Austrian Economic Service

BAK *Bundesarbeiterkammer*, Federal Worker's Chamber

BMVIT *Bundesministerium für Verkehr, Innovation und Technologie*, Federal Ministry of Transport, Innovation and Technology

BMWA *Bundesministerium für Wirtschaft und Arbeit*, Federal Ministry of Economics and Labour

BMWF *Bundesministerium für Wissenschaft und Forschung*, Federal Ministry of Science and Research

B-VG *Bundesverfassungsgesetz*, Federal Constitutional Law

BZÖ *Bündnis Zukunft Österreich*, Alliance for the Future of Austria

ECOplus *Wirtschaftsagentur des Landes Niederösterreich*, Business Agency of Lower Austria

FFG *Forschungsförderungsgesellschaft*, Austrian Research Promotion Agency

FPÖ *Freiheitliche Partei Österreichs, Freedom Party of Austria*

F-VG *Finanzverfassungsgesetz*, Fiscal Constitutional Law

HL-AG *Hochleistungsstrecken AG*, High-Performance Railway Line Corporation

IBE *Infrastrukturbenützungsentgelt*, Fee for Use of Infrastructure

KWF *Kärntner Wirtschaftsförderungs Fonds*, Carinthian Economic Promotion Fund

LHLK *Landeshauptleutekonferenz*, Conference of State Heads of Governments

ÖBB *Österreichische Bundesbahnen*, Austrian Federal Railways

OeNB *Österreichische Nationalbank*, Austrian National Bank

ÖGB *Österreichischer Gewerkschaftsbund*, Austrian Trade Union Federation

ÖPNRV-G *Öffentlicher Personennah- und Regionalverkehrsgesetz*, Local Public and Regional Transport Law

ÖRK *Österreichisches Raumordnungskonzept*, Austrian Spatial Planning Concept

ÖROK *Österreichische Raumordnungskonferenz*, Austrian Conference on Spatial Planning

ÖVP *Österreichische Volkspartei*, Austrian People's Party

PGO *Planungsgemeinschaft Ost*, Planning Association East

RIZ *Regionale Innovationszentren*, Regional Innovation Centres

SCHIG *Schieneninfrastrukturdienstleistungsgesellschaft mbH*, Railway Infrastructure Service Association

SPÖ *Sozialdemokratische Partei Österreichs*, Social Democratic Party of Austria

STRAT.AT *Nationaler Strategischer Rahmenplan Österreich*, National Strategic Reference Framework of Austria

TIP	*Technologie, Information, Politikberatung*, Technology, Information, and Policy Consulting
UVP	*Umweltverträglichkeitsprüfung*, Environmental Compatibility Assessment
VOR	*Verkehrsverbund Ostregion*, Eastern Region Transport Association
VORG	*Verkehrsverbund Ostregion Gesellschaft mbH*, Organisation Company of Eastern Region Transport Association
VVNB	*Verkehrsverbund Niederösterreich-Burgenland*, Transport Association Lower Austria–Burgenland
VVO	*Verkehrsverbundorganisationsgesellschaft*, Organisation Company of Transport Association
WIFO	*Österreichisches Wirtschaftsforschungsinstitut*, Austrian Institute of Economic Research
WKÖ	*Wirtschaftskammer Österreichs*, Austrian Federal Economic Chamber

Denmark

AKF	*Anvendt KommunalForsking*, Danish Institute of Governmental Research
BORNTEK	Regional Technology Centre Bornholm
DATI	see DEACA
DEACA	*Erhvervs- og Byggestyrelsen*, Danish Enterprise and Construction Authority; until 2004: *Erhvervs- og Boligstyrelsen*, National Agency for Enterprise and Housing (NAEH); until 2001: Danish Agency for the Development of Trade and Industry (DATI); until 1993: National Agency of Industry and Trade (NAIT)
DKK	*Danske Kroner*, Danish Crowns (currency)
DSB	*Danske Statsbaner*, Danish National Railways
EBST	see DEACA
ERT	European Round Table of Industrialists
HT	*Hovedstadsområdets Trafikselskab*, Greater Copenhagen Council Transportation Company
HUR	*Hovedstadens Udliklingsråd*, Capital Development Council
ITDC	*Erhvervsudlklingsråd*, Industry and Trade Development Council; 2001–2006: *Danmarks Erhvervsråd*, National Business Council; since 2006: *Danmarks Vaekstråd*, National Growth Council
KL	*Kommunernes Landsforening*, Local Government Denmark Association
NAEH	see DEACA
NORDTEK	Regional Technology Centre North Jutland
ØDC	*Ørestad Udviklingsselskabet I/S*, Ørestad Development Corporation
RGF	*Regional vaekstforum*, Regional Growth Forum
TIC	Technological Information Centre

Ireland

ABP	Area-Based Partnerships
ADM	Area Development Management Limited (now Pobal)
AMAI	Association of Municipal Authorities of Ireland
BMW	Border, Midlands and Western Regional Assembly
C/C	Counties and Cities
CDB	County Development Board
CEB	County Enterprise Board
CIÉ	*Córas Iompair Éireann* (state-owned group of transport companies)
CVS	Community and Voluntary Sector
DART	Dublin Area Rapid Transit
DoEHLG	Department of Environment, Heritage and Local Government
DTO	Dublin Transportation Office
FÁS	*Foras Áiseanna Saothair*, Employment and Training Authority
GCCC	General Council of County Councils
GDA	Greater Dublin Area
IDA	Industrial Development Agency
LDI	Local Development Initiatives
LGA	Local Government Act
LGF	Local Government Fund
NDP	National Development Plan
NRA	National Roads Authority
NSS	National Spatial Strategy
RAss	Regional Assemblies
RAuth	Regional Authorities
RPA	Railway Procurement Agency
RPG	Regional Planning Guideline
RTI	Rural Transport Initiative
RTP	Rural Transport Programme
SE	Southern and Eastern Regional Assembly
SPC	Strategic Policy Committee
SPU	Spatial Planning Unit

chapter one | introduction

Policy making is spatially structured. Although this is clear to political scientists as well as to public finance scholars, the two disciplines deal with the territorial organisation of the democratic state in completely different and, more problematically, unrelated ways. One might go so far as to say they seem to live in different worlds. This book aims to bring together the viewpoints of political science and public finance. By merging their concepts and analytical tools we open up a perspective from which we can critically analyse the policy consequences of different combinations of territorial state activity with regard to both decision making and policy implementation. The underlying question of this book is: Does federalism matter for effective policy making, and if so, in what way?

Political scientists distinguish between unitary and federal political systems according to the ways decision-making competences are allocated. While in unitary systems all powers to make authoritative decisions are concentrated at the level of central government, federally structured political systems consist of (at least) two levels of government and combine shared rule on the federal level with self-rule by the constituent states. The diverse arrangements found in federal structures can be reduced to two basic types: dual and joint federalism. Dual structures, as exemplified by political systems such as Canada or the United States, are characterised by a strict separation of powers and resources between the federal and the state levels, complemented by voluntary and ad hoc intergovernmental structures of negotiation and cooperation alongside a bicameral legislature that is the central access point for constituent states to influence federal legislation. Joint federalism, as in Germany and the European Union, does not so much separate powers and resources between levels as allocate functions. The federal level – with the participation of the states – makes most of the decisions; the state level implements them. Following from the need to cooperate, intergovernmental relations in this type of federal structure are fully institutionalised and compulsory.

There is an inbuilt assumption in political scientists' perspective on federalism that this arrangement goes along with highly decentralised policy implementation, whereas unitary systems are thought to be necessarily centralised. This book shows not only that this assumption is unfounded, but that it has crucial consequences in that spatial patterns of policy making are fundamentally misunderstood. One consequence is that political scientists mostly focus on the decision-making stage of policy making and do not pay enough attention to patterns of implementation – actor constellations, their respective resources, and the impacts on policy outputs and outcomes.[1] Another consequence is that political scientists have long preferred

---

1. There are, of course, exceptions such as the highly illuminating work of Fritz W. Scharpf (and his co-authors) on German joint federalism (Scharpf *et al.* 1976).

to analyse the input side of federalism – actors' demands and support in decision-making processes – instead of systematically assessing what impact federal and unitary arrangements have on the output in different policy areas. This last point has to be seen against the predominant normative view of federalism as helping to increase opportunities for participation and better include spatially defined units such as regions and national minorities without suppressing variety – 'e pluribus unum' can be read on the seal of the United States, the first federal political system in history.

Public finance, on the other hand, is preoccupied with the centralised or decentralised allocation of functions and – financial as well as administrative – resources. One source of misunderstanding between political scientists and public economists is the term 'federalism'. Whereas political scientists see federalism as a specific distribution of competences for decision making, economists are mainly interested in the budgetary reflections of the activities of different state levels and term this 'fiscal federalism'. Accordingly, economists largely ignore the institutional arrangements of the decision-making stage of policy making and focus on the centralised or decentralised provision of public goods and their consequences for public budgets.

In bringing together the analytical perspectives of political science and public finance, we combine their respective theoretical concepts and tools for empirical research. This allows us to examine the policy-output effects of different variations of federal and unitary arrangements at the decision-making stage and of centralised or decentralised allocation of resources at the implementation stage. Our central concern is whether multilevel arrangements systematically differ with regard to policy performance. As we are political scientists, we are particularly interested in whether federalism matters – a question that has only recently been seriously pursued and which so far has led to rather ambiguous answers (see Chapter Two). In order to study this question, we focus on a set of political systems that are similar in their political, social and economic contexts – the OECD countries. This way we can concentrate on institutional effects without having to worry too much about the impact of different levels of democratic stability and socioeconomic development. Clearly, our findings cannot be generalised and transferred to developing countries directly. However, we argue that as the group of OECD countries serves as the role model for efficient and effective policy making across territorial state levels, at least for a number of international donor organisations, this research has implications which transcend the OECD world.

Finding robust answers to the question of whether multilevel institutional arrangements matter for policy making in a systematic way is relevant both in academic and in real-world terms. Academically, the last two decades have seen a renewed interest in the role of institutions in political science. The 'new institutionalism' research agenda consists of three fundamental questions: (1) Why do we find specifically shaped political institutions in one political system, but not in others? (2) Why and under what conditions do political institutions change? (3) What are the effects of political institutions? Do they matter? This book contributes primarily to the third question. Up to now our knowledge has been very limited.

We therefore fill an important gap. However, gathering information on the effects of different institutional arrangements of the territorial state organisation is, of course, also highly relevant for policy makers. As mentioned, questions 1 and 2 on the new institutionalist research agenda imply that, at least to some degree, institutional arrangements can be a matter of choice and design. It is therefore indispensable for policy advice to be able to present robust empirical information as to what one can expect when a system changes from a unitary to a federal structure (as Belgium has done) or when implementation powers are delegated to the regional or local level (as international donor organisations have advised developing countries to do in recent decades).

The book is organised as follows. In Chapter Two we show that by distinguishing between two dimensions of the territorial state organisation, theories of federalism (originating in political science) and of decentralisation (as developed in public finance) can fruitfully be combined.[2] We derive a set of hypotheses on the policy-making consequences of these dimensions from a combined model of these theories. Chapter Three presents the research designs of both the quantitative and the qualitative parts of our study. Methodologically, we pursue a dual strategy of combining statistical analyses with case studies. Our statistical analyses focus on the OECD countries. We estimate cross-sectional models for average data from 1994 to 2002 and panel analyses for the period spanning the early 1970s to the early 2000s (see Appendix for information on the data sets). Our case studies explore two different policy areas – each in four countries representing different combinations of the federalism–unitarism and centralisation–decentralisation dimensions. We do this for two reasons: First, statistical findings are only correlations which may hint at causal directions but cannot prove them. Whether the causal mechanisms which we hypothesise are indeed in place is something that we study in detail in our case studies. The second reason is that we know from studies of the impact of political institutions that generally the effect of institutions is weak compared to socioeconomic factors. Hence a more fine-grained analysis is necessary to actually trace whether an assumed causal logic really holds. Chapter Four presents our statistical analyses. It first explains the designs of the cross-sectional and the panel approaches; then discusses the operationalisations of the independent, dependent, and control variables we use and demonstrates that the two dimensions of federalism–unitarism and decentralisation–centralisation are empirically independent; and finally presents our findings. Chapter Five has two main functions. The first is to establish the reasons for the selection of our cases. Secondly, we use our theoretical model of institutional logics to identify a number of criteria which we think lie behind the systematic effects of the two dimensions on performance. We can then test for these in the case studies. Chapters Six on decision making and seven on policy implementation encompass our case studies and are structured in a parallel fashion. After short country profiles of the

---

2. The theories which we combine derive partly from normative arguments originating in welfare economics, partly from formal models such as veto player theory. However, this is unproblematic as we are primarily interested in testing their empirical implications.

respective stage in policy making and a discussion of what we should expect to find if the assumed institutional logics hold, detailed case studies of two policy areas (regional development and transport policy) are presented, which aim at situating the material in a fully comparative perspective. We contrast our findings not only between the groups on the two dimensions – between federal countries and unitary ones in Chapter Six and between centralised and decentralised countries in Chapter Seven – but also within the groups – by comparing the two federal systems or the two unitary systems with each other – as well as across policy areas. The chapters close with short summaries of our findings. Chapter Eight summarises our main findings, but also poses a number of questions which should inform future research.

chapter two | theory and hypotheses

Studies evaluating the effects of territorial state organisation on the performance of democratic political systems are relatively rare. Most analyses place emphasis on explaining the effects of federalism on the input side of the political process, i.e. effects on democratic quality (Bednar *et al.* 1999). In contrast, our study deals with output effects of federalism. The underlying question of the book is: does federalism matter for effective policy making, and if so, in what ways? In this chapter we summarise existing theoretical arguments and empirical results as well as set out our own approach. It turns out that there are theoretical arguments for both improved and worsened performance, and that empirical evidence is ambiguous. We attribute this at least partly to an unclear conceptualisation of the two predominant concepts of territorial state organisation, federalism and decentralisation. We then develop our theoretical argument, which builds upon the disambiguation of the two concepts and the assumption that each of the two has an independent impact on performance. We furthermore assume the two factors to come into effect at different stages of the political process: federalism is expected to influence the political decision-making process and to have a slightly negative impact on performance, while decentralisation, according to our hypotheses, tends to improve performance via more efficient policy implementation.

Our approach is driven by an economic understanding of performance, borrowed from research on public finance. In this understanding, performance is equivalent to an efficient allocation of resources. This understanding, which embodies the core of public finance research, can be traced back to Musgrave's (1959) theory of public finance, which distinguishes between three interdependent branches of fiscal government: resource allocation, wealth distribution, and maintenance of economic stability. Efficiency considerations mainly occur within the allocative branch and refer to a provision of public goods and services that is in accordance with the resource needs of the population. The emerging concept of efficiency is thus an economic one that – at first sight – applies to patterns of policy implementation and largely ignores decision making as a distinct dimension of state activity (Beer 1977; Keman 2000). In contrast to public finance researchers, political scientists often apply the concept of efficiency to the analysis of decision-making processes and neglect its denotation as a process of spatial mapping of resource needs, preferences and public goods provision. However, the political performance of decision-making processes is conceptualised as 'the extent to which the political system generates appropriate solutions to problems of political guidance' (Wachendorfer-Schmidt 2000: 16). Such appropriateness may be judged both with regard to the efficiency of the decision-making process itself (measured as the intensity of conflict during negotiations as well as its duration) as well as the efficacy of its output in economic terms. So our dependent variable political performance theoretically builds upon the economic concept of allocative efficiency but can be applied to the stages of both decision making and policy implementation.

Having clarified our understanding of performance, we can now explicate the impact of multilevel state structures on it. We begin with a short literature review in order to highlight the heterogeneity of existing empirical findings before we turn to our own argument. Whereas some authors associate federalism with deficits in macroeconomic planning (Scharpf 1987), more recent approaches have qualified these findings (Lane and Ersson 1997; Castles 2000). However, Wibbels (2000) still corroborates a negative impact of federalism on macroeconomic policy in the case of developing countries. On the other hand, there is also evidence for the enhanced performance of federal countries: Lijphart (1999); Busch (1995) and Lancaster and Hicks (2000) detect a correlation between federalism and lower inflation rates; Busch (1995) also finds lower budget deficits in federal states. Moreover, some studies have shown that federalism leads to a lower share of government expenditure in GDP (Wilensky 1975; Cameron 1978; Castles and McKinlay 1979; Schmidt 1996; Crepaz 2002), to lower unemployment (Crepaz 1996), lower welfare spending (Kriesi 1994), or higher economic growth (Lancaster and Hicks 2000).

Regarding specific policy areas, the evidence is also mixed. Some scholars find no differences between federal and unitary states in the area of environmental protection (e.g. Scruggs 2003), while others perceive an interaction effect between federalism and corporatism (Wälti 2004; Lancaster and Hicks 2000). In health care, Gray (1991) finds no effect. By contrast, other scholars associate federalism with weaker performance, particularly in the areas of social policy and health care (Banting 1987; Pierson 1995). In the area of regional development, finally, positive consequences of federalism have been found (Wälti and Bullinger 2000). In sum, the effects that have been found so far are inconsistent. Thus, to date, political science seems unable to answer the question 'Does federalism matter?' (Kaiser 2004) in a coherent way. Empirical results are ambiguous and do not provide a clear picture of the effects different kinds of territorial organisations have on performance.

Confronted with the task of interpreting such ambiguous and disputed findings, we argue that existing research has mostly ignored the fundamental difference between federalism and decentralisation. Braun (2000b) and Keman (2000) were the first to stress the importance of distinguishing conceptually between a subnational entity's 'right to decide' on the one hand and its 'right to act' on the other. In other words, 'who may decide on *what* will be done (policy formulation and decision making) and who may decide on *how* it will be done (policy implementation)' (Braun 2000b: 29, emphasis in original). Formulated thus, it becomes obvious that the two aspects refer to different stages of the political process. The latter part of the phrase describes the competence to independently implement policies as disposed by some superordinated institution. It is this autonomy of subnational levels to allocate resources within their jurisdiction (Musgrave 1959; Oates 1972) that we define as *decentralisation*. The 'right to decide', on the other hand, refers to the competence to design and pass policies on its own or in cooperation with a superordinated institution. *Federalism* thus refers to a constitutionally guaranteed division of competences between territorially defined governmental levels (Lijphart 1999; Sawer 1969). In our view, federalism and decentralisation are hence two different dimensions of the territorial organisation of state activity, i.e. multilevel systems which exhibit independent as well as interdependent effects. Furthermore, they come into play at different stages of the political process: federalism affects the way political decisions are taken, decentralisation influences the implementation of policies.

Let us illustrate the importance of this distinction by highlighting ambiguities in existing approaches. Looking back at the history of federalism research, it is evident that these two dimensions have for the most part been analysed in a rather undifferentiated way. For instance, in an effort to challenge Riker's (1969) claim that federalism has no real effect except with regard to more complicated decision making, Ostrom (1973) assumes that federal countries are able to tap the full potential of a decentralised provision of public goods and services. In fact, though, Ostrom's argument, based upon findings from public finance literature (in particular Oates 1972), does not apply to federalism as such but rather ascribes anticipated effects to decentralised resource allocation. In a comparable manner, Weingast's concept of market-preserving federalism explicitly rests upon the condition that subnational autonomy encompasses the authority to adapt policies and to tailor the provision of local public goods and services to subnational circumstances as well as to set tax rates (Weingast 1995; Weingast and Qian 1997). Again, the theoretical argument refers to decentralisation rather than federalism itself. In the empirical literature cited above, various ways of operationalisation are present, while the two concepts have not always been differentiated properly[3] – which may provide an explanation for the contradictory empirical findings.

Having exemplified the need for a conceptual disambiguation, we now turn to our theoretical argument. Considering the broad theoretical arsenals of the political science and public finance literatures, it is not necessary to develop completely new theoretical arguments with regard to performance effects of federalism and decentralisation. Instead, we focus on merging existing theories in a consistent explanatory model.

Regarding independent effects of decentralisation, Oates's (1972) decentralisation theorem postulates that a decentralised provision of resources is more efficient than centralised supply – subject to specific conditions such as scale effects. The rationale behind the decentralisation theorem is that policy makers on the subnational level are better informed about local resource needs than policy makers on the central level. Hence resource supply is expected to vary efficiently between regions in decentralised states. Such an uneven supply, according to a different argument, is not always enforceable because it may violate

---

3. For example, Lijphart (1999) measures federalism and decentralisation on a single dimension, using decentralisation as a subcategory of federalism. For a more thorough assessment of operationalisations, see Chapter Four.

political perceptions of equal treatment (see Oates 2005). From a slightly different perspective (e.g. Tiebout 1956, 1961), keener competition between subnational entities is seen as promoting innovation and efficient solutions.

H 1a (Decentralisation hypothesis): Decentralisation is a more efficient mode of governance than centralisation, and therefore leads to better policy performance.

At the micro level, we can thus expect decentralised systems to induce subnational actors to gather detailed knowledge of resource needs, political preferences, and the local costs of providing public services in order to adapt their provision of public goods. Dealing with mobile citizens who may exit in case of inefficiencies, subnational actors will, according to the arguments of Tiebout and others, feel an incentive to invest in policy innovation as well as adopt best practices. As a consequence, decentralised countries will thus, in the aggregate, exhibit efficient variations in patterns of policy implementation.

On the other hand, several problems with decentralised provision of goods have been raised: enforced competition among regional entities, particularly tax competition, can lead to a 'race to the bottom' which leaves them all with insufficient resources for their tasks. Moreover, many effects of subnational policies are not restricted to their own territory; the resulting externalities and spillovers are difficult to compensate for (Oates 2002). Finally, decentralisation assigns tasks to inferior and necessarily smaller governmental bodies and territories. If a policy area is subject to 'economies of scale', efficiency gains emanating from informational advantages and increased competition might compensate for the disadvantages. The expectation of Oates's basic argument is hence subject to various conditions, like the existence of subnational discretion, the policy area under scrutiny, and the effectiveness of hard budget constraints (HBC). Let us turn to these points consecutively.

The decentralisation theorem is based upon the idea of efficient variation of resource supply. The central preconditions for such variance are discretion for subnational entities (in other words, sufficient staff and financial resources to ensure an adequate level of expertise and knowledge, precondition 1), sufficient own-revenue sources (or unconditional block grants) that establish a vertical fiscal balance (Weingast 2006, precondition 2), and discretionary leeway regarding policy formulation, i.e. only reasonable detailedness of national laws and administrative regulations (precondition 3). Potential effects of that discretion, however, may be moderated by patterns of vertical as well as horizontal interaction. On the one hand, a lack of own resources might affect the discretion level of subnational actors, since these are highly dependent on specific-purpose grants. Vertical influence may thus lead to a spatial harmonisation of policy implementation. On the other hand, subnational entities may face the need to horizontally coordinate policy implementation in order to internalise spillover effects. The capacity of subnational bodies to engage in horizontal coordination, however, may vary depending on their administrative resources. Finally, it may depend on the characteristics of the policy area under consideration whether coordination needs partly or completely counterbalance the predicted efficiency gains. This depends also on the existence of economies of scale and the magnitude of existing externalities. Following Braun (2000c: 19), we expect a positive effect of discretion foremost in space-related policy areas. Policy areas subject to huge externalities and dependent mainly on regulatory decisions, e.g. environmental policies, are less likely to gain advantages from decentralised resource allocation. Whether or not such policy-specific requirements impact the political efficiency of implementation processes is of specific interest with regard to the theory-building ambition of our case studies.

The last point to note is the relevance of hard budget constraints (HBC), which predominantly address the pathologies of excessive competition between regional or local governments. Recent public finance literature has increasingly shown that decentralised resource provision is not a superior mode of governance per se, but that additional institutional safeguards are necessary to guarantee fiscal discipline on the part of subnational governments. Such budget constraints frustrate incentives for subnational governments to provide more goods and services for their constituencies by overstretching their financial abilities. If subnational governments are not subject to such constraints, overspending may appear as a viable strategy, particularly when the central government is likely to step into the breach. This may cause the deficit burden to shift to residents of other subnational entities or to future generations (e.g. Goodspeed 2002). Likewise, the central government may only prevent welfare losses of subnational overspending if it can credibly put forward a no-bailout strategy. Accordingly, we advance the following qualification of the basic hypothesis:

H 1b (HBC hypothesis): The effects of decentralisation are subject to the hardness of budget constraints in a political system. For a given level of decentralisation, harder budget constraints are associated with superior policy performance.

Following a model by Inman (2003), we utilise the argument on HBC to establish a link between our two initial dimensions. The assumptions behind the HBC hypotheses can be represented as a game with sequential moves between the central and the subnational level (see Inman 2003). In the first period, a local government (LG) either overspends or does not. The respective strategy moves are denoted as O (overspending) and NO (no overspending). In one case the local government chooses NO and the game finishes after the first round. In the case that it chooses O, the central government (CG) then decides to provide a bailout (B) or to choose a no-bailout strategy (NB). The resulting payoff matrix is given in Table 2.1.

Table 2.1: Payoff matrix

Payoffs	(O, B)	(O, NB)	(NO, −)
CG	$P_{CG}(O, B)$	$P_{CG}(O, NB)$	$P_{CG}(NO, -)$
LG	$P_{LG}(O, B)$	$P_{LG}(O, NB)$	$P_{LG}(NO, -)$

The analysis of the game yields three conditions which must be met for decentralisation to lead to aggregate inefficiency. Firstly, the central government prefers to bail out the overstretched local government.

(1) $$P_{CG}(O,B) > P_{CG}(O,NB)^4$$

Secondly, the local government prefers to overspend in the case of a bailout, but would prefer not to overspend if the central government chooses a no-bailout strategy.

(2) $$P_{LG}(O,B) > P_{LG}(NO,-) \geq P_{LG}(O,NB).$$

The fulfilment of these two conditions makes the strategy combination (O, B) the dominant solution of this game. However, this solution only leads to aggregate inefficiencies if

(3) $$P_{CG}(O,B) + P_{LG}(O,B) < P_{CG}(NO,-) + P_{LG}(NO,-).$$

Therefore, inefficiencies may arise if the costs of overspending for the subnational government are low and/or if choosing a no-bailout strategy imposes significant costs on the central government. Hence, the effectiveness of HBC depends on the degree to which they increase the costs of overspending and/or reduce the costs of a no-bailout decision respectively. Inman (2003) and Rodden *et al.* (2003) show that this can be achieved principally using two different institutional mechanisms: market institutions such as capital markets and banking systems; and hierarchical oversight procedures and legislative restrictions in combination with independent monitoring agencies such as constitutional courts, central banks, and audit courts.

The institutional logic behind these arguments paves the way for theoretical propositions regarding interaction effects of federalism and decentralisation. Rodden *et al.* (2003) point out that subnational budget constraints are reflected either by subnational fiscal autonomy and unequivocal accountability of subnational governments or by hierarchical regulative authority from the central government. On this basis we establish a relationship between budget constraints and territorial state organisation (Rodden 2002). Countries with functioning democratic and economic institutions show the interaction effects between federalism, decentralisation and performance as depicted in Table 2.2.

Table 2.2: Interaction effects between federalism, decentralisation, and performance

		Central government's ability to regulate subnational government	
		Weak (Federalism)	*Strong (Unitarism)*
Subnational fiscal autonomy	No	Bailouts, soft budget constraints	Hierarchical mechanisms
	Yes	Unconstrained decentralisation	

---

4.   A no-bailout strategy may imply financial as well as distributive costs for the central government.

From this proposition, we derive the following hypothesis:

H 1c (Interaction hypothesis): The effects of decentralisation interact with the type of federalism. In federal countries with low subnational fiscal autonomy, i.e. the joint-federalism type, decentralisation is likely to have a negative impact on performance. In comparison, both unitary countries and federal countries with high subnational fiscal autonomy are expected to perform better.

In sum, positive effects of decentralisation are expected, but subject to various qualifications, such as the existence of subnational discretion, hard budget constraints, and the absence of a joint-federalism model with low subnational fiscal autonomy. We now turn to the last factor, being our second main concept under investigation.

Beyond the descriptive value that federalism adds to our *interaction hypothesis*, we expect it to have an additional independent influence on policy performance. Public finance literature entails the important insight that different arrangements of federalism may coincide with varying performance effects. Yet it neglects the effects of federalism by focusing solely on the implementation stage of the policy process. However, inefficiencies may arise not only in the course of implementing decisions on resource allocations, but also at the decision-making stage itself. At the decision-making stage of the political process, the federal or unitary character of a state's organisation becomes relevant. This primarily affects redistributive policies (Braun 2000b; Scharpf *et al.* 1976). Here we can expect negotiations between subnational entities on the allotment of resources to correspond to the logic of a prisoner's dilemma (Inman 2003): cooperation of all subnational governments with the central government would yield the most efficient allocation of resources, but the chance of reaching an efficient solution is diminished by the fact that any single subnational government has an incentive to deviate and demand a bigger slice of the pie. Since by definition subnational entities in federal states start with decision-making competences, the integration of subnational actors into negotiations at the national level is stronger in federal than in unitary countries.

This perspective is supported by other strands of literature. Veto-point approaches (Immergut 1992; Kaiser 1997) have highlighted the role of additional actors whose agreement is needed for a political decision. In this tradition, veto-player theory postulates greater policy stability in federal countries than in unitary states (Tsebelis 2002).[5] Moreover, game-theoretical considerations also imply that it is quite difficult to reach a welfare-optimising equilibrium in prisoner's dilemma situations with n>2 players (Ostrom 1990; Scharpf 1997).[6]

---

5. This is not exclusive to federalism but is an effect of power-sharing arrangements, like corporatism or presidentialism, in general. See, for example, Vatter (2005) for a debate on the equivalence of these institutions' impacts. In contrast to this view, Crepaz (2002) postulates different effects for various types of veto players.

6. On the other hand, it has been argued that the additional veto points provided by federal structures could ease the access of interest groups to the decision-making process. Since this access can serve as an additional source of information on societal preferences, it might improve the quality

We thus argue that *ceteris paribus* welfare-maximising policy reforms that reallocate between subnational entities are more difficult to achieve in federal countries than in unitary states. Subnational entities are expected to act in a weakly coordinated way and develop individual policy proposals that reflect their preference for resource maximisation.[7] This should lead to empirical evidence that it is difficult to reach political decisions which considerably change the status quo, that decisions taken do not solve the apparent problems adequately, and that the decisions are sometimes difficult to implement since a larger variety of possibly contradicting interests had to be integrated.

In sum, theoretical arguments support the notion that decision making in federal countries is *ceteris paribus* harder to achieve or at least slowed down. Slower decision-making processes, even if they correlate with higher decision-making costs, are not necessarily equal to lower efficiency of a political system.[8] However, a transaction-cost economics approach indicates that slower decision making parallels a reduced capacity for reacting to socioeconomic changes. Transaction costs (see, for examples, North 1990a, 1990b; Williamson 1985) basically entail all costs that arise due to the existence of institutions. In a market economy, such costs derive, for instance, from the need for information gathering before actual decisions, from negotiations and decision making itself, as well as from implementation and monitoring. According to Williamson (1991), hierarchical structures are clearly superior to other forms of governance if actors are dependent on one another and altered socioeconomic conditions require a coordinated response. This holds particularly in the redistribution of resources, according to Scharpf (1992). In territorial state organisation, hierarchy is clearly strongest in unitary states. Hence one can deduce a structural disadvantage of federalism compared to unitary structures, given that changing socioeconomic conditions force states to react.[9] This disadvantage should manifest itself in a prolonged decision-making process and a relatively higher conflict level during negotiations.

The increasing worldwide market integration that has taken place since the mid-1980s thus plays an important role in our argument, since the adaptation to the resulting changes in socioeconomic conditions has been assigned a prominent role on the political agenda in virtually all OECD countries (Pierson 1998). Hence we expect countries with a greater capacity for reaction to adjust better to the changing conditions and also therefore to exhibit better performance:

---

of the resulting policy.

7. This problem of cooperation is also empirically corroborated (e.g. Wälti and Bullinger 2000) and judged as crucial in the cases of environmental policy (Scruggs 2003) and health policy (Wyss and Lorenz 2000).

8. Some authors stress the role of federalism in finding more balanced policy solutions (Breton 1987) that cannot be changed so easily.

9. While a recent volume edited by Feiock and Scholz (2010) highlights various ways to reduce the higher costs associated with less hierarchical governance forms, for instance through informal policy networks, the basic notion remains undisputed.

H2 (Federalism hypothesis): In an environment of changing socioeconomic conditions, federalism tends to result in lower policy performance.

Hypothesis H2 is only formulated as a weak relationship and does not indicate a lower performance in federal countries per se. Instead, federalism tends to go hand in hand with negative effects only if accompanied by further institutional factors (Pierson 1995) and in cases where a strong pressure for reform exists. In the qualitative part of this volume, we identify the pressures for reform our cases were subject to.

We trace cumulative performance effects back to different institutional arrangements of resource allocation. Figure 2.1 visualises the hypothesised causal chains. The white arrows symbolise an (idealised) political process. The grey arrows show the hypothesised influence territorial state structures have on the political process and hence on performance or outputs. Efficiency gains are chiefly realised by decentralised resource supply (H1a). However, these gains are subject to institutional budget restrictions which prevent subnational governments from misapplying their discretion at implementation stage (H1b). The effectiveness of hard budget constraints itself depends on the type of federalism and the lack of subnational fiscal autonomy – which in combination soften the budget constraints subnational entities are subject to (H1c). Additionally, we expect federalism, at least in times of major socioeconomic change, to influence performance negatively via a prolonged decision-making process, especially when it comes to questions of redistribution between individual governments (H2). The influence of federalism on the input side – which is not subject of our research – is designated as a dashed arrow.

In this chapter, we have reviewed existing theoretical arguments and empirical work on the effects of multilevel state structures on the output side of the political process. The ambiguities in the existing empirical research are caused at least in part by the lack of differentiation between federalism and decentralisation as two distinct dimensions of state activity. We have then developed a theoretical argument,

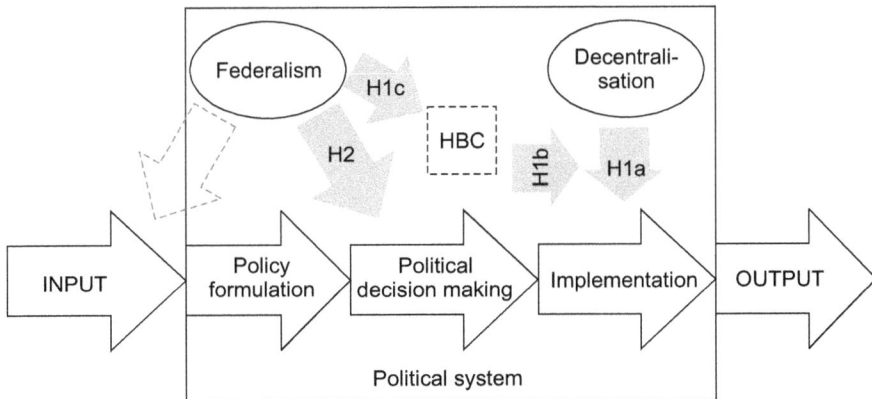

Figure 2.1: Hypothetical impact of federalism and decentralisation on the output performance of a political system

which hypothesises a positive impact of decentralisation on performance, while federalism is expected to have a slightly negative influence. In the next chapter, we will outline how we designed our research in order to test these theoretical propositions.

chapter three | research design

To evaluate the validity of our theoretical arguments, we apply a two-stage research design that consists of a quantitative and a qualitative part. In the first step (Chapter Four), we test for a systematic relationship between the vertical organisational structure of a nation state, i.e. federalism and decentralisation, and its policy performance at the macro level. Building on our theoretical framework, policy performance is thought to emanate both from patterns of economic efficiency during the stage of policy implementation and from an adequate capacity of governments to cope with external changes. A macro-quantitative analysis, however, cannot grasp the essence of the micro-level theoretical arguments and can only deal with rather rough indicators of policy and macroeconomic performance. This is particularly true for the evaluation of performance in different policy areas – for example, the number of teachers and PISA results are used as indicators for performance in education. However, our quantitative part does not aim to account comprehensively for the concept of performance but rather to detect whether systematic differences in the level or trend of performance exist between federal and unitary as well as decentralised and centralised countries. Moreover, owing to the theoretical premises of a stable democratic and economic context for policy making as well as considerations of data reliability, we restrict our statistical evaluation to OECD countries and apply a multifaceted strategy that combines cross-country and panel analyses (see Chapter Four for details). This allows us to cope with the challenges of a situation where there are only a small number of country cases but a potentially large number of factors to control for in addition to the institutions of state organisation which may impact policy performance.

The quantitative analysis yields three main findings. First, descriptive statistics show that federalism and decentralisation are indeed independent dimensions of territorial state organisation such that one may reasonably describe countries as belonging to one of four types: federal–decentralised, federal–centralised, unitary–decentralised, or unitary–centralised. Second, federalism tends to decrease policy performance as indicated by macroeconomic indicators, whereas decentralisation improves it. Third, once we compare across policy areas, federalism and decentralisation turn out to affect performance in divergent ways, though all areas that have been selected for the statistical analyses classify as spatially relevant and are thus, according to Braun (2000c: 19), most likely to exhibit the expected effects from a theoretical point of view.

The findings from macro-level relationships build the basis for the second step (Chapters Five to Seven) of our empirical enquiry in which we switch the level of analysis and focus on in-depth case studies. These seek to understand the causal connections between territorial state organisation and policy performance that underlie the visible macro effects. It is precisely at the crossover between quantitative and qualitative analyses that the main advantages of a mixed-methods research design kick in (Lieberman 2005; Gerring 2004; Rohlfing 2008). In our case, the quantitative results enable a two-step strategy of case selection (see Chapter Five for details). To begin with, our findings clearly suggest that the effects of federalism and decentralisation differ across policy areas and we seek to understand why this is the case. Accordingly, the case studies provide a detailed comparison of processes of decision making and policy implementation across two policy areas (regional development and transport policies), which exhibit divergent results in the quantitative analysis. On the one hand, the detailed analysis of regional development policies allows us to trace why both dimensions impact performance as expected; on the other hand, a comprehensive account of transport policies may detect why neither federalism nor decentralisation has shown significant effects in the course of our statistical analysis. In methodological terms, regional development policy thus classifies as a typical and transport policy as a deviant case. Beyond that, the quantitative findings allow for a non-biased selection of countries which are *representative* for each of the four country types and *average* with regard to those control factors that were shown to significantly influence policy performance in the selected policy areas.

The following chapters present the design as well as results of our quantitative and qualitative analyses in more detail.

chapter | quantitative analysis
four

Our quantitative analysis of policy performance in OECD countries faces the well-known methodological problem of a small-N design because there are many variables with a potential impact on performance, but only twenty to thirty cases accessible for analysis (depending on data availability). The principal problem regarding validity is that the central limit theorem that builds the indispensable assumption for statistical inference obviously does not apply in such a setting.[10] While this limitation may have contributed to the much-bemoaned lack of comparative studies on federalism and clear preference for case studies (Scharpf *et al.* 1976, Peterson 1995; Painter 1998), this does not necessarily mean that a systematic comparative analysis is impossible. However, it leaves us with a situation in which we have to carefully design models that withstand demanding robustness tests. We propose a twofold solution. On the one hand, we opt for cross-sectional analyses and restrict the factors incorporated in our models through different statistical selection procedures. We thus end up with a large number of multivariate regression analyses and infer an effect of federalism and/ or decentralisation only when we find stable and resilient effects in a majority of models for a specific causal relationship. In a strict sense, such evaluation of the relationship of interest is restricted to the empirical distribution of the OECD countries. We cannot and will not generalise beyond the confines of this group of countries, even if we believe that this research has implications which transcend the OECD world. On the other hand, we increase the number of observations by conducting a panel analysis wherever there is enough variation in the independent variables over time. Before we display the results of both approaches, the following sections discuss their technical properties in more detail.

4.1 Design of the cross-sectional analysis

In our cross-sectional analysis we need to control for a large number of factors that have been highlighted as influential for a country's policy performance. However, our capability to do so is greatly restricted by the low number of cases available, so that we must preselect factors we wish to incorporate in statistical estimations. We select indicators on the basis of statistical selection procedures, employing bivariate and t-test selections as well as stepwise regressions. In doing so, we identify a large number of statistically significant models with good explanatory power, which initially incorporate none of the federalism and decentralisation indicators.

---

10. The central limit theorem states that the sum of stochastically independent random variables is approximately normally distributed.

Instead, we add these indicators to the basic models afterwards, because this is the only way of making sure that the models account for the relevant combinations of control factors. Due to the non-applicability of the central limit theorem we cannot draw statistical inferences from any single model, but must instead consider the persistence of the federalism and/or decentralisation indicators across different models. Hence we infer an effect in cases where federalism and decentralisation turn out to significantly impact our performance indicators in a majority of the models. Furthermore, we test all resulting models for outliers.[11] Finally, we verify the stability of the models by adding all bivariately significant indicators. An exemplary step-by-step analysis of the impact of federalism and decentralisation upon one of our performance indicators – budget balance – is given in Section 4.5.

4.2   Design of the panel analysis

The feasibility of applying panel analyses as a solution to the small-N problem in comparative political economy has been debated at least since since Beck and Katz's article (1995). Panel analyses have indeed almost become standard in the discipline (Plümper *et al*. 2005). The idea behind these procedures is the incorporation of the time dimension, thus allegedly increasing the number of observations by the factor t (with t being the number of time intervals covered by the analysis). Yet panel designs are not without fallacies, and there is a growing awareness that panel analyses may not have such promising potential after all (Beck 2001; Plümper *et al*. 2005). Kittel and Winner (2005) point out that although using panel analyses is worth a try, they are not a full replacement for more basic cross-sectional methods. In this light the parallel approach of our study is additionally justified.

As time-series data are not available for policy-area variables, the evaluation of performance effects in the course of the panel analysis is confined to the macroeconomic indicators of economic growth, unemployment, price stability, and budget balance. Models for the size of government and for spending on welfare are not analysed due to an insufficient data basis. Additionally, the panel analysis incorporates fewer control variables owing to non-availability of time-series data. We therefore conducted supplementary estimations with and without considering government size because panel data for the size of the public sector are available only for a shorter period of time. In addition, as our federalism indicators generally do not vary over time (with the exception of Belgium) the analysis is restricted to the impact of decentralisation where we do find variation over time.

Pre-tests show that most of the macroeconomic indicators are non-stationary and moreover (partly) auto-correlated over time. Accordingly, it is appropriate to include all independent variables as lagged ones (t-1 periods) and to estimate

---

11.   Mexico and Turkey turn out to be outliers in most of the models. As they are the two countries with the lowest levels of development, this finding underlines the importance of a stable democratic and economic context for our analysis. At the same time, it corroborates our decision to restrict the analysis to OECD countries.

panel models both with and without the lagged dependent variable respectively. Moreover, our data structure requires the incorporation of time and country dummies (so-called fixed effects) and a correction for the specific characteristics of the error terms via panel corrected standard errors (Beck and Katz 1995). As a consequence, the focus of our panel analysis is not on the effects of decentralisation regarding the absolute level of the dependent variable, but rather on the effects with regard to short-term shifts of the respective macroeconomic indicators (Kittel and Winner 2005).

To summarise, we estimate four different models for each macroeonomic indicator (economic growth, unemployment, price stability, and budget balance) as these models either include or exclude government size and are estimated on grounds of either a regular or a lagged dependent variable.

4.3 Operationalisation

Even a brief glance at the literature reveals that there are a number of diverging indicators which capture different aspects of both federalism and decentralisation.[12] We therefore refrain from specifying a single indicator or a combination of indicators in an index, but choose six different indicators for each of the dimensions (plus an additional dummy for the federalism type which accounts for the *interaction hypothesis*). In the case of federalism, these are a dummy variable (federal system or unitary system) (Elazar 1987), indicators from Keman (2000), Lijphart (1999), Treisman (2000), Gerring and Thacker (2004), and an indicator from Maddex (1998). For decentralisation we consider the ratio of subnational expenditure to total expenditure as well as the respective revenue ratio (average values for 1994–2003 calculated from the Government Finance Statistics yearbooks of the International Monetary Fund, IMF), three different indicators from Rodden (2002, 2004), and an indicator measuring the ratio of subnational to total administrative personnel (Schiavo-Campo *et al.* 1997).

Turning to the control variables, indicators which capture fiscal aspects of a political system and control for the influence of budget constraints as depicted in our *HBC hypothesis* are set apart. We incorporate the proportion of new debts to subnational expenditure (International Monetary Fund) and an index of budget constraints that has been developed by the Inter-American Development Bank (1997), as well as a slightly modified version of the relevant data from Rodden (2002) as fiscal indicators.[13] Furthermore, we use an indicator for the proportion of grants to subnational revenue (Rodden 2004) as well as subnational expenditure (International Monetary Fund), and finally two additional indicators measuring the vertical fiscal imbalance of the political system (average values for 1994–2003

---

12. For the measurement of federalism and decentralisation, see Levin (1991), Baldi (1999), and Rodden (2004).

13. Rodden (2002) provides data for the hardness of budget constraints for all subnational levels separately. We have modified these data by taking the average values for the state and local level in the case of federal countries.

calculated from the International Monetary Fund).

Additional control factors are population size, the size of the country in terms of area, and population density (Central Intelligence Agency 2005), age distribution (United Nations 2004), income distribution (United Nations Development Programme 2004), ethnic (Levinson 1998) and religious fragmentation (Encyclopedia Britannica 1997), and the degree of urbanisation (United Nations 2001). We also control for the level of development, measured by the Human Development Index (United Nations Development Programme 2004), the number of 'democratic years' 1900–2003 as given by the Polity IV Dataset (Marshall and Jaggers 2002), the legal culture (La Porta *et al.* 1999), and the institutional configuration of the political system (Lijphart 1999).[14] By including the values of Lijphart's executive-parties dimension we are able to control for the overall consensus character of the political system without inflating the number of variables in our small-N design. Such control is especially important, as recent studies have, for example, pointed at a systematic relationship between the effects of corporatism and federalism upon political performance (Wälti 2004).

As dependent variables, we chose macroeconomic performance indicators based on the literature (see Chapter Two). Federalism supposedly has an effect on government size, welfare spending, inflation rates, unemployment rates, budget balance, and economic growth. These indicators come from the OECD (OECD various years). Analogous with the previous independent indicators, the macroeconomic indicators for the cross-sectional analysis are average values for the years 1994–2003.

Besides the macroeconomic indicators, we have collected indicators for performance in different policy areas to evaluate the assumption that federalism and decentralisation may have divergent effects depending on policy area (Benz 1998, 2001). Before selecting these indicators, however, we must put forward a number of additional considerations. Firstly, in view of the theoretical arguments of Musgrave (1959) and Oates (1972) one can expect efficiency gains only in policy areas with allocative functions. Secondly, Braun (2000a) points out that divergent subnational policy outputs are particularly likely in space-related policy areas as well as in such areas that affect subnational identities. We therefore focus on the policy areas of public order and safety, education, recreation and culture, economic policy, infrastructure, and environment, while distinguishing between output and outcome indicators. The output of a political system is related to policy results which can be directly influenced by policy making, whereas the outcome is also influenced by external factors outside the policy-making realm. An analysis of the relationships between institutional arrangements and policy-area performance must therefore focus on output indicators or – if such indicators are unavailable – at least on outcome indicators for which a close connection with output is highly plausible. Accordingly, we have chosen the number of police officers per 1000 inhabitants in the area of public order and safety (United Nations 2002), in the

---

14. Macroeconomic indicators are also incorporated as potential influence factors.

area of education the number of teachers (United Nations Educational Scientific and Cultural Organization 2001) as well as PISA results (OECD 2001), for culture the number of library officials (United Nations Educational Scientific and Cultural Organization 2001), for economic policy an index which captures the extent to which technical, scientific, and human resources meet the requirements of the economy (International Institute for Management Development 2005), for the environment compliance with international environmental conventions (Porter *et al.* 2001) and, finally, for infrastructure the size of road networks (United Nations Economic Commission for Europe 2005) as well as three indicators from the Global Entrepreneurship Monitor 2002[15] regarding regulations, the quality of public funding, and physical infrastructure for start-up enterprises. It is important to recall that we do not strive to capture a country's performance in a specific policy area with a single indicator. Rather, we seek to grasp systematic level differences, leaving an all-embracing operationalisation of policy performance to the subsequent case studies (see Chapter 5.2 for details).

A description of all indicators, their minima and maxima as well as their respective sources, can be found in Tables 1 (cross-sectional data) and 2 (panel data) in the appendix. Additionally, the raw data is available at http://www.vergl-polwiss.uni-koeln.de/10604.html.[16]

4.4   Differentiation of federalism and decentralisation

The basic assumption underlying our theoretical argumentation (see Chapter Two) is that federalism and decentralisation represent distinct dimensions of territorial political organisation. The first step of our quantitative analysis therefore is to test this assumption empirically.

Table 4.1 displays the results of a correlation analysis between all federalism and decentralisation indicators. As apparent, the analysis points to a moderate but in no case perfect relationship between federalism and decentralisation. The highest correlation of .74 is between the Keman index of federalism and the Government Finance Statistics indicator of expenditure decentralisation. Aside from that, there are only seven correlations with values greater than .60 and even one indicating a negative relationship. The exact relationship between federalism and decentralisation thus remains unsettled. However, this is not unexpected, because the various indicators capture different aspects of federalism and decentralisation. Yet the correlation analysis does verify the theoretical difference between the two dimensions. Taking individual countries, for any combination of indicators there are always some which do not fit the assumption that federalism and decentralisation, unitarism and centralisation, go hand in hand – in particular

---

15. Expert survey in the course of the Global Entrepreneurship Monitor (GEM) 2002; for methodo-logical details see Sternberg and Bergmann (2003).

16. In the event of data usage, please refer to Biela, J., Hennl, A. and Kaiser, A. (2012) *Policy Making in Multilevel Systems: Federalism, Decentralisation, and Performance in the OECD Countries* Colchester: ECPR Press.

Table 4.1: Correlation analysis between all federalism and decentralisation indicators

Correlations	dezrev2	dezrev3	dezrev4	snadm	dezrev1	dezexp
feddummy	0.46	0.14	0.52	0.41	0.57	0.64
fedlijp	0.46	0.13	0.61	0.43	0.60	0.71
fedkeman	0.58	0.31	0.63	0.48	0.65	0.74
fedtreis	0.30	0.12	0.54	0.41	0.46	0.50
fedgth	0.25	−0.03	0.43	0.45	0.47	0.58
fedmadx	0.44	0.24	0.63	0.47	0.61	0.67

Note: Any abbreviations are listed in Tables 1 and 2 in the appendix.

the unitary Nordic countries with high levels of decentralisation. The conventional assumption of a strong relationship between federalism and decentralisation can thus be safely rejected. Policy making in multilevel systems takes place in more combinations than just federal-cum-decentralised and unitary-cum-centralised arrangements.

4.5 Results of the cross-sectional analysis

The central result of our cross-sectional analysis is a confirmation of the *decentralisation hypothesis* and the *federalism hypothesis* with regard to the majority of our macroeconomic performance indicators. Broadly, decentralisation exhibits a positive impact, and federalism tends to show negative effects. As set out in Section 4.1, the strategy of analysis that yields such results is quite complex and builds upon several stages of enquiry. Before we display a summary of our results, we therefore exemplarily delineate the single steps for the analysis of budget balance in order to increase traceability.

The analysis that seeks to discover whether federalism and decentralisation systematically impact a country's budget balance consists of five main steps:

First, we run bivariate regressions of budget balance to any of the decentralisation indicators. Only Rodden's (2004) indicator of revenue decentralisation and the one for expenditure decentralisation display a significant correlation.

In a second step, we conduct a T-test to see whether federal and unitary countries systematically differ with regard to their budget balance. The difference is not significant.

The third step is the main part of the analysis. At the beginning, we develop a basic model that consists of only those control variables that significantly influence budget balance in bivariate regression analyses and are still significant after a stepwise reduction of the model. The resulting basic model includes the unemployment rate, trade balance (proportion of exports to imports), government size, and the median age of the population as independent variables. Afterwards, we add fiscal control variables to the basic model and, if one of them is significant, the indicators for federalism and decentralisation. In doing so, we generate four models that possess predictive power and can be classified as significant:

The first model includes the unemployment rate, trade balance, and Rodden's (2004) indicator of revenue decentralisation as significant predictors of budget balance; the second model includes trade balance, the proportion of grants in subnational revenue (Rodden 2004), the index of budget constraints as developed by the Inter-American Development Bank (Rodden 2002), and the indicator for federalism and bicameralism that was developed by Gerring and Thacker (Gerring and Thacker 2004); the third displays significant effects of trade balance, the index of budget constraints as developed by the Inter-American Development Bank (Rodden 2002) and Rodden's (2004) indicator of revenue decentralisation; and the fourth shows trade balance, the index of budget constraints as developed by the Inter-American Development Bank (Rodden 2002) and the own-source subnational revenue as share of total subnational revenue which is corrected for rate and base autonomy by Rodden (2004). In the first, third and fourth models, the decentralisation indicators positively impact the budget balance, whereas in the second model Gerring and Thacker's (2004) federalism indicator has a negative effect upon the budget balance.

Each model is then specified further by the exclusion of outliers[17] (in this case Norway and the United States of America for all the models, and additionally Canada in model 4). Finally, we seek to test the robustness of these models and add each of the federalism indicators to models 1, 3, and 4; and the decentralisation indicators to model 2. In the former case, the models classify as robust and including federalism does not add any predictive power. In the latter case, however, adding any of the decentralisation indicators to model 2 deletes the negative effect of federalism. The second model is thus not robust.

The fourth step is broadly similar to step 3. However, instead of using bivariate regressions to set up a basic model, we conduct a stepwise regression. This alternative approach to construct a reduced model is supposed to be especially sensitive in order to avoid missing relevant model specifications (Smith and Young 2001). It yields a basic model that includes unemployment, trade balance, population density, and the median age of the population as independent variables. Adding indicators of federalism and decentralisation reveals that only the subnational proportion of government employees has a significant positive impact on budget balance. The resulting model is robust against adding the federalism indicators.

In the fifth step we add all bivariately significant control variables to the models that were developed in steps 3 and 4. This re-iterated model testing displays the same results as the tests in step 3 and 4. The decentralisation indicators continue

---

17. Outliers were excluded if they reached a Cook's d value larger than $4/(n-(k+1))$.

Table 4.2: Selected cross-sectional regression models for macroeconomic indicators

Macroeconomic indicators											
Economic growth		Unemployment		Inflation		Government size		Welfare spending		Budget balance	
unemp	0.0007*	budgdef	-8.2308***	hdi02	-0.5284***	budgdef	-54.030***	hdi02	-0.5710*	unemp	-0.0075***
medage	-0.0018**	incineq2	-0.0727**	growth	0.9598***	incineq1	-0.5707**	urban	0.2334***	tradebal	0.2289***
fedkeman	-0.0060***	medage	-0.1100**	grants	0.0385	legscan	9.2216***	feddummy	-0.1023***	medage	-0.0176***
dezexp	0.0372**	fedmadx	-0.0523	fedgth	0.0028**	legfren	3.9141*	dezrev1	0.3031***	fedmadx	-0.0010
_cons	1.0739***	dezrev1	0.7052	snadm	-0.0271**	fedgth	-0.9366	_cons	0.4594*	snadm	0.0701*
		_cons	7.3657***	_cons	0.5539**	dezexp	4.4382			_cons	0.4311***
						_cons	56.324***				
#obs	17	#obs	26	#obs	21	#obs	25	#obs	21	#obs	22
Prob > F	0.0010	Prob > F	0.0042	Prob > F	0.0001	Prob > F	0.0001	Prob > F	0.0009	Prob > F	0.0000
R-squared	0.7084	R-squared	0.5522	R-squared	0.9357	R-squared	0.7757	R-squared	0.6693	R-squared	0.8465

* significant at the .10 level; ** significant at the .05 level; *** significant at the .01 level.

Note: Any abbreviations are listed in Tables 1 and 2 in the appendix.

to have a positive effect upon budget balance, but the impact of federalism loses significance once we include additional indicators. Finally, we assess the predictive power of all models on basis of the Akaike information criterion (Akaike 1973).

In sum, we find that decentralised countries exhibit a more balanced budget than centralised ones, whereas there is no systematic difference between the budget balance of federal and unitary countries. Later on (Table 4.3) we refer to this finding by assigning a '+' to the impact of decentralisation, and a 'o' to the federalism column. However, while this table may appear to be rather simplistic, these symbols derive from a detailed analysis that, in the case of budget balance, rests upon 557 different model specifications that have been tested.

Such complex strategies of analysis have been conducted for each of the macroeconomic indicators. However, instead of giving a lengthy description for each, Table 4.2 displays a single selected cross-sectional model specification for each of the macroeconomic indicators, and Table 4.3 gives a summary of all findings using a '+' for a significant positive effect, a '–' for a significant negative effect, and a 'o' in case that no robust effect was found.

The model specifications selected for Table 4.2 present those results that we found in the majority of our specifications (see Table 4.3). Federalism dampens and decentralisation fosters economic growth. Additionally, the expected relationships are predominantly supported in the case of price stability, although this finding must be qualified inasmuch as a stable effect can only be verified for the indicator of personnel decentralisation. The analysis confirms no effect regarding unemployment rate and government size. In the area of social policy, however, the findings indicate that decentralisation leads to higher spending on welfare, whereas federalism correlates with less spending.

In a second step, we conduct similar analyses for varying indicators of policy-area-specific performance. Our analysis corroborates the assumption of the literature (Benz 1998, 2001) that the effects of federalism and decentralisation

Table 4.3: Relationships between federalism, decentralisation, and macroeconomic performance

Performance indicators	Federalism	Decentralisation	Federalism type
Economic growth	−	+	o
Unemployment	o	o	o
Price stability	−	(+)	o
Government size	o	o	o
Welfare spending	−	+	o
Budget balance	o	+	o

+ signals a significant positive, − a significant negative relationship; o indicates that there is no significant relationship

Table 4.4: Selected cross-sectional regression models for policy area performance

	Policy area indicators										
Public order (policemen)		Education (teachers)		Culture (librarians)		Economy (resources)		Infrastructure (for start-ups)		Environment (importance)	
democ	-0.0212**	infl	4.3208**	govsize	0.0112**	pop	0.00007	growth	-24.242***	govsize	0.0255**
fedmadx	0.6242	legscan	0.3350**	legfren	-0.2036**	hdi02	391.494***	area	1e-07***	religion	1.6583***
dezrev1	-4.8555***	medage	-0.0281*	area	-6e-07***	feddummy	5.9006	tradebal	1.9521***	area	-9e-08***
_cons	4.1645***	fedtreis	0.1421	hdi02	2.1548*	dezrev2	66.264***	fedmadx	-0.0301	legscan	0.9582***
		dezexp	-0.5511	feddummy	-0.0557	_cons	-314.62***	dezrev1	-0.2010	fedgth	0.0435
		_cons	-6.4741***	dezrev1	0.5443			_cons	26.669***	dezexp	2.1870**
										_cons	3.1922***
#obs	18	#obs	19	#obs	21	#obs	19	#obs	18	#obs	24
Prob > F	0.0336	Prob > F	0.0230	Prob > F	0.0021	Prob > F	0.0000	Prob > F	0.0001	Prob > F	0.0000
R-squared	0.5179	R-squared	0.5974	R-squared	0.7321	R-squared	0.8422	R-squared	0.8679	R-squared	0.7954

* significant at the .10 level; ** significant at the .05 level; *** significant at the .01 level.
Note: Any abbreviations are listed in Tables 1 and 2 in the appendix.

differ from policy area to policy area.[18] Again, we display a table (Table 4.4) that shows selected regression specifications for each policy area.

Our findings point to a positive effect of decentralised resource supply in the areas of economic policy and environment. Moreover, decentralisation tends to have positive effects in the area of recreation and culture, albeit these are ambiguous due to instability in some models. The analysis yields no effects with respect to the policy areas of education and infrastructure. In the area of public order and safety, however, regression models actually point to a relationship that runs counter to the theoretical argument. Decentralised countries tend to have fewer police officers per 1,000 inhabitants than centralised countries, whereas federalism exhibits no persistent effect. However, this finding is confirmed only for some models. In Table 4.5 we summarise the findings for policy-area-specific effects of federalism and decentralisation.

With respect to the *HBC hypothesis* concerning the influence of institutional budget constraints, the analysis is at first glance not altogether decisive. The relevant indicators are significant in several regression models, but we do not find a persistent and stable effect across the models. We are thus left without a clear confirmation of influence. One explanation may be the relatively low degree of variance in the budget constraint indicators for the OECD countries, or alternatively the small number of available cases for them. In interpreting the results, it is moreover necessary to take into account that, for our purpose, the budget constraint indicators serve primarily as control factors. Hence the incorporation of these indicators in the analysis is predominantly relevant for a correct interpretation of the effects of federalism and decentralisation, whereas significant effects of the budget constraint indicators themselves are only of secondary importance.

Table 4.5: Relationships between federalism, decentralisation, and policy area performance

Performance indicators	Federalism	Decentralisation	Federalism type
Public order and safety	o	(−)	(+)
Education	o	o	(−)
Recreation and culture	o	(o/+)	o
Economic policy	o	+	o
Infrastructure	o	o	o
Environment	o	+	o

+ signals a significant positive, − a significant negative relationship; o indicates that there is no significant relationship.

18. In assessing the effects of federalism and decentralisation one must consider that the distribution of competences and resources in individual policy areas may be different from the overall distribution in the country. Precise statements about the causes of deviating findings in specific policy areas are therefore not possible on the basis of a quantitative analysis.

With regard to the type of federalism, there is no confirmation for a persistent effect either. Thus we find no clear corroboration of our *interaction hypothesis*. However, the regression models indicate that Germany (as the sole case of joint federalism in the analysis) differs from the remainder of the OECD countries with respect to the number of police officers (positively), the PISA results (negatively), and public funding (positively).

Overall, the cross-sectional analysis suggests that the empirical relationships between federalism, decentralisation, and performance in the case of the macroeconomic variables are mainly compatible with our theoretical propositions. Decentralisation leads to improved policy performance for a majority of indicators, whereas federalism exhibits no or negative effects. Moreover, the effects of federalism and decentralisation show varying effects once we compare across individual policy areas. This is in line with the relevant predictions in the literature. We find areas where the results fit our prediction (economic policy and environmental policy) as well as those where none of the dimensions exhibits a significant impact (infrastructure, education, and partially, recreation and culture). Moreover, the effects of territorial state organisation upon policy performance in the area of public order and safety actually run counter to our expectations as we find a positive influence of federalism. Results with respect to the institutional budget constraints and the type of federalism are unclear, and accordingly the respective hypotheses are neither confirmed nor rejected. In order to put our findings on more solid ground, the following chapter also conducts a panel analysis.

4.6   Results of the panel analysis

Taking into account the time dimension, the first insight is the surprising stability of OECD countries with regard to decentralisation over time for both revenue and expenditure decentralisation.

Table 4.6 shows the degree of revenue and expenditure decentralisation as of 1975 and 2000. It turns out that for those older OECD countries, for which data are available since the 1970s, the only countries that have strongly increased the degree of decentralisation are Belgium (expenditures), Italy (revenues), and Spain (revenues and expenditures). In these countries, the driving forces behind these trends have been subnational efforts to gain more room for political manoeuvre rather than mere efficiency considerations. In the younger, predominantly Central–East European OECD member countries we do not find a clear trend towards decentralisation either, only Poland and the Slovak Republic are exceptions. However, as these two countries start from a rather low level, and the steps towards more decentralisation are not very pronounced, it is too early to really confirm such a trend. We can conclude that, at the end of the period covered by our analysis (2003), decentralisation does not represent a strategy adopted by the OECD countries to adjust to increasing market integration, which means that they – in contrast to less developed countries – have not participated in the worldwide 'wave of decentralisation' (Rodden *et al.* 2003: 3).

As there is no intertemporal variation on the federalism dimension (with the

Table 4.6: Decentralisation 1975 and 2000

| | Decentralisation | | | | | |
| | Revenue | | | Expenditure | | |
	1975	2000	Δ	1975	2000	Δ
Australia	0.20	0.22	2.0%	0.41	0.40	−1.0%
Austria	0.22	0.21	−1.0%	0.31	0.33	2.0%
Belgium	0.05	0.09	4.0%	0.13	0.31	18.0%
Canada	0.41	0.46	5.0%	0.58	0.57	−1.0%
Denmark	0.30	0.33	3.0%	0.46	0.48	2.0%
Finland	0.30	0.22	−8.0%	0.35	0.33	−2.0%
France	0.08	0.09	1.0%	0.17	0.16	−1.0%
Germany	0.31	0.31	0.0%	0.44	0.40	−4.0%
Greece	0.01	0.01	0.0%	0.04	0.04	0.0%
Iceland	0.21	0.23	2.0%	0.20	0.26	6.0%
Ireland	0.07	0.01	−6.0%	0.28	0.25	−3.0%
Italy	0.03	0.14	11.0%	0.20	0.25	5.0%
Luxembourg	0.07	0.06	−1.0%	0.16	0.12	−4.0%
New Zealand	0.07	0.07	0.0%	0.14	0.11	−3.0%
Netherlands	0.01	0.05	4.0%	0.27	0.28	1.0%
Norway	0.23	0.18	−5.0%	0.40	0.34	−6.0%
Portugal	0.04	0.06	2.0%	0.07	0.11	4.0%
Sweden	0.25	0.31	6.0%	0.43	0.41	−2.0%
Switzerland	0.43	0.34	−9.0%	0.55	0.46	−9.0%
Spain	0.04	0.17	13.0%	0.10	0.29	19.0%
United Kingdom	0.11	0.05	−6.0%	0.30	0.22	−8.0%
USA	0.35	0.31	−4.0%	0.46	0.50	4.0%

Source: International Monetary Fund (various years).

exception of Belgium), the panel analysis cannot yield any results concerning the prediction of the hypothesis that federal states adapt to external changes at a slow rate.[19] The results of the panel estimations, moreover, should be interpreted cautiously because the relative stability of decentralisation values increases the sensitivity of the estimations with regard to small data variations (and possibly data errors).

Nevertheless, conducting panel analyses as described in Section 4.2 yields findings that point to a significant effect of decentralisation. In analogy to the

---

19. This follows from the incorporation of dummy variables for the individual countries in the panel models. Use of dummies is confirmed by tests of significance subsequent to the panel estimations. A separate interpretation of the federalism indicator is therefore not possible.

Table 4.7: Panel effects of decentralisation on macroeconomic performance

	Without LDV; with govsize		Without LDV; without govsize		With LDV; with govsize		With LDV; without govsize	
	dezrev	*dezexp*	*dezrev*	*dezexp*	*dezrev*	*dezexp*	*dezrev*	*dezexp*
Economic Growth	o	o	o	o	o	o	o	o
Unemployment	−	o	−	o	−	o	−	o
Price stability	−	o	o	+	−	−	o	+
Budget Balance	o	o	+	−	o	o	+	o

Note: LDV stands for 'lagged dependent variable', i.e. the dependent variable of the previous period is included in the estimation as an additional independent variable; govsize: indicator for the size of government.

illustration of cross-sectional results, Table 4.7 provides a summary of the revealed panel effects of decentralisation on macroeconomic performance.

The most striking finding is that decentralisation on the revenue side positively influences macroeconomic performance, whereas expenditure decentralisation tends to have a negative influence. To explain this seemingly surprising result, one must remember that revenue decentralisation in the context of federalism research means that a country behaves like an ideal-typical dual system. However, there are unitary countries, such as Denmark, Finland, Iceland, and Sweden, which also exhibit a comparatively high level of revenue decentralisation. Measuring decentralisation on the expenditure side, however, is more problematic because one additionally needs to consider the degree to which subnational governments are able to dispose of financial resources (Rodden 2004). In this context, there is no control for the budget constraint indicators in the course of the panel analysis, as respective time-series data have not been available. The indicator for revenue decentralisation is therefore theoretically clearly preferable, whereas the indicator for expenditure decentralisation may be distorted in case of expansive spending by subnational governments.[20] Importantly, the focus of the analysis does not lie at the level of the dependent variables, but rather on short-term shifts. The results of the panel estimations therefore complement the findings of the cross-sectional estimations so that even opposite signs of the coefficients do not necessarily contradict the relevant findings.

In a more detailed perspective, Table 4.7 shows that none of the panel models reveals any effect of decentralisation on economic growth. However, decentralisation (on the revenue side) leads to a reduction in unemployment. These two findings are probably the most reliable results with regard to the persistence of the models. The panel results again reflect the inconsistency of the cross-sectional models in the case of the inflation rate. The models that incorporate the size of

---

20. This proposition is corroborated by the fact that the additional inclusion of an indicator for subnational debts heavily influences the coefficients of expenditure decentralisation, without affecting the coefficients for revenue decentralisation.

government, for instance, show a positive effect of decentralisation (on both the revenue and expenditure sides); however, when we drop government size from the analysis (which increases the number of observations by approximately 270), the effect of revenue decentralisation disappears and the sign of the coefficient for expenditure decentralisation is actually reversed! With respect to budget balance, revenue decentralisation again has a positive effect (for the model without government size) and expenditure decentralisation a negative effect. If the lagged budget balance is added to the model, only the positive effect of revenue decentralisation remains valid.

All in all, decentralisation of revenues tends to have a positive effect on macroeconomic performance, whereas the results for expenditure decentralisation imply a negative effect. Most notably, the estimated effects of revenue and expenditure decentralisation are out of line with each other in almost all panel models. As it is not possible to control for budget restraints in the course of the panel analysis, focusing on the revenue decentralisation indicator is clearly preferable in interpreting the findings.

4.7   Summary of the quantitative analysis

So far, we have developed a theoretical model of the causal relationships between federalism, decentralisation, and performance, and have tested its hypotheses by means of a quantitative analysis of OECD countries. The findings show, first, that federalism and decentralisation are not only theoretically but also empirically distinct dimensions of state activity. Second, the analysis basically confirms the expected positive effects of decentralisation (*decentralisation hypothesis*) and slightly negative effects of federalism (*federalism hypothesis*) on policy performance as measured by macroeconomic indicators. The panel analysis additionally underlines the importance of controlling for subnational budget constraints, and thus indirectly points at a confirmation of the remainder of the hypotheses derived from the theoretical model. Third, our analysis reveals divergent effects of federalism and decentralisation in different policy areas, which have previously been noted by very few scholars (Benz 1998, 2001). It thus yields fresh insight into the interplay of institutional arrangements with regard to the territorial organisation of politics in individual countries.

Our quantitative analysis confirms that territorial state organisation is a two-dimensional phenomenon and that each dimension affects a country's policy performance at the macro level independently. Our theoretical reasoning and complex statistical design yields robust findings in a research area that has so far been plagued by ambiguous results and conceptual confusion. However, up to this point, we are not able to substantiate our research findings in the sense of causal explanations because a quantitative study cannot tell us *why* these differences accrue. A plausible causal explanation lies within our theoretical arguments that build upon the assumption that macro effects emanate from the intentional behaviour of political actors who are responsive to incentives set by the institutional design of territorial state organisation. The indispensable next step therefore is to conduct in-depth case studies that trace whether it is indeed the case that expectations and actions of political actors systematically differ between federal–centralised, federal–decentralised, unitary–centralised, and unitary–decentralised countries and account for varying patterns of policy performance. The following chapter shows that the combination of sound theoretical reasoning and the encompassing evaluation of empirical macro relationships conducted so far allows us to base such case studies upon a clear-cut and solid research design.

chapter five | qualitative analysis

The qualitative analysis focuses on the causal mechanisms underlying the relationships between federalism and policy performance on the one hand, and decentralisation and policy performance on the other. The case studies thus aim to detect how exactly the theoretically ascribed and quantitatively approved macro relationships are rooted in the micro level. In line with our theoretical model, we assume that federal structures set incentives for actors' behaviour in decision-making processes, whereas decentralisation structures behaviour regarding policy implementation. Moreover, the effectiveness of budget constraints may vary depending on the overall type of territorial state organisation and is expected to influence subnational actors' decisions to engage in or abstain from extensive debt financing.

Our case studies thus, first, set out to test the validity of three different institutional logics which influence actors' behaviour at different stages of the policy-making process. Building upon our quantitative analysis, we can clearly identify economic policy as a most likely, and thus a typical case for such a *theory-testing* endeavour. However, in light of the varying effects of federalism and decentralisation across policy areas, our case studies pursue a second goal. The careful selection of a policy area where none of the dimensions displays an influence on policy performance (infrastructure policy) allows us to additionally pursue a *theory-modifying* case study, one that strives to reformulate and enhance our theoretical arguments (Lieberman 2005). We then compare the dynamics of decision making and policy implementation in both policy areas across four countries that are most representative for each of the country types and additionally display average values with regard to important control factors. This leads us to a comparison of regional development and transport policies in Switzerland (federal–decentralised), Austria (federal–centralised), Denmark (unitary–decentralised), and Ireland (unitary–centralised).

Consequently, both the limitation of our cases – that is, the selection and definition of policy areas – and their spatial delineation, which encompasses the selection of countries, are based upon the findings of our quantitative analysis. Accordingly, we are able to tap the full potential of a mixed-methods or nested design. The following sections delineate the logic of case selection in more detail and specify our qualitative research design with regard to the elaboration of expected micro-level mechanisms as well as the concept of policy performance that underlies our case studies.

5.1   Case selection

In order to locate our cases properly, we define them on a substantive, a spatial, and a temporal dimension (Rohlfing 2012: 24–28). Accordingly, our first step is to substantively delineate two policy areas for in-depth analysis by selecting both a typical and a deviant case on the basis of our macro-quantitative analysis. Given approved relationships between federalism and decentralisation on the one hand and the macroeconomic performance of countries on the other, the quantitative analysis drew attention to the separation of effects across varying policy areas (Chapter 4.5). It discovered that the effects of decentralisation and federalism vary between area-specific indicators of policy performance. Because all policy areas included in the quantitative analysis display allocative functions and are space-related, they qualify as most likely cases; the multifaceted results displayed in Table 4.5 allow us to select both a most likely (and thus typical) case that met our theoretical expectations and a deviant case.

The former is represented by the area of economic policy in which a decentralised allocation of resources has a positive impact upon performance whereas federalism displays a null effect. However, since the statistical analysis is based on an index that captures the extent to which technical, scientific, and human resources meet the requirements of the economy (International Institute for Management Development 2005), we need to further specify the policy area for qualitative analysis. Given our focus on the relevance of territorial organisation to performance, it is reasonable to delimit our case studies to the realm of *regional* economic policies. These are best understood as the sum of spatially relevant policies (Glassmann 2007) that aim at actively influencing economic processes in distinct areas of a state (Maier *et al.* 2006). Regional economic policy is thus a broad area including several fields such as labour, social, educational, environmental, and transport policies. However, such a definition is still far too broad, given our aim of comparing processes of decision making and implementation across countries. Consequently, we restrict ourselves to an even narrower focus and analyse those strategies fostering investment, growth, and competitiveness to reduce regional disparities. This goal is, albeit to varying degrees, part of official policy in almost every European country (Yuill *et al.* 2007), so that the strategies applied to achieve it provide a fruitful ground for cross-country comparison. It is these strategies, the sum of which we call *regional development policy*, which lie at the heart of our case studies when we seek to detect the micro-level dynamics underlying the approved typicality of federalism's and decentralisation's effect upon policy performance.

A failed most likely case, in contrast, is the area of infrastructure policy. Though it is clearly space-related and encompasses the allocation of resources, the quantitative analysis detected no influence either of decentralisation or of federalism upon its performance. The latter was in this case measured by two distinct indicators – the size of road networks (United Nations Economic Commission for Europe 2005) as a straightforward output indicator and three indicators from the Global Entrepreneurship Monitor 2002 that assess regulations, public funding, and physical infrastructure for start-up enterprises. Our quantitative indicators thus put emphasis upon the material or physical dimension of infrastructure, which refers to

> 1. the totality of all earning assets, equipment and circulating capital in an economy that serve energy provision, transport service and telecommunications; [...] 2. structures, etc. for the conservation of natural resources and transport routes in the broadest sense and 3. buildings and installations of public administration, education, research, health care and social welfare (Jochimsen 1966: 103, translation by Buhr 2009).

For the purpose of our case studies, it is again necessary to delimit the object of study more clearly. We thus focus on the first of Jochimsen's aspects, yielding a definition of infrastructure policy that contains the sum of those policies that fall into the areas of transport, energy, and telecommunications policies (Sager 2006). In order to allow for a cross-country comparison that builds upon cases which are most similar on a substantive dimension (but differ with regard to their spatial location and thus their territorial state organisation), we narrow down further and compare only processes of decision making and policy implementation in the realm of *transport policy* that concern public as well as private transport on roads and railways.

Subsuming, our quantitative results lead us to select two distinct policy areas – regional development policy and transport policy – as a preliminary delineation of our cases on a substantive dimension. Nevertheless, our theoretical arguments regarding the effects of federalism (and decentralisation) pose the challenge to select distinct reform initiatives (and implementation processes, respectively) for in-depth comparative analysis. But such a selection, which touches upon both the substantive and the temporal dimension, requires extensive country-specific knowledge. We therefore base our selection on secondary sources and a number of pilot interviews with country and policy experts. Chapters Six and Seven which present the results of our case studies thus encompass a more detailed location of our cases in both the substantive and the temporal dimension.

With regard to the spatial dimension of case selection, we strive to select countries that are *representative* for each of the four country types and *average* with regard to those control factors that have been shown to significantly influence performance in the selected policy areas. Given two independent dimensions of territorial state organisation, one may reasonably classify countries as being federal–decentralised, federal–centralised, unitary–decentralised, or unitary–centralised. Again, our quantitative database allows for a clear-cut classification of countries with regard to the two dimensions of multilevel politics. Each of the federalism indicators is plotted against each of the decentralisation indicators. Using the mean of the OECD countries as a separating device, a country's position in one of the four quadrants serves to classify it. To give an example, Figure 5.1 shows the scatter plot for the Keman federalism indicator and revenue decentralisation.

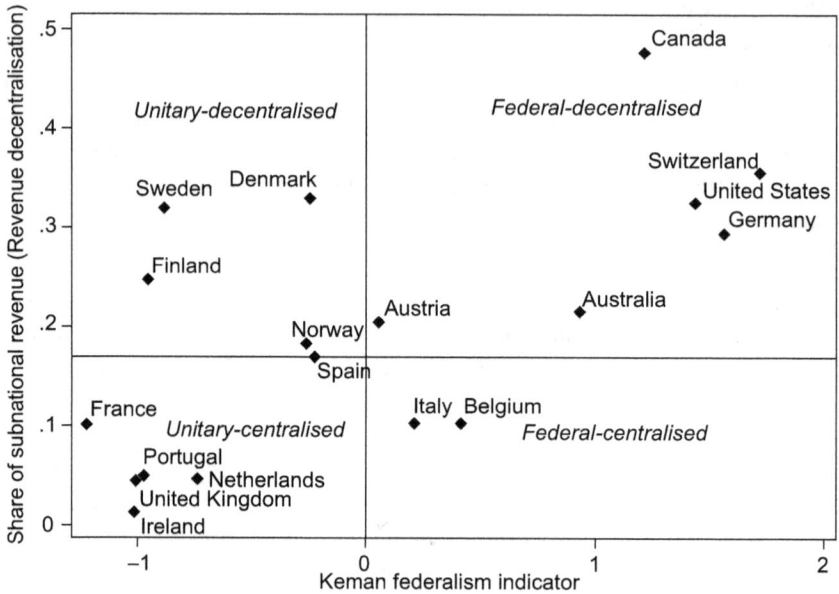

Source: International Monetary Fund (various years, see 'dezrev1' in Appendix, Table 1); Keman (2000).

Note: The lines indicate the mean of the OECD countries.

Figure 5.1: Scatter plot between federalism and decentralisation

From this, it can be seen that, for example, Sweden, Denmark, Finland, and Norway fall into the category of unitary–decentralised countries, whereas France, Portugal, the Netherlands, the United Kingdom, and Ireland are unitary–centralised countries. Spain seems to split the difference. However, given the variety of diverging indicators which capture different aspects of both federalism and decentralisation, we do not rely upon such snapshots of country types but rather plot each indicator of federalism against each of the decentralisation indicators. This gives us, depending upon data availability, a maximum of thirty-six classifications for each country. The frequency with which a country appears in each of the four quadrants is shown in Table 5.1. The most common classification is indicated in **bold**, allowing us easily to select cases for qualitative studies. A case study of a federal–centralised country can, for example, focus on Austria; one of a federal–decentralised country on Australia, Canada, Switzerland, or the US. In order to analyse policy processes in a unitary–centralised country one can pick France, Greece, Ireland, or Poland; and a unitary–decentralised pattern of policy making may be predominantly observed in the Scandinavian countries.

Table 5.1: Classification of countries

Country	UC	UD	FC	FD	Country	UC	UD	FC	FD
Australia	0	0	0	24	Korea	0	4	0	0
Austria	**4**	**2**	**20**	**10**	Luxembourg	8	0	2	0
Belgium	3	2	12	8	Mexico	0	0	12	8
Canada	0	0	0	36	Netherlands	24	0	12	0
Czech Rep.	8	0	0	0	New Zealand	15	0	0	0
Denmark	**6**	**30**	**0**	**0**	Norway	18	18	0	0
Finland	6	30	0	0	Poland	20	4	0	0
France	24	0	0	0	Portugal	36	0	0	0
Germany	0	0	18	18	Slovak Rep.	12	0	0	0
Greece	15	0	0	0	Spain	9	9	9	9
Hungary	20	0	0	0	Sweden	6	30	0	0
Iceland	10	10	0	0	**Switzerland**	**0**	**0**	**0**	**36**
Ireland	**24**	**0**	**0**	**0**	Turkey	4	0	0	0
Italy	8	0	16	0	U.Kingdom	30	6	0	0
Japan	0	4	0	1	United States	0	0	0	36

Source: own calculations.

Note: UC unitary–centralised; UD unitary–decentralised; FC federal–centralised; FD federal–decentralised. Countries selected for our case studies are in bold.

For our purpose, it is, however, fundamentally important that the cases selected for comparison are average with regard to those factors that additionally influence policy performance in the areas of regional development and infrastructure policy. The quantitative analysis tells us that, next to federalism and decentralisation, these are a country's surface area and its population. Further, French legal tradition, as measured by La Porta (1999), has been found to negatively impact policy performance. Hence a comparison of Switzerland, Austria, Denmark, and Ireland is adequate, as each unambiguously belongs to one of the distinct country classes (see Table 5.1) and is an average case with regard to the relevant control factors. The last of these is assessed by comparing the surface area and population size of each country to the overall distribution of the sample. While the cases analysed in the quantitative study display a minimum population size of 281,000 (Iceland) and a maximum one of 279,245,000 (USA), a minimum area of 2,586 (Luxembourg) and a maximum of 9,984,670 square kilometres (Canada), our cases prove to be moderately large and populated, as can be seen in Table 5.2.

In sum, our case studies compare processes of decision making and policy implementation in the areas of regional development policy and transport policy across a federal–decentralised country (Switzerland), a federal–centralised country (Austria), a unitary–decentralised country (Denmark), and a unitary–centralised country (Ireland). Additionally they test whether the effectiveness of budget constraints systematically differs between these countries. Consequently, the case studies are arranged alongside three theoretically ascribed institutional logics which generate diverging expectations regarding micro-level dynamics. The following section presents these theoretically derived expectations in more detail and provides a set of hypothetical statements that guide the qualitative analyses. Furthermore it specifies an operationalisation of our dependent variable – political performance – that builds upon the theoretical framework and is suitable for qualitative analysis.

Table 5.2: Characteristics of Switzerland, Austria, Denmark, and Ireland

	Switzerland	*Austria*	*Denmark*	*Ireland*
Subnational revenue as share of total revenue[a]	0.41	0.19	0.35	0.03
Subnational expenditure as share of total expenditure[a]	0.54	0.29	0.51	0.13
Inhabitants (million), total	7.18	8.02	5.36	3.61
Area (sq km)	41,290	83,858	43,094	70,182

Source: International Monetary Fund 2008, Central Intelligence Agency 2005.
[a] Data for all countries refer to 2006, except for Switzerland (2005).

5.2   Institutional logics and theoretical expectations

The set of hypothetical statements regarding behavioural patterns at the micro level is derived from the three institutional logics suggested by our model.

(1) Reform capability of federal and unitary arrangements. This refers to the incentives that federal or unitary structures set for the dynamics of political decision making in times of strong pressure for reform. In a nutshell, the model builds upon the prisoner's dilemma as a heuristic device for the behaviour of subnational actors in federal states and yields the following expectations: subnational actors in federal states will act in a weakly coordinated way[21] and develop individual policy proposals that reflect the subnational entities' preferences for resource maximisation. As the integration of subnational actors into negotiations at the national level is stronger in federal than in unitary countries, welfare-maximising policy reforms that reallocate between subnational entities are then *ceteris paribus* harder to achieve. With regard to national decision making in federal countries, we thus expect to detect a strong integration of subnational actors that adopt divergent policy positions leading to comparatively high transactions costs. As

---

21. Where subnational actors in federal states are highly coordinated horizontally and develop joint policy positions via co-decision, it is plausible to assume that policies reallocating budgets between the layers of government are hard to reform. In this case, the logic of negotiations between the central and the coordinated subnational level may either evolve into a zero-sum game that inhibits centralising (or decentralising) policies or set incentives for an externalisation of costs, e.g. to municipalities or future generations (Wachendorfer-Schmidt 2000).

a consequence, reform processes may either be protracted or yield only minor policy changes.

However, federalism is a broad concept and political scientists have tried to capture its core by a variety of indicators. These, in turn, display how multiple access as well as veto points may allow subnational actors in federal states to influence national policies. Our case studies will thus investigate in a qualitative fashion whether and to what extent subnational actors make use of such access and veto points in federal and in unitary countries. Moreover, they might contribute to the debate on whether such venues of influence are used interchangeably (Vatter 2005; Kaiser 1998).

The performance of decision-making processes is then mainly defined as the capacity to react properly to external changes and will be systematically compared according to the following operationalisation. In line with our theoretical arguments we analyse (a) whether subnational actors are involved in the respective decision-making process and what access or veto points they use (precondition for federalism's negative effect), (b) whether the transaction costs are high or low (duration of negotiations and level of conflict), (c) to what extent a change of status quo is achieved, (d) whether the new policy is judged an adequate reaction to the main challenges, and, finally, (e) to what extent it provides the structures and guidelines necessary for successful implementation of the policy.

(2) Decentralised and centralised policy implementation. The second institutional logic presupposes that patterns of policy implementation are influenced by the degree of decentralisation. According to our model, decentralised systems induce subnational actors to gather detailed knowledge of resource needs, political preferences, and the local costs of providing public services in order to adapt their provision of public goods to it. Facing mobile citizens who may exit in case of inefficiencies, subnational actors will, moreover, feel an incentive to invest in policy innovation as well as adopt best practices. Patterns of policy implementation are thus, in aggregate, expected to vary in decentralised countries in an efficiency-enhancing way. However, if policy implementation is mostly conducted by the central administration, difficulties may arise. The actors engaged may lack the local knowledge necessary to design efficient policies or be unable to realise an uneven supply of resources since this contradicts political perceptions of equal treatment. As seen in the variety of quantitative indicators used for operationalising decentralisation, the concept, in its most basic sense, builds upon the discretion of subnational actors. Full discretion requires sufficient own revenue sources (or unconditional block grants) that establish fiscal balance, as 'revenue independence is a central part of subnational government policy independence' (Weingast 2006: 28), personnel to engage in knowledge accumulation, and policy discretion. Revenue discretion is determined by both the fiscal system and the tax base available in the respective entity. Policy discretion is influenced by the degree of detailedness of the policy to be implemented as well as by administrative regulations.

However, patterns of vertical as well as horizontal interaction may influence discretionary leeway and thus the efficiency of implementation processes. Where subnational entities have insufficient own resources, the central level might severely encroach on their policy discretion by providing specific-purpose grants. Vertical influence might thus lead to a spatial harmonisation of policy implementation. On the other hand, subnational entities might face the need to horizontally coordinate policy implementation in order to internalise spillover effects. While their capacity to engage in horizontal coordination may vary depending on their administrative resources, the type as well as extent of coordination needed might differ between policy areas. To what extent the trade-off between an efficient variation of policies and necessary coordination across space impacts implementation patterns in varying policy areas is of specific interest with regard to the theory-modifying ambition of our case studies.

In accordance with the discussion above, we assess the performance of implementation processes throughout our case studies on the basis of (a) the extent to which subnational units possess financial and personnel resources (precondition 1 for decentralisation's positive effect), (b) the vertical fiscal balance of the respective implementation process (precondition 2 for decentralisation's positive effect), (c) the policy discretion given during implementation processes (precondition 3 for decentralisation's positive effect), (d) the degree of subnational variance arising from implementation processes, (e) the degree and adequacy of horizontal cooperation, and (f) an overall assessment of its efficiency in economic terms.

(3) Budgetary discipline of subnational units. The third institutional logic refers to differences of budget discipline between the four country types and emanates from the insight that decentralisation entails the danger of irresponsible fiscal behaviour on the part of subnational governments. Our case studies thus shed further light on processes of budgetary decision making and patterns of subnational indebtedness. The game-theoretical bailout model introduced in Chapter Two allows a clear derivation of causal mechanisms to be tested for. We assume that actors engaged in subnational budgetary processes take into account the perceived probability of a central level bailout, regulative mechanisms, and the incentives set by financial as well as electoral markets. Our model further expects that the extent to which these budget constraints apply varies depending on the country's territorial organisation. In unitary countries governments may strongly constrain the budgetary leeway of subnational units via regulative measures, thus impeding extensive debt financing. In federal but decentralised countries the central level may rely on market forces as well as electoral accountability to increase the cost of debt finance to a subnational entity. National governments in federal but centralised countries, however, face a dilemma. According to the bailout model presented in Chapter Two (Inman 2003), they will be too weak to put in force regulatory measures, but too engaged in subnational finance to let subnational entities freely interact with financial markets. Moreover, given their engagement, accountability becomes blurred and anticipated strategies of blame shifting increase central level costs of denying a bailout.

Our case studies aiming to detect dynamics of the bailout game will thus systematically compare whether (a) national governments in unitary states use mechanisms of hierarchical control in order to prevent subnational units from overspending, (b) subnational units in federal-decentralised states are subject to market pressures and thus refrain from overspending, (c) subnational units in federal countries with high fiscal imbalance tend to overspend their budget in anticipation of a central government's bailout. Alternatively, they might put pressure on the federal government to provide inefficient amounts of funding as compensation for not overspending.

Our case studies compare the validity of three theoretically derived institutional logics across four countries and two policy areas. The data required for qualitative inference alongside the indicators were generated by documentary analysis, interviews conducted with policy and country experts, and secondary literature.

The case studies are presented in the following way. Chapter Six seeks a deeper understanding of the dynamics of decision making (*federalism hypothesis*) and emphasises the comparison of reform dynamics in federal (Switzerland and Austria) and unitary countries (Ireland and Denmark). It starts by surveying the multilevel institutional settings that the four countries provide (6.1), then focuses on the opportunities these structures provide for subnational interests to impact national level policy negotiations (6.2). Having established this general foundation, we turn to detailed analyses of distinct reform processes in the area of regional development policies (6.3), followed by an evaluation of negotiations in the realm of transport policies (6.4). Section 6.5 subsumes the findings and additionally provides a comparative interpretation of the dynamics across the two policy areas.

Chapter Seven deals with the effects of decentralised and centralised patterns of resource allocation. It starts with an overview of general patterns of policy implementation and assesses the extent of discretion granted to subnational actors in Switzerland, Austria, Denmark, and Ireland (7.1). Before turning to a detailed analysis of implementation processes in both policy areas, it provides a systematic comparison of those factors that underlie subnational indebtedness in these countries (7.2). It thus sheds light on the third institutional logic and assesses the applicability of the bailout game (*HBC hypothesis*). The qualitative analysis of the second institutional logic (*decentralisation hypothesis*) is then to be found in Sections 7.3 to 7.5 focusing on implementation patterns in decentralised (Switzerland and Denmark) and centralised (Austria and Ireland) countries. Following the lines of Chapter Six, we first focus upon patterns of implementation of regional development policies (7.3), followed by analysis of the implementation of transport policies (7.4). Finally, Section 7.5 subsumes the findings regarding the effects of decentralisation and additionally provides a comparative assessment of the dynamics across the two policy areas.

chapter six | decision making in federal and unitary countries

This chapter provides a focused comparison of decision-making processes in federal and unitary countries in order to evaluate micro-level mechanisms underlying the negative impact of federalism upon policy performance found in our statistical analysis. It locates the comparison in two policy areas which we have classified as typical (regional development policy) and deviant (transport policy) cases based upon quantitative results.

Section 6.1 provides short country profiles that focus on the institutional underpinnings of multilevel politics in our four countries. As discussed in Section 5.1 the countries chosen for in-depth analysis vary systematically: Switzerland and Austria are classified as federal and Denmark and Ireland as unitary countries. We outline the institutional set-up underlying this classification for each of the countries in more detail. In line with our theoretical reasoning, Section 6.2 pays special attention to the extent of subnational involvement in national politics. It is only on the basis of such knowledge that a systematic and targeted comparison of policy-area-specific negotiation processes can evolve. We provide such a comparison for regional development policies in Section 6.3 and turn to transport policies in Section 6.4. We bring together our findings in Section 6.5, highlighting the dynamics across the two policy areas.

6.1   Multilevel country profiles

Let us turn to the federal countries first. Switzerland, where sovereignty constitutionally lies with the cantons, is undoubtedly federal. It is divided into 26 cantons (including six half-cantons) and 2,715 communes.[22] According to article 3 of the Swiss Constitution (*Bundesverfassung der Schweizerischen Eidgenossenschaft*, BV) sovereignty and all residual powers reside with the cantons. The realm of federal authorities is restricted to those tasks explicitly enumerated. Local autonomy is warranted by cantonal jurisdiction (art. 50.1, BV). Swiss cantons differ enormously with regard both to structural characteristics like population, area, cultural and linguistic differentiation, socioeconomic and geographical conditions[23] and also to central components of their political systems, such as their party systems, the number of municipalities, the degree of intracantonal decentralisation, administrative organisation, the extent and use of

---

22.   Given their small size, many Swiss communes are involved in processes of fusion. The website http://www.bfs.admin.ch/bfs/portal/de/index/infothek/nomenklaturen/blank/blank/gem_liste/03. html gives an overview of current developments.

23.   The homepage of the Swiss Statistical Office provides a comparative database. See http://www. bfs.admin.ch/bfs/portal/de/index/regionen/regionalportraets/comparator.html.

direct democratic instruments, and the degree of consociationalism (see Bochsler *et al.* 2004, Vatter 2002).

Regarding multilevel dynamics, cantonal interests are systematically integrated into 'nearly every stage of the policy-making process, either by influencing policy formulation, decision making or implementation' (Vatter 2005: 12). Thus these stages are heavily influenced by patterns of horizontal as well as vertical interaction. Note that policy processes in many areas are characterised by a functional division of tasks, so that decision making rests with the federal level but most policy implementation is carried out by cantons. This is the case in nearly all policy areas that ascribe exclusive decision-making competencies to the federal authorities and in those of concurrent jurisdiction. Our study will demonstrate that this mutual dependency of federal and cantonal authorities, which has been referred to as 'administrative federalism', is also the basis for interaction effects between the stages of policy formulation and implementation.

Turning to Austria, the federal character is also constitutionally fixed in article 2 (*Bundes-Verfassungsgesetz,* B-VG)[24], which states that Austria consists of nine federal states (*Länder*).[25] Additionally, within Austrian national territory there are 2,357 municipalities (*Gemeinden*)[26] in 81 districts (*Bezirke*).[27] However, Austrian federalism displays quite different characteristics from the Swiss version. Until the end of the era of 'grand coalitions' between Conservatives and Social Democrats, centralism was predominant. From 1964 onwards, the *Länder* have increasingly developed their own demands (Berchtold 1988). In 1974, the principle of 'co-operative federalism' was anchored in the constitution (Dachs 1996). Hence the competencies of federal and state levels of government are highly integrated. One can distinguish at least four different types of competence distribution.[28] (1) Decision making and implementation are federal competencies; (2) decision making is a federal, implementation a state competence; (3) framework legislation (*Grundsatzgesetzgebung)* is a federal, executive decision making (*Ausführungsgesetzgebung)* and implementation state competencies; (4) decision

---

24. Article 3 B-VG assigns veto power to the *Länder* on decisions regarding territorial changes at the state level, article 44 veto power on decisions regarding shifts of competencies between the levels of government.

25. Burgenland, Carinthia, Lower Austria, Upper Austria, Salzburg, Styria, Tyrol, Vorarlberg, and Vienna.

26. The Austrian municipalities are comparatively small (mean average approx. 3,500 inhabitants). Organisational features, like division of municipalities, frequency of elections or number of delegates in the municipal council (*Gemeinderat)*, are fixed by the respective *Land*. With the exception of *Statutarstädte* (Eisenstadt, Graz, Innsbruck, Klagenfurt, Krems, Linz, Rust, Salzburg, Steyr, St Pölten, Villach, Waidhofen an der Ybbs, Wels, Vienna, and Wiener Neustadt), the *Länder* are allowed to abolish, split up or merge municipalities.

27. The 81 districts are purely administrative units, relevant in some centralised policy areas (e.g. police) and for monitoring of local governments. Fifteen statutory towns (*Statutarstädte*) do not belong to a district but still have the same competencies. Vienna has a special status as municipality and state at the same time.

28. Articles 10–15 B-VG.

making and implementation are state competencies (Gamper 2000).

Although the constitution assigns a residual competence to the *Länder*, the regional level is relatively weak, especially for a formally federal country. Exclusive competencies of the states (type 4) are rare.[29] Legally, most of the competencies belong to the first type (Thorlakson 2003). In many of these tasks,[30] notwithstanding the federal right to implement, *Länder* are incorporated into the implementation by indirect federal administration (*mittelbare Bundesverwaltung*). In these cases, the *Länder* administration headed by the state head of government (*Landeshauptmann*) is subordinated to the relevant national ministry (Fallend 2005). Another Austrian particularity is the *Privatwirtschaftsverwaltung* that allows private, non-governmental (although government-financed) agencies to perform tasks beyond the limits of decision-making competencies of the financing governmental level (Gamper 2000).[31]

Austrian federalism has frequently been criticised. Bußjäger calls it 'sclerotic' (Bußjäger 2002). *Länder* are characterised as more 'administrative subunits [...] rather than retaining their position as constituent members of a federal union' (Erk 2004). Watts describes Austrian federalism as 'one of the most centralised with the constituent units often serving mainly as "agents" and "subordinates" of the federal government' (1999: 25). The residual competence clause in the constitution is considered as 'rather symbolic' (Fallend 2005: 1028). The felt irrelevance of the federal structure is partly also provoked by the *Länder* themselves, who frequently do not use their competencies to the full extent. They make no use of their residual competence for new policy areas (Erk 2004)[32] and have rejected offers of more competencies by the federal state (interview Fallend).

Despite widely acknowledged weaknesses, recent attempts to initiate a reform of Austrian federalism failed (Bußjäger 2002, Bußjäger 2006, Bußjäger *et al.* 2005).[33] Some authors see a clear trend to even more centralisation (Gamper 2000, Erk 2004). Austria can reasonably be depicted as 'a unitarian federal state or a federal state with centralistic traits' (Dachs 2002: 32).[34]

The two federal countries chosen for in-depth analyses thus vary considerably

---

29. Only in construction law, regional planning, tourism, nature conservation, hunting, agriculture, forestry, sports, and childcare (Fallend 2005; Watts 1999) are the *Länder* completely independent from the federal government.

30. For instance, in the areas of transport, water, and business law.

31. In this way, the state governments manage to run facilities like hospitals or finance regional development measures, even though these are federal competencies. On the other hand, the federal level uses the same trick for its own purposes (Fallend 2005).

32. This does not hold for every single case: when Lower Austria introduced a new tax on mobile phone poles (*Niederösterreichisches Sendeanlagenabgabengesetz*), the federal level pressured the *Land* to waive it.

33. The last two initiatives were the *Perchtoldsdorfer Paktum* of 1992 and the *Österreich-Konvent* 2003.

34. 'dass man heute [...] von einem unitarischen Bundesstaat bzw. einem Bundesstaat mit zentralistischen Zügen sprechen kann', translation by authors.

with regard to the extent of decision-making competencies constitutionally granted to as well as *de facto* executed by the subnational level. Notwithstanding these contrasts, our theoretical argument leads us to expect both countries to display similar dynamics of negotiating policy reform at the national level when compared to unitary countries. Accordingly, the next section outlines general characteristics of national decision-making processes with a special focus upon the extent to which subnational actors are integrated, establishing the basis for the policy-area-specific case studies we aim for. First, however, the multilevel set-up of our two unitary countries needs to be introduced.

Denmark's territorial state organisation is based on the constitution of 1953 which established a parliamentary monarchy, with Queen Margrethe II as formal head of state. The unicameral parliament,[35] the *Folketing,* is elected every four years by means of a proportional representation system. Below the national level, there is a two-tier structure of subnational authorities. From 1970 to 2006, there existed fourteen counties (*Amter*) and 275 municipalities (*Kommuner*).[36] Effective from 1st January 2007, the Local Government Reform Act reduced the then 270 municipalities to 98. The *Amter* were abolished and replaced by five regions: Jutland was split up horizontally, the northern and central parts forming two regions (*Nordjylland, Midtjylland*) and the southern part combined with Funen Island forming the new region of Southern Denmark (*Syddanmark*); while Zealand was divided into a capital region (*Hovedstaden*) and the rest of the island (*Sjaelland*).

Article 82 of the Danish constitution guarantees the self-government of the municipalities 'under State supervision'. The national government is allowed to assign or withdraw subnational governments' tasks. All competencies remain at the national level as long as they are not shifted down to subnational levels. In contrast to other Scandinavian countries the municipal competencies have never been fixed in a written statute (Page 1991). According to our criteria, then, Denmark clearly represents a unitary state.

A similar assessment is valid for the Irish case. Ireland is a unitary state and the core decision-making competencies in all policy areas rest at the national level. Parliament's[37] unique role in law making is constitutionally guaranteed: 'no other legislative authority has power to make laws for the State' (article 15.2.1 of the Constitution of Ireland). There is, however, a long-standing tradition of local government (Haslam 2003) whose main responsibility – next to the democratic representation of local interests – is the provision of public services in eight tightly restricted policy areas. The functions of Irish local authorities are thus located

---

35. The second chamber of parliament, the *Landsting*, was abolished in 1953.

36. The merger of the five municipalities on the island of Bornholm into a 'regional municipality' in 2003 reduced the total to 271. In 2006, the founding of the second regional municipality on the island of Ærø reduced the number of municipalities to 270. The cities of Copenhagen and Frederiksberg were simultaneously municipalities and counties.

37. The *Oireachtas* is a bicameral legislature consisting of the first chamber (*Dáil Éireann*) and the second chamber (*Seanad Éireann*).

on the dimension of decentralisation. The same holds for Irish regional bodies, even though their remit is mainly restricted to monitoring the implementation of EU funding policies. Contemporary Ireland is divided into two Regional Assemblies (RAss): Southern and Eastern Regional Assembly (SE) and Border, Midlands and Western Regional Assembly (BMW). In addition there are eight Regional Authorities (RAuth),[38] twenty-nine counties and five cities (C/C),[39] and, finally, 80 local government towns.[40] The last two categories are referred to below as local authorities. Even though the role of local government was eventually constitutionally recognised in 1999, it is important to note that all local competencies are subject to assignment by national law or statute, most notably a number of Local Government Acts.[41] The national level can thus at any time reduce local government's remit to a minimum.

Each of these four countries exhibits some form of administrative territorial substructure; however, the clear distinctions between Switzerland and Austria on the one hand and Ireland and Denmark on the other arise from the fact that subnational entities possess constitutionally guaranteed decision-making competencies in the first two cases but not the latter ones. Thus the concept of federalism successfully distinguishes the two pairs. According to our line of argument, we assume that such characteristics are decisive for quite general patterns of decision making, as we expect a federal constitution to systematically accompany increased opportunities for subnational actors to impact or even block processes of national decision making. The following section thus delineates the extent to which subnational interests play a role in national decision making. Again, we will focus upon the federal cases first and turn to the unitary ones afterwards.

---

38. Border; Dublin; Mid East; Midlands; Mid West; South East; South West; West.

39. 26 historical counties, 2 counties in Tipperary, 3 counties in Dublin. The five cities are Cork, Dublin, Galway, Limerick, and Waterford. The terminology regarding subnational government structures in Ireland has been changed a number of times in the last century. We use the terms that were established by the Local Government Act 2001 (Oireachtas 2001). For a guide to former terminology, see O'Sullivan (2003).

40. The functions of the local government towns vary between C/C but are in most cases limited to the adoption of statutory orders and, more generally, the representation of local interests. The borough councils Clonmel, Drogheda, Kilkenny, Sligo and Wexford constitute an exception and exercise a number of functions in the areas of housing, roads and development control.

41. Most recently, the Local Government (Business Improvement Districts) Act 2006 (Oireachtas 2006), the Local Government (No. 2) Act 2003 (Oireachtas 2003), and the Local Government Act 2001 (Oireachtas 2001). All Government Acts can be accessed online at http://www.Irishstatute-book.ie/acts.html.

6.2   Subnational interests and national decision making

Patterns of national decision making in Switzerland are markedly influenced by the overall consensual character of its institutional configuration. The Swiss political system has been characterised as a paradigmatic case of consensus democracy and thus a political system that 'tries to share, disperse and limit power in a variety of ways' (Lijphart 1999: 2). The alternatively used term 'negotiation democracy' (Kaiser 1997: 434) indicates that processes of national decision making in Switzerland are marked by extensive bargaining. The system's inclusiveness, which is enforced by the incentives of direct democracy, is *inter alia* reflected in the multiparty composition of the Federal Council (*Bundesrat*) as well as a high impact of organised interests on policy formulation. Despite recent changes – the

> decreasing fragmentation and increasing polarisation in the party system [...] the rise of the SVP [*Schweizerische Volkspartei*], acting in the classic oppositional style as the most powerful party; the government acting less and less like a cooperative body; and [...] the increasingly pluralistic interest group system (Vatter 2008: 31–2)

– Switzerland is still considered a consensus democracy, though more an average than an extreme type.[42] Besides government parties and interest groups, federal agencies as well as experts influence policy formulation (Sager and Rüefli 2005).

Cantonal interests are highly integrated into the stages of policy formulation and decision making, though they hold bargaining rather than veto power. Their influence is strongly formative as 'voice' during the pre-parliamentary process,[43] that is, in extra-parliamentary expert commissions and the formal consultation procedure (Braun 2003, Linder and Vatter 2001; Vatter 2005).[44] During the consultation procedure, cantonal statements often exhibit considerable variance in content (Sager and Steffen 2006) and individual cantons' influence varies according to their resources, expertise, and integration into the implementation process. Whereas larger cantons 'in some cases come to play a crucial role in the pre-parliamentary process' (Linder and Vatter 2001: 103, see also Sager and Rüefli 2005, Vatter 2005), small and structurally weak cantons are dependent on cooperation. They often rely on interest groups' opinions (Linder and Vatter 2001) or adopt the position of a larger canton (Armingeon 2000: 123).

---

42. Vatter's re-analysis of the Swiss case compares the period 1997–2007 to 1945–1996 and shows that Swiss democracy exhibits slightly stronger majoritarian features than before. However, these changes are located on the executive-parties dimension and do not affect the federal–unitary dimension of Lijphart's conceptual map (Vatter 2008; Lijphart 1999).

43. Other options for active cantonal participation in decision-making processes emerge from the systematic representation of cantons inside the Federal Council, the rarely used cantonal initiative, and the extraordinary summoning of parliament available to at least five cantons which, however, has never, to date, been used (see Wälti 1996).

44. Though cantons are integrated into almost all consultation procedures, their actual participatory power has been assessed as weak in comparison to interest groups or federal agencies (see Sager and Steffen 2006).

Compared to other federal systems like Canada, the United States or Spain, coordination between cantons is highly institutionalised and integrated (Bolleyer 2006b), but less so than in Germany (Vatter 2005: 10). Nonetheless, two mechanisms of intercantonal cooperation, concordats[45] and organisations/conferences, have gained importance over time whereas instruments of individual representation have lost impact (Wälti 1996: 18–9; Vatter 2005: 12–3). Intercantonal organisations/ conferences are bodies mainly engaged in developing joint policy positions and compiling coordinated problem definitions. They often fulfil a consultative role in decision-making processes (Wälti 1996; Bochsler *et al.* 2004; Linder and Vatter 2001: 104–5) and have increased in importance with the establishment of the Conference of Cantonal Prime Ministers (*Kantonale Ministerkonferenz*) in 1993. Regional conferences of cantonal governments also play an influential role, e.g. the *Zentralschweizer Regierungskonferenz* (Freiburghaus and Vital 2003). However, the scope of influence of intercantonal conferences is systematically constrained. They yield only non-binding recommendations as they lack the right of co-decision over common tasks[46] and even though these might be considered as 'rather effective instruments to coordinate policy' (Bolleyer 2006b: 493), it remains to be seen within our case studies whether cantons develop and maintain a joint policy position during decision-making processes.

The stage of actual decision making is characterised by the equal footing of the National Council and the Council of the States (article 148, BV); each bill has to pass both houses. The Council of the States, whose members are directly elected and have a free mandate (article 161, BV), is thus formally vested with veto power. However, State Councillors do not necessarily represent genuine territorial interests to a larger extent than national councillors. Both Councils vote for federal interests, but State Councillors tend to incline more towards conservative rural interests (Linder and Vatter 2001: 99–100) which is *inter alia* attributable to the over-representation of rural cantons (Vatter 2005). The State Council thus effectively represents party interests as well as those of the cantonal electorate[47] rather than cantonal governments' interests.[48] An effective cantonal veto position

---

45. Concordats are mainly relevant for horizontal coordination in implementation matters.

46. In light of the new financial equalisation system (see Section 7.1), this assessment has to be slightly modified as it establishes two new instruments of obligatory cantonal cooperation in some areas of cantonal jurisdiction (cantonal universities, hospitals, cultural facilities of transregional relevance, crime control, and transport in conglomerations). A majority of cantons (18 or 21) can ask the federal authorities to declare intercantonal agreements binding for all (*Allgemeinverbindlichkeitserklärung*). A similar mechanism entails the obligation of individual cantons to enter into regional contracts (*Beteiligungspflicht*). These mechanisms were established to ensure an equalisation of financial burdens and avoid free-riding. See http://www.efv.admin.ch/d/dokumentation/downloads/themen/finanzausgleich/faktenblaetter/11-NFA_Faktenblatt_11_IKZ_d. pdf for details.

47. These are tied together by a strongly decentralised party system (Braun 2003).

48. The connection between State Councillors and the respective cantonal government is further weakened as deliberations within parliamentary commissions are confidential. Possibilities for cantonal executives to participate directly in central level decision-making processes have been

is vested in the instruments of direct democracy. First, a group of eight cantons can call for a popular referendum (*Kantonsreferendum*) concerning any legislative reform. In fact this has only been used once, over tax reform in 2004, subsequently attracting renewed attention (Fischer 2006). Second, constitutional amendments require a majority of both the voting citizens in the federation and the voters in a majority of the cantons (*Doppelmehr*). Empirically, the *Doppelmehr* has benefited the interests of the 'small and medium-sized, generally catholic and conservative cantons in the German-speaking parts' (Vatter 2005: 6).

National decision making in Switzerland is further influenced by the fact that Swiss cantons are described as having an 'exit' or 'veto' option via policy implementation (Wälti 1996: 10; Armingeon: 122; Braun 2003: 70–1). Policy implementation may, in cases of incongruent preferences, vary significantly across cantons and individual cantons may even completely refuse to implement (Braun 2003: 76–7). The effects of this discretion on decision making[49] are, however, ambiguous. Alongside increasing flexibility in decision-making processes (Wälti and Bullinger 2000: 81–2), inconsistent policy implementation causes huge uncertainties and a reduction in the federal government's governance capacity (Braun 2003; Linder and Vatter 2001; Vatter 2005). Federal laws are often specified as framework legislation, leaving plenty of discretion in executive decision making[50] as well as administrative action to the cantons (Fleiner 2002: 116–7; Thorlakson 2003). They 'are often formulated in a less coercive or ambiguous way' (Wälti 1996: 10), rely on 'incentive rather than regulatory measures' (Wälti and Bullinger 2000: 102), and set minimal standards via negative coordination. Overall, our literature review suggests that patterns of Swiss decision making are markedly influenced by the cantons' strong position, arising from the interplay of institutionally granted access, veto opportunities and their extensive administrative and political resources.

Turning to Austria, the first thing to note is that its national decision-making characteristics are also influenced by consensual practices. Austria is a parliamentary political system with proportional representation (PR); within the universe of real-world PR systems, it is 'closer to the end of full proportionality' (Müller 2005: 397). Party politics dominate the Austrian political arena (Obinger 2002). For a long time, the Austrian party system was dominated by the two largest political parties: the Austrian People's Party (*Österreichische Volkspartei*, ÖVP) and the Social Democratic Party of Austria (*Sozialdemokratische Partei Österreichs*, SPÖ).[51] Decision making in Austria is strongly influenced by the

---

partly strengthened by the Constitutional Reform of 2000. For details see Fleiner (2002).

49. Its impact on the efficiency of policy implementation will be scrutinised in Chapter Seven.

50. The Swiss process of policy making has for this reason been described as including not only one but 27 stages of decision making (Sager and Rüefli 2005).

51. In 1945–66, 1986–2000, and from 2007 on, a so-called 'grand' coalition of both parties governed the country, in 1966–70 (ÖVP) and 1970–1986 (SPÖ) single-party governments were in charge. Only in 1983–6 and 2000–7 did another party – the right-wing Austrian Freedom Party (*Frei-heitliche Partei Österreichs*, FPÖ), later the Alliance for the Future of Austria (*Bündnis Zukunft*

need for consensual agreements between them. Additionally, in a neocorporatist arrangement, the so-called social partners[52] are involved in political decision making relating to economic and social policies. The predominance of consociationalist practices developed largely because of the high societal fragmentation that had its origins in the first half of the twentieth century. In times of 'small' coalitions (such as the ÖVP/FPÖ and ÖVP/BZÖ coalitions 2000–7) the influence of the social partners on the decision-making process is blurred (Pelinka 2008).

The process of legislative decision making is formally divided into a 'parliamentary' and a 'pre-parliamentary' stage. The highly formalised pre-parliamentary phase includes law formulation by the relevant federal ministry and its administration, as well as statements by other ministries (particularly the Ministry of Finance), all *Länder* and the social partners within the appraisal proceeding (*Begutachtungsverfahren*).[53] Conflicts are dealt with at the levels of government heads, ministers, and administration and it is here that subnational influence on national decision making is exerted. The formal Second Chamber, the *Bundesrat*, is not involved in the pre-parliamentary process (Weber 1992). The results of these proceedings are 'more or less' (Pelinka 1997: 488)[54] taken into account when drafting a bill and passing it to cabinet (*Ministerrat*). During the parliamentary process, the bill is discussed in committees and the plenum and subsequently amended. Generally speaking, approval of the bill is highly likely, given strong party discipline and the consensual tradition within the political arena. Next the *Bundesrat* deals with the bill. Then it is formally enacted by the signatures of the president, the chancellor, and the appropriate minister (Pelinka 1997).

Subnational interests in Austria come into play through both formal and informal institutions. Let us first turn to the (rather weak) formal institutions (members of Parliament (MPs), the *Bundesrat*, formal agreements) and then deal with informal channels of influence, like the Conference of State Heads of Governments (*Landeshauptleutekonferenz,* LHLK) which regularly coordinates the *Länder*'s position and communicates it via party channels.

The 183 seats of the *Nationalrat* are distributed among the nine *Länder* and 43 regional districts. Seats are assigned according to a three-tier system on the regional, state, and federal level. Due to strong parties and quite large electoral districts, regional representation through national MPs is not assured. However,

---

Österreich, BZÖ) – form part of the governing coalition.

52. The social partnership (*Sozialpartnerschaft*) includes the Austrian Federal Economic Chamber (*Wirtschaftskammer Österreichs*, WKÖ), the Austrian Trade Union Federation (*Österreichischer Gewerkschaftsbund*, ÖGB) and the Federal Workers' Chamber (*Bundesarbeiterkammer,* BAK), representing the employees' interests. The presidential conference of the Farmers Unions (*Land-wirtschaftskammern*) also takes part.

53. The federal government can influence the extent and length of the appraisal proceeding. More majoritarian-style 'small' coalitions tend to set tighter deadlines for the proceedings (Pelinka 2008).

54. 'Die Ergebnisse des Begutachtungsverfahrens werden dann [...] mehr oder weniger berücksich-tigt', translation by authors.

office accumulation is possible: in 1997, 42 of 183 national MPs still stuck to their local office (Aigner *et al.* 2001). This provides an additional possibility of representing interests at a higher level of government.[55]

The *Bundesrat* consists of delegates elected proportionally by the state parliaments just after their election, for the duration of the legislative term.[56] The chamber decides by absolute majority or, in cases when a reduction of state competencies is at issue, with a two-thirds majority. Only in these cases is the affirmation of the *Bundesrat* obligatory. In all other cases, its veto power is suspensive and can be overridden by the *Nationalrat* (*Beharrungsbeschluss*). The *Bundesrat* is thus a weak second chamber (Lijphart 1999; Fallend 2000; Tsebelis and Money 1997). Its competencies and composition hinder an effective representation of regional interests at the national level (Dachs 1996), as does its lack of involvement in the pre-parliamentary formulation process of bills. It mostly agrees with the *Nationalrat* (Pelinka 2008),[57] not least because of the extent to which it is dominated by party interests (Gamper 2000; Erk 2004).[58]

Parties in the Austrian system are powerful and also provide channels for regional interests. Their internal organisation is democratic and federally structured; the regional party associations enjoy a high degree of autonomy (Fallend 2005).[59] As the two major parties frequently form grand coalitions and in most *Länder* a proportionally composed all-party government is obligatory,[60] there are several direct relations between core executives at *Land* and federal level. This holds especially for the ÖVP, being traditionally strong in the Austrian provinces. The *Länder* are therefore expected to have greater influence on federal politics when the ÖVP forms part of federal government (Bußjäger 2007).

---

55. At the subnational level, office accumulation is more common. In 1997 almost 50 per cent of *Länder* parliamentarians in Upper Austria, Styria, and Vorarlberg also held offices at the local level (Wolfgruber 1997).

56. The number of delegates varies between three and twelve, depending on the size of the state's population (article 34.2 B-VG). At present, Burgenland and Vorarlberg send three, Salzburg and Carinthia four, Tyrol five, Styria nine, Vienna and Upper Austria eleven and Lower Austria twelve delegates to the *Bundesrat*.

57. Between 1945 and 2002, the *Bundesrat* vetoed only 111 (1.75 per cent) of a total of 6,337 bills. In only eleven cases (0.17 per cent) did the veto bring about a change in the original proposal (Fallend 2005, authors' calculations).

58. This is also symbolised by the seating plan of the *Bundesrat*: delegates are placed not by state but by party.

59. The most influential regional party branches are the Lower Austrian one within the ÖVP and the SPÖ's Viennese branch (Dachs 2003).

60. Proportional governments are still required in Lower Austria, Upper Austria, Styria, Carinthia, Burgenland, and in all Austrian municipalities. Until 1999, the governments of Tyrol and Salzburg were also formed proportionally. In Vorarlberg, there is no legal obligation, but *de facto* an oversized coalition of ÖVP and FPÖ governs the state. In Vienna, there is a division between 'governing' and 'non-governing' (*amtsführende* and *nicht amtsführende*) *Stadträte*. This disputed rule leads *de facto* to a coalition government facing an opposition, which is paradoxically integrated into the local executive.

Despite the strong consociationalism in Austrian political life in general, associations play only a minor role in the intergovernmental relations between national and state levels. This holds both for the members of the social partnership and for the local government associations (*Österreichischer Städtebund* and *Österreichischer Gemeindebund*). The latter take part in the fiscal equalisation negotiations and have a right to be consulted over municipally relevant law proposals. This stems from the newly established consultation mechanism (*Konsultationsmechanismus*), granting *Länder* and municipalities veto power if national decisions affect them financially (Pernthaler and Wegschneider 2000; Rosner 2000; Fallend 2001; Bußjäger *et al.* 2005). Sometimes authors refer to the influence of the *Länder* administrations on the decision-making process, deriving from the federal obligation to leave policy implementation to the *Länder* within *indirect federal administration* (Bußjäger 2007). The only legal instruments for vertical and horizontal cooperation provided by the constitution are agreements according to article 15a B-VG. These 'classical instruments' are well established and effective when it comes to long-term agreements, but described as slow and clumsy (Bußjäger 2007: 92–3).

Since the formal instruments of influence over national-level policy making, especially the *Bundesrat*, are ineffective, over the years informal arrangements have taken over relevant coordination functions (Weber 1992). The most important one for the representation of regional interests at the national level is the *Landeshauptleutekonferenz* (LHLK) (Erk 2004). It basically consists of the nine state heads of government (*Landeshauptleute*) and decides by unanimity, either in regular meetings or through so-called *Umlaufbeschlüsse* (Rosner 2000: 24).

The *Landeshauptleute* have a crucial position in the administrative process: as heads of the state governments, they have control over their *Land*'s administration. They are generally also heavyweights within their *Land* party branch. Being democratically elected representatives, they can draw on high regional legitimacy and privileged access to regional media (Pelinka 2008) for the formulation of their interests at the national level. All these factors contribute to their strong position and, hence, the strength of the LHLK in national decision making. Its extent varies depending on the political situation, but in general a virtual veto power is assigned to the conference (Bußjäger 2007). The LHLK along with other conferences[61] is described as '*the* vital element of Austrian cooperative federalism' (Weber 1992: 414, emphasis in original).[62]

---

61. The *Landeshauptleute* are from time to time substituted by their *Landesamtsdirektoren* (state chiefs of staff) or *Landeshauptmannstellvertreter* (deputy state prime ministers). The chair of the LHLK changes every six months, the LHLK meets at least twice a year and is organised by the Liaison Office of the *Länder (Verbindungsstelle der Bundesländer)*. Other important conferences are the *Landesamtsdirektorenkonferenz* (Conference of the State Chiefs of Staff, prepares meeting of the LHLK and is responsible for administrative coordination) and the *Referentenkonferenzen*, of which the *Finanzreferentenkonferenz* (prepares the fiscal equalisation negotiations with the federal finance minister) is the most relevant.

62. '*das lebendige Element des kooperativen Föderalismus in Österreich*', translation by authors.

Internal coordination of LHLK is fair, as unanimity is the precondition for being heard at the federal level. The unanimity needed for a formal decision makes the settlement in the presence of diverging interests difficult at first glance, but also promotes the LHLK's internal coherence. It has been identified as the 'glue' sticking the *Länder* together (Rosner 2000: 30) and thereby assuring a predominance of state interests over party interests (Fallend 2003). Although the formal decisions are legally non-binding, they are – as the result of the consensual position of all state governments – still a trump card up the *Länder*'s sleeve, which is normally brought onto the national agenda through the internal party organisation. However, the LHLK's influence is obstructive rather than formative. Bußjäger assigns it a blocking capacity (Bußjäger 2007: 85).[63] The common position of the *Länder* is softened, when it comes to financial issues, for example in negotiations on fiscal equalisation. Here, the rich *Länder* (Vienna, Upper Austria, Vorarlberg) are frequently opposed to the poorer ones (Carinthia, Styria, Burgenland). In some cases, the federal government managed to break the *Länder* phalanx by offering generous co-financing (Fallend 2005).[64] It seems that the individual *Länder* prefer additional resources to a common strategy – which fits with our theoretical model of a prisoner's dilemma in *Länder* coordination.

In sum, subnational influence on national decision making is stronger than the formal competencies of the *Länder* and especially of the *Bundesrat* would suggest. The *Landeshauptleute* have an important role in Austrian politics due to their strong position within their *Land*, within their party and within public administration. They exert their influence mainly through the *Landeshauptleutekonferenz*, which has considerable impact on national decisions. The *de facto* veto power of the LHLK, the predominance of 'grand coalitions' and the resulting coercion towards consensual agreements lead to a specific problem-solving strategy: 'muddling through [*durchwursteln*] attained the valor of a pragmatic method of conflict resolution and crisis management. Backroom deals in para-public institutions came to be regarded as acts of statemanship' (Markovitz 1996: 16).

Both federal countries, then, display significant representation of regional-level interests in national-level decision-making processes. Although it is not necessarily formal institutions driving such impact, although points of access differ between Switzerland and Austria, and although various access and veto points may be used interchangeably, one important insight is that both federal countries display frequent and lasting interaction between regionally defined interests and the federal level. To comparatively assess the importance of this characteristic, we now turn to an evaluation of patterns of decision making in Denmark and Ireland. However, given the unitary character of these countries, we do not expect multilevel negotiations between regional entities and the national level to be

---

63. 'Blockadefunktion', translation by authors.

64. The close personal relationship between Chancellor Kreisky (SPÖ) and the Tyrolean Lande-shauptmann Wallnhöfer led to intense federal infrastructure investments in return for substantial co-financing by Tyrol. This precedent was the starting point for a more and more common pattern of state co-financing of federal tasks, as for example motorway construction since the 1970s.

highly formalised. Accordingly, it is appropriate to further broaden the enquiry and explore whether the systematic impact of regional or local interests shapes negotiations at the national level in unitary countries. The following sections on decision making in Denmark and Ireland thus explicitly scrutinise those bodies that might serve as building blocks for the formation of a regional political interest and furthermore shed light on the role of local government associations.

Turning to the Danish case first, it is clear that the typical dynamics of national decision making differ markedly from the federal ones described above. The Danish constitution states that legislative power is exercised jointly by the government and the parliament. Constitutional amendments and authority transfers to international bodies have to be approved by referendum. In addition to laws, ministers have legislative powers through statutory orders. The ministers' right to license these statutory orders must be according to law. In general, national ministers have great independence within their departments and neither other ministers nor the prime minister – whose role therefore can be described as *primus inter pares* – are in a position to interfere in their portfolio (Nannestad 2008).

Complex reforms are often tackled by expert commissions appointed by the relevant minister. The interest groups affected are also frequently involved in these commissions. Generally, Danish politics is structured by corporatist agreements. After 1973, when the number of parties represented in parliament doubled,[65] minority governments became the rule rather than the exception. This development forced the government to be more flexible with regard to negotiations in parliament and also reduced the influence of public administration and interest groups. Legislative acts, like the annual budgeting law, are now regularly part of larger package deals with the opposition parties (Nannestad 2008). Denmark has become 'less unitary and more pluralist [...] As a consequence, corporatist negotiations get complicated' (Christiansen and Rommetvedt 1999: 216). The Conservative government in office until 2011 has partly broken with this negotiation style – having a *de facto* majority in parliament,[66] it is less interested in brokering deals with lobby groups and opposition parties and exercises a more majoritarian politics style (interview Pallesen, Nannestad 2008).

As there is no second chamber in Denmark, subnational interests are promoted at national level either through members of the *Folketing* or through regional and local government associations. The Danish electoral system induces a relatively strong interrelation between the individual representative and the local electorate.

---

65. From the 1971 to the 1973 elections, the effective number of parties (Laakso and Taagepera 1979) in parliament almost doubled from 3.93 (a value relatively stable for the entire period from 1913 to 1970) to 6.85. Since the 1973 election, never fewer than seven parties have held seats in the *Folketing* (effective number of parties: 4.94) (authors' calculations based on Scocozza and Jensen 2005).

66. The government of Lars Løkke Rasmussen consisting of his Liberal Party (*Venstre*) and the Conservative Party (*Det Konservative Folkeparti*) has regularly been supported by the right-wing Danish People's Party (*Dansk Folkeparti*) in parliament. The three parties together hold a majority in the *Folketing*.

National elections take place every four years. 135 of the 175 Danish MPs[67] are elected in multi-member constituencies; the remaining 40 seats are compensatory and are disseminated by a multi-stage process in order to ensure proportional representation of parties and regions in the parliament (for details see Elklit 2005). Regional interests, notwithstanding high party discipline, are part of the MPs' rationale. This is assured by a complex system of personal voting[68] which invests local party branches with strong influence on their respective representatives (Blom-Hansen 1999a). In contrast, the degree of office accumulation is quite low by international comparison (Page 1991).[69] Additionally, regional interests are reflected through the Danish party system. The Liberal Party is traditionally strong in rural areas, whereas Conservatives and Social Democrats find their electorate largely in urban regions. The party system hence represents the main cleavage gaping between Jutland and the Greater Copenhagen area. Lobbyism and pork-barrel politics have increased in the last decades (Christiansen and Rommetvedt 1999), but have not become crucial factors in Danish politics (Kristinsson 1996).

Apart from this individual representation of local areas,[70] the Danish Local Government Association (*Kommunernes Landsforening*, KL) organises horizontally coordinated representation of municipalities in the national decision-making process. Today, all municipalities are members of the KL.[71] It is democratically structured: after every local government election, all newly elected mayors plus several members of the local councils (in order to reflect the relative party strength indicated by the election results) meet to elect an executive committee. Subsequently, the committee elects a chair. In all three instances, the relevant political parties are represented proportionally based on the local government election results (www.kl.dk).[72] Within the KL, actors follow the

---

67. The 179 seats in parliament are completed by two delegates each from Greenland and the Faroe Islands.

68. Denmark is divided into three electoral regions, seventeen multi-member constituencies, and 103 nomination districts. The voter has to choose between a party or a personal vote. Based on all votes, the mandates are assigned to the different parties. Afterwards, the mandates are assigned to individual candidates, either by party lists (on constituency level) or – if the candidate passed a certain threshold – by personal votes on nomination-district level. For a more detailed description, see www.folketinget.dk/BAGGRUND/00000048/00232623.htm.

69. 44 per cent of MPs and 26 per cent of national ministers had come from the local level during the 1980s.

70. Denmark's local government was traditionally run by the fifteen county governors (*Statsamts-mand*) and their administrations (*Statsamter*) (OECD 1997, Bjorna and Jenssen 2006). In 2004, they were merged into five new state county administrations (*Statsforvaltninger*) with a state county prefect (*director*) at the top (www.statsforvaltning.dk). The county governors also perceived their role as representatives of regional interests at the national level (Bogason 1987) and must therefore be included as a further channel of subnational interest representation.

71. Prior to 2005, only the cities of Copenhagen and Frederiksberg had not been members of the organisation.

72. The chairman normally either belongs to the Social Democrat or the Liberal Party. As of 2008, the executive committee consisted of seven Social Democrats, five Liberals, two Conservatives,

interests of their local entities (interview Mouritzen). The KL can only take formal decisions unanimously.

In almost all cases the KL is involved in the national decision-making process at an early stage (Lidström 2001), regardless of the topic (interview Blom-Hansen). The KL represents local interests on the national level and plays a decisive role in the annual budget negotiations with the Ministry of Finance (see Chapter 7.2.1).[73] The strength of the KL in bargaining situations depends mainly on its internal coherence and its strategic position in the political game. It is therefore important to highlight fields of potential conflict among municipalities. As Blom-Hansen's (2002) investigation showed, the KL's internal coherence is quite high, except on redistributive issues: 'the more redistributive among municipalities the policy areas are, the weaker the association is' (interview Blom-Hansen). Potentially conflictual are the relations between the capital region and Jutland municipalities and among economically diverging local governments. A minority government increases the KL's influence: minority governments have historically been more likely than majority governments to negotiate with the KL. This is the result of a circumventing strategy by the national government: rather than taking on the national opposition, it frequently negotiates an agreement with the KL and hence with local representatives of all parties. The national opposition is then confronted with the alternatives of voting for the agreement or opposing it against the wishes of their local fellow party members (Blom-Hansen 1999a, interview Pallesen).

Since the Local Government Reform of 2007, the new municipalities have become more homogeneous and their relations over economic issues are possibly less conflictual. However, there have been several occasions on which a small group of large municipalities (Aarhus, Aalborg, Vejle, Odense, among others) circumvented both the KL and the regional level in order to negotiate directly with the national government (Lidström 2001). If this strategy became the rule rather than the exception, the role of the KL would be weakened; the experts we interviewed disagree on the likelihood of such a scenario.

On the regional level, there is an organisation similar to the KL: the former counties were organised in the *Amtsradsforeningen*, while the consortium of the new regions constitutes the association *Danske Regioner* (www.regioner. dk). However, these organisations have always been less important than the KL and their relevance has decreased even more since 2007 because of the reduced competencies of the regional level.

So processes of decision making in Denmark are mainly shaped by national-

---

and one member each of the Social Liberal, the Socialist People's and the Danish People's Party. The Liberal chairman was complemented by three Social Democrat and one Social Liberal vice-chairmen.

73. In addition to its core competence of representing municipal interests on the national level, the KL represents the municipalities as employers in wage bargaining with the trade unions and supports local governments with expertise in planning and public relations. It also provides municipal liaison committees (*Kommunekontaktrådene*) for regional cooperation among municipalities (www.kl.dk).

level dynamics of party competition, the majority or minority status of the government in charge, and by corporatist agreements with interest groups. While local or regional interests partially enter the game via electoral incentives, the most interesting role seems to be played by the local government association KL. Subnational entities in federal countries are assumed to protract reform processes because they pursue *separate* strategies, whereas the KL's influence depends essentially upon its internal *coherence*. It thus remains to be seen in the course of our case studies whether its existence did in any way affect the negotiations preceding regional development or transport policy reforms.

The process of law making in Ireland is very similar to the traditional Westminster one. It shares the characteristics of a dominant government relative to parliament as well as an adversarial relationship between government and opposition (Connolly 2005; Saalfeld 2008). Accordingly, cabinet is 'the arena where the major allocative decisions are taken' (Laffan 1996: 323). A decisive role inside government is played by the *Taoiseach*, based upon his or her departmental resources, public reputation, and position within the government party. This is enforced by the doctrine of collective accountability that limits public awareness of intra-cabinet dissent. It would, however, be misleading to underestimate ministerial leeway in shaping legislation. Individual ministers have technical, area-specific expertise, 'unparalleled access to departments of state and the wider public service' (Laffan 1996: 323), and are able to pursue their own policy agenda (Chubb 1992a; Mitchell 2006: 436). In addition, ministerial bureaucracy affects cabinet decision making in interaction with the local orientation of national politicians (Collins and Butler 2001: 122; Saalfeld 2008) and is especially influential in shaping incremental policy change (Collins and Quinlivan: 343).

In contrast, there is hardly any genuine policy formulation in parliament (O'Halpin and Connolly 1999). Its agenda is controlled by cabinet, and parliamentary parties lack specialisation, even in important policy areas, due to a weak committee system (Connolly 2005; Saalfeld 2008: 11) as well as time constraints resulting from extensive constituency work (Gallagher and Komito 2005). Given these characteristics, Irish interest groups seek to influence policy on a national scale mainly through government, the governing parties and ministries. The *Dáil*'s members largely serve as a 'centre for information, access, and publicity' (Murphy 2005: 370) and groups representing local interests are likely to lobby all local parliamentarians on a cross-party basis (O'Halpin and Connolly 1999: 130–1).

The characteristics of Irish bicameralism, moreover, reflect the fact that regional interests are not systematically integrated into national level decision making. The *Seanad Éireann*, the Irish second chamber, is not elected on territorial grounds but rather composed of 60 members, partly elected by five panels representing vocational interests (43 senators), by college graduates of two universities (6 senators) and partly nominated by the *Taoiseach*, the Irish prime minister (11 senators). Moreover, the *Seanad's* role in law making is clearly subordinate to the *Dáil* (Braune 2000). Consequently there is no institutional veto power emanating from territorial state organisation in Ireland.

Regional interests play hardly any role in national decision making; both the RAuth and RAss and those associations that horizontally coordinate local authorities' interests prove very weak. The RAuth and RAss play only a marginal political role beyond their ascribed administrative functions. This even applies to the preparation of Irish National Development Plans (NDP) that are subject to the partnership principle in EU structural funding policy and therefore require regional input (Barry 2005).[74] RAuth are 'quite ineffective as political fora' (interview Callanan) and their 'input [...] into the process of formulation of the development plans is virtually zero' (interview Breathnach). This missing impact is mainly attributable to their limited financial and personnel resources as well as to a lack of regional identity in Ireland.

There are three political associations responsible for horizontal coordination of local authorities' services and interests: the Association of City and County Councils, the Association of Municipal Authorities of Ireland, and the Local Authorities Members Association 'which is more like a trade union [...] than a representative body' (interview Callanan). Though the first two occasionally publish policy papers,[75] their policy influence is diminutive. None of our case studies on processes of decision making came across any instance of these organisations affecting negotiations.

Nevertheless, local interests do systematically influence national decision making, as politicians are highly responsive to their constituents. There are four main reasons for this: the political culture, the small scale of society, the electoral system including patterns of candidate selection, and the nature of the Irish administrative system (Collins and Butler 2001: 117; Gallagher and Komito 2005; Mitchell 2006: 427–8). Incumbents' incentives to nurse local interests are further strengthened because national politicians are frequently elected to local offices (Kenny 2003). By representing local interests *Dáil* deputies might act as 'welfare officers' or 'local promoters', depending upon their own status as backbencher or government minister (Collins and Butler 2001) and the government's status as a minority or majority government (Gallagher and Komito 2005; O'Halpin and Connolly 1999). Whereas 'welfare officers' largely act as advisers or mediators over contacts with the civil service, 'local promoters' influence decision making in a way that serves the constituency's collective needs (Searing 1994). Local pressure groups rather than individuals play an important role in lobbying for benefits (O'Halpin and Connolly 1999: 136–7; Murphy 2005) and the deputies are 'expected to fight to increase the constituency's share of whatever cakes exist' (Gallagher and Komito 2005: 249). It is this type of local lobbying that is important with regard to our research question, as it might impede the efficiency of negotiation processes or their output. Apart from the danger of degenerating into outright corruption (O'Halpin and Connolly 1999: 139–40), it might protract

---

74. For a slightly different assessment, see Laffan (1996) and Adshead (2003).

75. These papers focus mostly on issues of local government or administrative reform. See http://www.councillors.ie/Publications.html.

processes of decision making or yield package deals based on brokerage or clientelism[76] rather than considerations of efficiency (Gallagher and Komito 2005: 249–50).

6.3 Decision making in the area of regional development policy

Building upon our theoretically and empirically guided case selection as well as the country-specific information presented in the preceding sections, we are finally ready to turn to detailed analyses of decision-making processes in the area of regional development policy. However, instead of delving into an assessment of distinct reform processes right away, let us first develop country-specific overviews of the policy area under study (Section 6.3.1). On the one hand, it is necessary to evaluate whether the countries chosen feature policies that match the definition of regional development policies proposed above. On the other hand, our theoretical argument requires a delineation of the extent to which decision making in the depicted policy area takes place at the national level as it is here that we assume federalism's incentives operate most obviously. To be sure, in a policy area with purely regional competencies, a reform may be protracted when changing socioeconomic conditions demand a joint and coordinated policy shift by regional subunits. However, in order to increase the validity of comparison across cases, our aim is a focused comparison of *national* negotiations. As will be seen, delineating areas of national negotiations is quite easy in Switzerland as well as both unitary countries, but a more complex task in Austria.

Once we have outlined national policies of regional development in each of the countries, we are all set to identify the core challenges that the countries face (Section 6.3.2) and, finally, to provide a critical assessment of their reaction and reform capacity (Section 6.3.3).

6.3.1 Regional development as a national policy area

In Switzerland, the constitutional basis of a regional policy carried out by the federal government is article 103,[77] BV. It enables federal authorities to support economically disadvantaged regions as well as branches of the economy. Moreover, the federal constitution assigns the responsibilities for economy (industry and trade) and physical planning (including regional development) to both the cantons and the federal authorities. Physical planning is additionally partially delegated to the cantons by federal laws (Wälti 1996: 9–10). To date, all cantons have, though to varying extents,[78] advanced their own strategies for economic development

---

76. According to Gallagher and Komito the 'main difference between brokerage and clientelism is that clientelism implies a more intense, more permanent relationship' (Gallagher and Komito 2005: 253). In either case, the allocation of resources is affected by such behaviour.

77. Some instruments of regional policy are based on article 104, which enables the federal government to support agriculture.

78. Expenditure on the economy accounts for up to 15–17 per cent of total cantonal expenditure in

alongside federal regional policy (Veraguth 2003). However, in accordance with our research focus, the following chapter focuses on processes of national decision making that are based upon article 103, BV, and more specifically the negotiations preceding the Swiss New Regional Policy (NRP). It is here that we expect to detect the incentives of federal decision making at work most clearly.

In Austria, where the constitution remains silent on regional development policies (Österreichische Raumordnungskonferenz (ÖROK) 2002), we find a more ambiguous and labyrinthine picture. Following the residual clause (article 15.1, B-VG), the competence stays with the *Länder*; in practice, however, this encourages both federal and provincial governments to take action. As a consequence, regional development policy in Austria is understood as a broad cross-sectional policy including all spatially relevant areas, e.g. infrastructure, energy, transport, labour market, and local economic policies (Huber 2002). The federal level holds many sectoral competencies, such as transport, mining, forestry, and laws pertaining to water and waterways. Following a 1954 constitutional court's decision, regional planning is a *Länder* task and local planning belongs to the municipalities (interview Mayerhofer). Local and regional planning guidelines are supposed to be coordinated with the other levels (Gamper 2000). Furthermore, all levels are allowed to develop activities through state-owned but outsourced agencies (*Privatwirtschaftsverwaltung*). Consequently 'it is actually extremely difficult to isolate a clear regional policy in Austria as is possible in many other western European countries' (Downes 2000: 248). Among the many actors in the policy area are three federal ministries, nine state governments, the local government associations and the social partners. Both federal and state levels operate a number of agencies for the implementation of their policies (see Chapter Seven).

In effect, binding agreements on many spatially relevant issues like planning and regional development can only be attained by unanimity between *Bund* and *Länder* (Schindegger 1999). Despite existing agreements according to article 15a B-VG between various states on the one hand,[79] and on the other between all *Länder* and the federal government (Kanonier 2003),[80] an effective coordination of regional development and planning efforts is necessary. This is provided by the Austrian Conference on Spatial Planning (*Österreichische Raumordnungskonferenz*, ÖROK). When the ÖROK was founded in 1971, its core

---

smaller and rural cantons; some urban cantons spent less than 3.3 per cent on economic development in 2003 (Bochsler *et al.* 2004: 143–4).

79. At present, there are cooperation agreements in force between Salzburg, Styria, and Carinthia (Lung-Murau-Nock-Grenzgebiet), between Salzburg and Upper Austria, between Upper and Lower Austria, and between Vienna, Lower Austria, and Burgenland (*Planungsgemeinschaft Ost*).

80. The most important being the agreement for joint implementation of the regional programmes financed by the EU structural funds. These are the European Regional Development Fund (ERDF), the European Social Fund (ESF), and the European Agricultural Guidance and Guarantee Fund (EAGGL).

task was the coordination of regional planning.[81] Since the 1990s it has accrued more and more responsibilities pertaining to regional economic development policy. Nowadays it plays a crucial role in the joint implementation of EU programmes and the formulation of the National Strategic Reference Framework of Austria (STRAT.AT).[82]

In the course of our case studies, we approach the quite complex Austrian situation by concentrating on two different processes. First, we focus upon processes of decision making with regard to EU structural funding, as it is here that decision-making competencies lie mainly at national level but subnational governments are strongly involved. We thus assume that processes of decision making match our theoretical model in this case. Second, we contrast the respective findings with a more general analysis of regional development initiatives that were mainly undertaken by the Austrian *Länder* during the 1990s. Such within-case comparison may yield insights that go beyond the basic theoretical argument presented above.

Turning to the unitary countries, we see that regional development policies are an entirely national competence both in Denmark and Ireland. However, according to Danish planning law, physical planning has to be a process involving all political levels (Bogason 1982). Moreover, ad hoc and standing committees like the National Growth Council[83] regularly act as agenda setters and regional development policies have been subject to fundamental changes regarding both the strategies and the distribution of competencies. The first programmes were strongly selective and not sustainable (Kristensen 1990).[84] After 1973, the strategy changed to giving subsidies, soft loans, and technical assistance to small and medium-sized enterprises (Jensen-Butler 1992; Amin and Thomas 1996). In the 1980s, programmes fostering endogenous growth by providing basic infrastructure and consultancy services became popular. These programmes were mainly provided by regional and local authorities without legal basis (Halkier 2000), using their right of 'self-government' (Jensen-Butler 1992).[85] In 1991, these 'grey area' programmes became legal and remained the only ones existing after the central government abolished all national development measures in the same year. For our purposes, the shifting paradigms and strategies as put forth by the national level are of main interest.

---

81. In the form of the Austrian Spatial Planning Concept (Österreichisches Raumordnungskonzept, ÖRK, 1981 and 1991) and the Austrian Concept for Regional Development (Österreichisches Raumentwicklungskonzept, 2001).

82. From *Nationaler STRATegischer Rahmenplan* and the Austrian WWW country code.

83. Before 2006, it was called the National Business Council. It consists of representatives of economy, science, and associations, as well as political members from national ministries and municipalities. In the National Growth Council the heads of the five Regional Growth Forums are also members.

84. The granting of subsidies depended strongly on the individual ability of local governments to adopt the goals of specific national programmes. The policy effects were rather unspecific and not sustainable.

85. Examples of the latter are regional technology centres like NORDTEK for North Jutland and BORNTEK for the island of Bornholm.

In Ireland, all decision-making competencies for a policy of regional development rest at the national level. However, Irish economic policy has long neglected the regional dimension (Adshead and Quinn 1998; Barry 2003) and instead focused strongly on the industrial policy that was designed to attract foreign direct investment, making Ireland one of the most globalised economies in Europe (Eustace 1982; Hardiman 1992; Morgenroth 2006).[86] Though this had indirect effects upon regional development (Killen and Ruane 1998; Meyler and Strobl 2000; Frenkel *et al.* 2003), the economic recession of the 1980s brought about a marked shift back to a national focus (Boylan 2002), most prominently the Irish social partnership approach (Allen 2000; House and McGrath 2004; Hardiman 2002). Consequently, during this period there were scarcely any decision-making processes that substantially match our definition of regional development policies.

In the 1990s, however, policies aiming explicitly at regional development were put on the agenda. On the one hand, the economic boom of the 'Celtic Tiger' (O'Donnell 1998; Murphy 2000; Boylan 2002) brought about growing economic and social disparities between the regions, especially a monocentric dominance of the Greater Dublin Area (GDA) (O'Leary 2003b; Davoudi and Wishardt 2005).[87] On the other hand, the external influence of EU policy via funding, directives, informational input, and technical cooperation led to a completely different political environment that especially affected regional development policies (Carroll and Byrne 1999; Walsh (2000); Adshead 2005; Barry 2005). It is here that we are able to detect debates on policy reform that constitute a valuable research subject in the course of our study.

Summarising the country-specific profiles, regional development constitutes a discrete policy area in Switzerland, Denmark, and Ireland, but less so in Austria. Moreover, regional development has formed an integral part of the national-level policy agenda in Switzerland and Denmark since the 1970s, but has only gained attention in Ireland since the 1990s. In Austria, where responsibilities are distributed between all state levels, coordination efforts were quite feeble, until the national focus on regional *development* was greatly sharpened in the course of EU structural funding programmes in the 1990s. Since then, the ÖROK has gained a crucial role in the political process.

However, with regard to our theoretical argument, it would be misleading to descriptively analyse the comparative evolution of the policy area only since it gained importance on the national agenda. Rather, our argument presumes that differences in negotiation patterns of federal and unitary countries gain relevance to policy performance only in cases of changing socioeconomic conditions that induce strong pressure for policy reform. The final step in substantively defining our cases therefore is to isolate core challenges that the Swiss, Austrian, Danish, and Irish governments faced with regard to the task of regional development.

---

86. For a critical assessment, see Smith 2004.

87. The Greater Dublin Area comprises Dublin City, Dun Laoghaire, Rathdown, Fingal, South Dublin, Kildare, Meath and Wicklow.

6.3.2 Core challenges in regional development policies

In the realm of regional development policy, the national governments of all four countries felt a strong need to redesign their strategies throughout the 1990s. From a very general perspective, these challenges accrued from the interactive pressures of a globalised market competition and country-specific structural characteristics relating, for example, to industrial or geographic profile.

For Switzerland, the main structural component influencing patterns of regional development is its mountainous terrain. Accordingly, the explicit regional policy that was developed during the 1970s was mainly directed at helping mountainous regions through financing infrastructure, supporting individual enterprises in monostructural regions and the tourist industry (Buser 2005; Scherer and Schnell 2008). However, in the course of the late 1980s and 1990s these instruments were increasingly perceived as being insufficient for contemporary challenges. In light of the economic recession, growing disparities of income between the cantons, and debates about the impact of globalisation, the Swiss federal government, in line with those of many other OECD countries, perceived a necessity to redesign instruments of regional policy. In an effort to strengthen regions' capacity to successfully stand up to increasing regional competition (Wälti and Bullinger 2000: 90–1), the resulting reorientation of regional policy in 1996 partially revised existing instruments and established a series of new policy instruments.[88] These new instruments were, however, based on temporary resolutions intended to expire in 2007. This additionally increased the pressure to comprehensively rethink the strategy set of regional policy and finally led to a wholesale reform of Swiss regional policy, the *Bundesgesetz über Regionalpolitik*, called *Neue Regionalpolitik* (NRP) (Bundesversammlung der Schweizerischen Eidgenossenschaft 2006b), that was adopted in October 2006. The negotiations preceding the NRP, as well as its adequacy, lie at the heart of the following case study.

In Austria, the focus of regional development policies shifted from a neoclassical, mobility-oriented strategy in the 1960s to capital transfers and infrastructure improvement in the 1970s. Following a strategy of 'decentral concentration', the *Bund* aimed for regional development centres and equalisation (Huber 2002). Nonetheless, politically motivated sectoral promotion measures were often poorly coordinated (Aigner *et al.* 2001) and dissipated labour forces from rural areas (interview Mayerhofer). With the extension of cooperative federalism in 1974, the *Länder* gained more control over regional economic policy and tried to raise their endogenous potentials (Dirninger 2003; Downes 2000; Heintel 2004). The situation changed radically over the 1980s. Increasing globalisation intensified regional competition between the *Länder*, whose economic structure changed dramatically. The 'fall of the Iron Curtain' accelerated this process, as the Austrian economy was confronted not only with new markets, but also with low-cost

---

88. Like Regio plus (Bundesversammlung der Schweizerischen Eidgenossenschaft 1997a) and In-notour I/II (Bundesversammlung der Schweizerischen Eidgenossenschaft 1997b). Switzerland also participates in the European Inititative INTERREG (see Buser 2005: 18–9 for details).

competitors (Schremmer and Tödtling 1996; Huber 2002). Existing structures of regional development proved to be ineffective (Huber 2002). The economic crisis hit Austria hard and forced the federal level to reduce industrial policy subsidies. Because of their dependence on federal transfers, *Länder* governments now had to struggle hard for resources. A further promoter of change in regional economic policy was accession to the European Union in 1995, which made adaptation to European structural fund guidelines necessary (Schwarz 2003).

As seen, rethinking regional development policies was a highly debated topic in Austria at the turn of the 1990s. However, given the vagueness of competence distributions in the policy area, we cannot focus on a single reform process in the case of Austria. Rather, our case study pursues a two-fold strategy as indicated above. On the one hand, we examine how Austria tackled the need for stronger intergovernmental coordination that was brought about by the (imminent) EU accession. On the other hand, we investigate the diversity of regional development initiatives that were independently undertaken by the national as well as subnational governments during the 1990s.

The most serious challenges Danish governments have faced since the changes of global economic markets in the 1980s arise from its structure as a small, open economy (Katzenstein 1985). Heavy industries closed down, causing high unemployment and rising budget deficits. The Conservative-led government of the time tried to manage the structural changes by cutting public expenditure in order to lower tax levels and public indebtedness. Countermeasures taken during the decade did not reach the core of the Danish problems: the predominance of low-tech exports and slow-growing industries (Amin and Thomas 1996). At the turn of the 1990s, the Danish government was eager to find new strategies to promote economic growth in the country.[89]

Until 1990, the administration of grant schemes had been firmly centralised. As the 1990 study *On the Competitive Advantage of Nations* (Porter 1990) attested, Denmark had an unbalanced economic structure, based on small and medium-sized enterprises and little heavy industry. The study made a significant impact on Danish economic policy (Amin and Thomas 1996; Boekholt and Thuriaux 1999; Drejer *et al.* 1997), albeit Danish economists had developed similar recommendations in the 1980s (Lundvall *et al.* 2002). It was also widely acknowledged that deficits in research and development and technological competitiveness (Kluth and Andersen 1994) and 'slow-growing markets and a general lack of adaptive and innovative capacities in Danish industry' (Kjaer and Pedersen 2001: 235) were structural problems for the Danish economy. In light of these prominent debates revolving around economic development, Denmark witnessed a number of quite radical policy shifts throughout the 1990s. The basic aim of the Danish case study

---

89. 'In '91 the EU made their evaluation of where development will take place in Europe – it was called the Blue Banana. And the Blue Banana was south of Denmark. Then you as a minister can't sit back and say "Oh well development is heading this direction and there is nothing we can do about it." Then you have the damned duty to figure out how you bend the Blue Banana' (Per Stig Møller, Danish Environment Minister 1990–3, quoted by Larsen 1999: appendix, p. 46).

therefore is to detect the dynamics underlying such activism.

Lastly, the core challenge for contemporary Irish development policy is regional disparities. This is especially visible with regard to output measures (Boyle *et al.* 1999) though less so in the case of unemployment (see Table 6.1).

The relative position for the index of per capita Gross Value Added is twice as high in Dublin as it is in the weakest region, Border. Differences in the relative position regarding per capita income are smaller (113 per cent in Dublin, 89.5 per cent in South-East), though still visible. Accompanying these hard economic indicators is a growing perception of the Irish public and policy makers that current disparities constitute a major threat for further development. The Irish government now sees the necessity of redesigning spatial policies in an effort to manage functional areas emerging around regional centres (Government of Ireland 2002). It is important to note, however, that the challenge for Ireland consists of more than designing policies that entail a greater regional balance. Though the establishment of the RAuth and RAss is in itself part of this new focus on regional policies, their extremely weak position entails a need to devise 'institutions or processes that are flexible enough to allow regions to develop their own capacity and their own appropriate decision-making processes' (interview Ò Broin). The ability to achieve far-reaching institutional reform is thus another, more fundamental challenge.

Consequently, the debate on adopting an economic policy that enhances regional clusters of economic activity returned to centre stage in the 1990s and has been prominent ever since (Keane 2002; O'Leary 2003a). The strongest reflection of this emphasis is the National Spatial Strategy (NSS), a central policy document launched in 2002 providing an investment framework for a twenty-year period. It was 'designed to achieve a better balance of social,

Table 6.1: Key indicators of Irish regions

Regional authority	Population, 2006	Area in sq km	Per capita gross value added (per cent of national average), 2004	Per capita income (per cent of national average), 2004	Unemployment rate, 2006	Persons at work (thousands), 2006
Border	468,375	12,345.61	74.3	91.6	5.0	205.2
Midlands	251,664	6,625.38	66.3	91.4	4.0	115.2
West	414,277	14,286.87	74.8	93.8	4.2	195.5
Dublin	1,187,176	920.66	133.3	113.0	4.8	595.4
Mid East	475,360	6,061.34	73.8	98.9	3.3	225.6
Mid West	361,028	8,248.64	93.2	100.5	3.9	174.2
South East	460,838	9,451.51	81.6	89.5	5.0	213.6
South West	621,130	12,242.23	122.3	97.4	3.7	292.3
Ireland	4,239,848	70,182.24	100.0	100.0	4.3	2,017.0

Source: Morgenroth 2007, partly corrected.

economic, physical development and population growth between regions' (National Spatial Strategy, section 1a).[90] The following chapter will therefore provide a detailed analysis of the decision-making process preceding its formulation and scrutinise its efficiency as well as the adequacy of its output.

6.3.3 Negotiating regional policy reform

Having clarified and narrowed down the reach and focus of our case studies, we will now pursue in-depth, country-by-country analyses of the selected reform processes in the area of regional development. In line with our theoretical arguments we aim to detect whether there was a systematic difference in the capacity of federal and unitary governments to tackle the challenges just described. And given our focus upon multilevel politics, several questions provide a guideline for the comparative endeavour. To what extent were subnational actors involved in the relevant decision-making processes and what access or veto points did they use? Were negotiations lengthy or quite short? Was reforming regional development policies a highly conflictual or fairly consensual issue? To what extent was the status quo changed? Can the new policy be judged an adequate response towards the main challenges and, if so, on what grounds? Finally, does the policy enacted provide the structures and guidelines necessary for its successful implementation? While each of the following country studies touches upon these questions separately, Section 6.3.4 consolidates the findings from a comparative perspective.

6.3.3.1 Switzerland. Negotiating the New Regional Policy

The process of decision making preceding the New Regional Policy in Switzerland lasted almost six years and was characterised by a high level of conflict. Its policy debate was thereby linked to the federal government's agglomeration policy as well as to the comprehensive reform of the fiscal equalisation system called NFA.[91] The federal government's agglomeration policy (based upon article 50.3 of the constitution) was launched in December 2001 and aims at integrating metropolitan areas mainly by means of providing financial support for innovative projects that foster vertical and horizontal collaboration (see Eidgenössisches Volkswirtschaftsdepartement 2006 for details). It is implemented by the newly established Federal Office for Spatial Development (*Bundesamt für Raumentwicklung*, ARE). As will be seen, the federal government unsuccessfully strove for an integration of its agglomeration and regional policy.

---

90. Beforehand, the NDP 2000–6 included the government's commitment 'to achieve balanced regional development' and to prepare the NSS (Government of Ireland 1999: 46). However, it did not provide details on the distribution of funding by programme to the eight regions.

91. The NFA mainly encompasses a decoupling of federal and cantonal tasks as well as a reform of the equalisation system that aims at increasing own resources of the cantons. See Chapter Seven for details.

Table 6.2: Decision-making process NRP in Switzerland

Date/Period	Event	Main Actors
January 23 and March 1 2001	Requests for a federal report upon efforts and achievements in regional policy	Committees for Economic Affairs and Taxation of the National Council and State Council
2001 to February 6 2003	Expert commission, initiated by federal government Report: Evaluation and Conceptual Revision of Regional Policy	Representatives of SECO, universities, tourist industry, ARE, City Zurich, Canton Vaud, SAB[a], Sierre-Région
April 2004	Draft: Federal Law on Regional Policy (*Bundesgesetz über Regionalpolitik*)	EVD
April 28 to August 31 2004	Consultation procedure	All cantons, six parties, economic associations, regional actors, interest groups
November 2004	Report: Results of the Consultation Procedure	EVD
December 2004 to June 2005	Working Group New Regional Policy (AG NRP) Report for the EVD: Optimization of the draft for the Federal Law On Regional Policy	Five federal representatives (SECO, EFV[b]) and nine cantonal directors of economy (UR, ZH+1secretary, SG, FR, GR, NE, AG, BE)
November 16 2005	Draft and Federal Message: Federal Law on Regional Policy (*Botschaft über die Neue Regionalpolitik*)	Federal Council
June 2006 to October 6 2006	Parliamentary debate	State Council
	adoption of bill: *Bundesgesetz über Regionalpolitik*	National Council

Source: Sekretariat für Wirtschaft. Seco, *Pilotprojekte zur neuen Regionalpolitik.*
[a] *Schweizerische Arbeitsgemeinschaft Berggebiete* (Swiss Consortium for Mountainous Regions);
[b] *Eidgenössische Finanzverwaltung* (Federal Finance Administration); Abbreviations of cantons : AG Aargau; AI Appenzell Innerrhoden; AR Appenzell Ausserrhoden; BS Basel-City; BL Basel-Country; BE Berne; FR Fribourg; GE Geneva; GL Glarus; GR Graubünden; JU Jura; LU Lucerne; NE Neuchâtel; NW Nidwalden; OW Obwalden; SH Schaffhausen; SZ Schwyz; SO Solothurn; SG St. Gallen; TG Thurgau; TI Ticino; UR Uri; VS Valais; VD Vaud; ZG Zug; ZH Zurich.

The regional policy's link to the NFA is more pronounced. The NRP was from the very beginning framed as a supplement to the NFA. The idea is that the latter develops distributive objectives and provides a partial harmonisation of cantonal financial capacities and thereby enables the former to place emphasis on control tasks.

Table 6.2 provides an overview of the major stages of the NRP's decision-making process. As shown, the interests of cantonal governments were only marginally represented in the expert commission, but strongly relevant in the consultation procedure and the following working group. During the consultation procedure, the first draft[92] of the Federal Department of Economic Affairs (*Eidgenössisches Volksdepartement*, EVD) was highly criticised by many cantons as well as regional actors. Table 6.3 displays their positions as indicated by their written statements.

Though most cantons generally approved the aims of fostering entrepreneurship, innovation and added value systems, there were at least three highly debated topics. First, many cantons rejected the idea of promoting greater functional areas within the framework of regional policy and requested a clear demarcation between the NRP and the agglomeration policy. Second, almost half of the cantons rejected the proposal to establish a foundation that would build upon cantonal contributions for its capitalisation and allocate support for small-scale regions. Third, the proposed end to tax reductions for small businesses was opposed by the eight cantons that had so far mostly benefited from it (see Chapter Seven). Individual cantons as well as representatives of mountainous regions additionally requested an overall increase in federal contributions or individual benefits, like support for border regions. Seven cantons (including many of the French-speaking cantons) as well as the conference of cantonal directors of finance actually rejected the draft *in toto*. The results of the consultation procedure thus confirm our theoretical expectation: Swiss cantons are strongly integrated into processes of federal decision making and pursue policy proposals that would favour their own territory.

Confronted with such manifold criticisms, the federal government decided to initiate a working group (AG NRP) that included cantonal representatives far stronger than the first expert commission. Its explicit assignment was to 'optimise' the draft in a way acceptable to a majority. As the resulting second draft was adopted in parliament quite quickly and not challenged by a popular referendum, it is safe to say that the AG NRP succeeded in fulfilling this brief. However, cantonal involvement negatively affected the extent to which the change of status quo aspired to was achieved. Table 6.4 contrasts the major characteristics of the first draft and the NRP.[93]

The comparison shows that major parts of the first draft were withdrawn in reaction to cantonal resistance. The final law neither provides for promotion of greater functional areas, and thus agglomerations, nor does it employ cantonal contributions for the establishment of a foundation. Moreover, the NRP retains a number of previous instruments, though their applicability is often more restricted than before (see annotation b in Table 6.4). The NRP thus exhibits characteristics of policy stability and might be described as a politics-dominated solution, though

---

92. Its major characteristics are illustrated in Table 6.4.

93. Given the patchwork of instruments applied in the first and second generation of Swiss regional policy, it is hard to comprehensively define the *status quo ex ante*. The comparison of the first draft and the NRP thus acts as an indicator for the policy-stabilising effect of regional interests.

Table 6.3: Cantonal positions during the NRP consultation procedure in Switzerland

Statement	Cantons	Characteristics
Promotion of greater functional areas?		
No support for projects whose effects are restricted to agglomerations	BE, OW, NW, SG, TI, NE, SAB[e]	Mountainous regions, mainly semi-rural cantons
Request for clear demarcation NRP – Agglomeration Policy	AR, UR, AG, TG, VS	1 urban, 2 semi-rural, 2 rural cantons
Establishment of a foundation under public law that operates on a small-scale level?		
Refusal	ZH, BS, BL, AI, SG, GR, AG, TG, VD, VS, NE, JU, FDK[a], NWRK[b]	4 urban, 4 semi-rural, 4 rural cantons
Request for an increase in cantonal competences in case of a foundation	BE, OW, AR, TG	3 semi-rural, 1 rural canton
End of support for small businesses		
Approval	ZH, LU, SZ, OW, NW; BL, GR, AG, TG, GE	4 urban, 4 semi-rural, 2 rural cantons
Refusal	TI, BE, UR, GL, AR, VD, NE, JU	3 rural, 5 semi-rural cantons
Requests		
More federal resources	UR, NW, GL, FR, GR, TG, VD, VS, JU	5 rural, 4 semi-rural cantons
Clear definition of regions	FR, AR, SG, VS, SAB[e]	Mountainous regions
Priority of NRP: Periphery → Main responsibility: Federal level	NE, ZH, UR, SAB[e]	Mountainous regions
Recognition of border regions	BS, GE, NWRK[b]	Border regions
No regional policy alongside NFA	AI, ZH	-
Aim to foster entrepeneurship, innovation and added value systems?		
Approval	SH, LU, UR, SZ, OW, NW, GL, ZG, SO, BS, BL, AR, SG, GR, AG, TI, NE, GE, RKGK[c], KoSeReG[d], Association of Cities	Most cantons, mountainous regions, cities
Overall Assessment		
Refusal draft	ZH, FR, AI, TG, VD, VS, JU, FDK	Most of Romandie + ZH, AI

Source: Eidgenössisches Volkswirtschaftsdepartement 2004a.
[a] *Konferenz der kantonalen Finanzdirektorinnen und Finanzdirektoren* (Conference of Cantonal Finance Directors); [b] *Nordwestschweizer Regierungskonferenz* (Conference of North-Western Cantonal Governments); [c] *Regierungskonferenz der Gebirgskantone* (Conference of Mountainous Cantonal Governments); [d] *Konferenz der Sekretäre des Schweizerischen Bergregionen* (Conference of Executive Directors of Mountainous Regions); [e] *Schweizerische Arbeitsgemeinschaft Berggebiete* (Swiss Consortium for Mountainous Regions); For abbreviations of cantons, see Table 6.2.

Table 6.4: Changing the status quo? Comparison of first draft and adopted NRP law in Switzerland

	Draft EVD	NRP
Aim	Regional competitiveness [→ job creation → reduction of regional disparities]	Regional competitiveness [→ job creation → reduction of regional disparities]
Strategies[a]	(1) promote initiatives, programmes, and projects that foster entrepeneurship, innovation, added value systems (via cluster building), cooperation between public and private intitutions, and **within and between** agglomerations **no** investments in basic infrastructure **no** federal tax reductions for individual businesses	(1) promote initiatives, programmes, and projects that foster entrepeneurship, innovation and added value systems (via cluster building), cooperation between public and private intitutions, and **with** agglomerations; (2) promote regional associations that design or coordinate development strategies;[b] (3) promote, in a restricted way, cross-border cooperation;[b] (4) grant, in a restricted way, interest-free loans for investments in basic infrastructure;[b] (5) provide, in a restricted way, federal tax reductions for individual businesses[b]
Criteria for eligibility	(1) anticipated benefit for rural and mountainous regions; (2) functional areas with greatest potential (agglomerations)	(1) innovative character and anticipated benefit for rural and mountainous regions
Executive decision making	(1) multi-annual federal programms for promotion of greater functional areas (agglomerations) (2) establishment of a *Foundation for Regional Development (Stiftung Regionalentwicklung)* under public law that operates on a small-scale level in mountainous regions (substitution of IHG)	(1) multi-annual federal programmes
Actors implementation	Seco; cantons; Foundation for Regional Development	Cantons, Seco (decisions over tax reductions)
Characteristics implementation	Cantons develop innovation strategies that have to be negotiated with the EVD (programmes with exit option) and can be financed either by the Federation (cantonal co-financing) or by the *Foundation for Regional Development*	Cantons develop innovation strategies that have to be negotiated with the EVD (programmes with exit option) and are financed by the *Fonds for Regional Development* (former IHG Fonds) All financial support is subject to a co-financing mechanism, is awarded as a global grant, and based upon programmatic agreements

Source: Eidgenössisches Volkswirtschaftsdepartement 2004b, Bundesversammlung der Schweizerischen Eidgenossenschaft 2006b.

[a] Both the draft and the law additionally enact strategies to enable synergies of federal sectoral policies, and to develop a knowledge system for regional development; [b] These strategies perpetuate mechanisms used on the basis of the IHG, INTERREG, BWE.

it successfully shifts the regional policy's overarching objective from reducing disparities to increasing the competitiveness of regions and almost completely withdraws from financing basic infrastructure by replacing four existing writs.[94]

6.3.3.2 Austria. Negotiating regional policy at the turn of the 1990s

From the 1970s on, Austrian *Länder* governments became increasingly involved in regional development policy. Mostly they ran their own initiatives, financed by federal grants, but the federal subsidies dried up by the end of the 1980s. The ending of the 'sprinkler principle' (*Gießkannenprinzip*) meant the *Länder* now found themselves in competition for scarce water. This hampered intergovernmental cooperation (e.g. the fiscal equalisation negotiations) and enforced parochial thinking (*Kirchturmsdenken*) by the states: 'The model of vertical co-operation between the different levels of government has come under pressure as joint decision making has turned out to be less effective, sometimes even unproductive' (Bauer 1991). The instruments used were ultimately ineffective. This 'finally brought about a shift from the old model to a new philosophy of regional development in Austria' (Steiner and Jud 1998: 49).

At the turn of the 1990s, two different developments emerged: firstly, new instruments and strategies were developed to replace the old, ineffective ones. Austrian national and subnational governments tried to cushion the impact of global competition. Secondly, imminent EU accession stimulated better intergovernmental coordination. We treat the two topics consecutively.

With regard to the first problem, the *Bund* reacted to research results attesting to Austria's deficit in innovation transfers between science and industry (interview Mayerhofer), and founded coordinating agencies for this purpose. The goal was to promote modernisation, international cooperation and application-oriented research (Peneder 1999). Meanwhile the *Länder* developed individual regional strategies. The beginning of the 1990s saw a considerable change in the instruments used, including infrastructure measures such as technology parks, consultancy agencies, promotion of regional cooperation and a focus on regional strengths. These cluster initiatives began almost immediately after the influential Porter study (1990) was published (interview Seidl). '[R]egional economic promotion activities no longer aim[ed] at the transfer of capital between regions, but tr[ied] to increase the competitiveness of regional economies by developing the regional innovation potential' (Steiner and Jud 1998: 52).[95] The high level of autonomy enabled both governmental levels to react quickly and flexibly to the changing environment.

Intergovernmental cooperation, on the other hand, was harder to generate. But with the approaching EU accession, Austria faced demands for coordinated Single Programming Documents to get access to EU Structural Funding. Since Austrian

---

94. The IHG, BWE, Regio plus and INTERREG. See Chapter Seven for details. The NRP thus renders the future of the IHG regions uncertain.

95. See also Schwarz 2003.

regional policy was until that point 'flexible to chaotic' (Aigner *et al.* 2001: 14),[96] the centrally planned process of European funding (Huber 2002) brought about a new logic as it posed high demands for compromise. Nevertheless, all actors managed to find common agreement (Huber 1999). The reasons are twofold. First, they all agreed the top priority was to make full use of the funds available (Huber 2002), as Austria expected to be a net payer into the European Union. The negotiations on the Programming Documents for the 2000–6 and 2007–13 periods were characterised by fast decision-making processes (interviews Mayerhofer, Seidl). It can be assumed that such rapid agreement supports the character of the topic as a positive-sum game on additional resources from the supranational level. Second, the national programmes are a clear case of negative coordination (Scharpf 1993): the agreement was made possible through 'very tolerant' (interview Mayerhofer)[97] operational programmes.

In sum, Austrian regional development policy relatively rapidly adopted new principles. The quick reaction of the Austrian government was possible mainly because both *Bund* and *Länder* tiers of government were able to react independently – as long as cooperation is not necessary or at least not essential, individual strategies may lead to an adequate overall strategy. Indeed, *Bund* and *Länder* levels developed a large variety of different instruments and goals (Heintel 2004). On the other hand, governmental tiers are able to react relatively speedily to new circumstances, if necessary. In the context of adaptation to EU funding, Austrian regional policy experienced drastic changes involving cooperative behaviour by the actors. However, this cooperation arose mainly from the will to extract maximal funding, and was thus a pareto-superior solution. The resulting agreements are very broad, leaving substantial discretion to the Austrian states (Kanonier 2003), which further facilitated approval.

6.3.3.3 Denmark. Negotiating paradigm shifts throughout the 1990s

Until the end of the 1980s, economic policy in Denmark had been mainly an issue of sector-specific subsidies. However, this changed dramatically at the beginning of the 1990s as the years 1990 and 1991 saw a far-reaching paradigm shift in Danish economic policy: 'The *raison d'être* of regional policy changed from addressing interregional inequalities to boosting the contribution of every region to national economic competitiveness' (Halkier 2001: 328). In 1990, the government passed a new Business Promotion Act, predicated on innovation and competitiveness as the main remedies for the Danish economy (Kluth and Andersen 1994). Simultaneously, national industrial policy programmes dealing with specific sectors or industries were merged or discontinued. Out of 26

---

96. 'flexibel bis chaotisch', translation by authors.

97. 'Da gibt es die übergeordnete Koordinationsleitlinie auf EU-Ebene. Dann gibt es den nationalen Rahmenplan. Der ist sehr geduldig. Dann gibt es darunter die operationellen Programme. Die sind sehr geduldig. […] Und dann unten, bei den Maßnahmen führt jedes Bundesland das ein, was es mag', translation by authors.

programmes in 1994, only nine remained by 1996,

> focusing on the framework for business development rather than on direct subsidies to business and industry. [...] Instead a number of core priorities were identified and supported with increasing funds (Cornett 1997: 8).

The national government retreated completely from regional development policies in 1991. The European Structural Programmes were shifted down to the regional level, only a supervisory role remaining with the central government (Halkier 2000). It was decided to legalise the 'grey area' programmes established by regional and local authorities in the course of the 1980s (Halkier 2000), using their right of 'self-government' (Jensen-Butler 1992). These programmes, which received resources exclusively from EU structural funding, were the only forms of regional development policy in Denmark between 1991 and 2003 (and are dealt with in more detail in Chapter 7.3.2).

The decision to reform Danish economic policy in such a dramatic way was mainly driven by

> short-term factors like party-political manoeuvring in connection with the yearly budget negotiations in late 1989, [...] a significant decrease in the traditional polarisation of core and periphery on a range of key indicators and [...] a generally waning support for financial subsidies to individual firms as a political instrument (Halkier 2001: 328).

It was developed by a commission, established by the Danish Ministry of Industry, the Industry and Trade Development Council (ITDC) and its secretariat, the National Agency for the Development of Trade and Industry (DATI).[98] The commission was an influential body consisting of state (national, regional, local) and non-state actors (unions, business, finance, and science) (Amin and Thomas 1996). It is typical for the agencies of the Danish 'negotiated economy' (Pedersen 2006). Within the commission, strategies were contentious. Porter's cluster approach was ill-reputed among conservatives as 'left-wing politics' (Kluth and Andersen 1994: 15). The committee's report presented in 1993 represents, hence, a mixture of different concepts: it defines eight clusters (Økonomi- og Erhvervsministeriet 1993)[99] but at the same time underlines that 'the analyses are supposed to comprise the bulk of the Danish business sector and therefore not merely a fraction of specially selected sectors' ('The Business Economics of Resource Areas in the Danish Business Sector – Analyses and Perspectives', ITDC report 1992, p. 4, quoted by Kluth and Andersen 1994: 16). The adopted cluster approach lacked any regional differentiation between centre and periphery (Cornett 1997) and was negotiated mainly at the national level between parties and

---

98. This agency has frequently changed its name and is currently known as the Danish Enterprise and Construction Authority (DEACA). For details, see the list of abbreviations at the outset of this book.

99. Meat and dairy products, medicine and medical equipment, sea transport, housing and construction, craft or designer consumer goods, alternative energy, tourism, and services.

corporatist groups. While subnational interests were represented, the subject was largely uncontroversial between the national and local levels. Since the reform granted a substantial amount of additional discretion to local governments which were empowered to pursue individual local development strategies (see Chapter 7.3.2), the KL took a positive stand on the reforms (Claus Ørum Mogensen, September 1, 2011, e-mail message to authors). The clear cut between national economic policy and regional equalisation funded by the European Union led to a strategy shift of the associations of local and regional bodies, striving for influence on EU policies via the Committee of the Regions (Cornett 1997).

In 2003/2004, the whole strategy took another radical turn caused by the new Conservative/Liberal government. A new regional development strategy (Økonomi- og Erhvervsministeriet 2003) stressed the importance of equalising regional disparities while the strong accentuation of competitiveness was somewhat softened. Along with the restructuring of subnational units, the regional entities became responsible both for establishing regional development plans and for equalisation within their area.[100] The Jutland regions include all rich (East coast) and underdeveloped (West coast) areas. This forced their Regional Growth Forums to compromise on the best development strategy.[101] The competitiveness goal of the 1990s is pursued only through 10 per cent of the funds held back by the national government (Neubauer et al. 2007).

In sum, paradigms of Danish regional economic policy shifted radically at the beginning of the 1990s. The old instruments, subsidies and regional development funds, were completely abolished: 'When the new planning law was passed in 1992, the former objective of uniform and equal development for the country was changed to appropriate development in the country as a whole and in the individual counties and municipalities' (Enemark and Jorgensen 2001: 161). On the other hand, the introduction of a new industrial policy was more difficult and subject to political controversies. These, however, were carried out between national party factions, with minor influence of subnational interests. Simultaneously, regional development was left to the counties and municipalities, funded by the European Union. In 2003, equalising economic disparities returned to the top of the agenda.[102] Taken together, decision-making processes are fast, but sometimes short-lived. Economic policy in Denmark is mainly driven by corporatist networks, coming together in ad hoc commissions. Bargaining occurs mainly between these actors, while the influence of subnational interests varies. In the decision-making process under investigation, local interests did not play a major role. However, subnational interests were represented in the reform commission and satisfied by granting additional discretion, which argues for their bargaining potential also at the national level.

---

100. Apart from the persisting fiscal equalisation schemes.

101. This was one of the reasons for drawing the regional borders in Jutland horizontally despite the vertical economic structure (interviews Halkier, Christoffersen).

102. At the same time, the EU enlargement implied a reduction of ERDF funding for Danish regions. This probably led to the need of a new national equalisation strategy.

6.3.3.4 Ireland. Negotiating the National Spatial Strategy

According to our theoretical model and in light of the general characteristics of Irish decision-making processes, the Irish government should be able to tackle the challenges described both fast and in an appropriate manner.

The preparation phase of the National Spatial Strategy began with the establishment of a Spatial Planning Unit (SPU) within the Department of the Environment, Heritage, and Local Government (DoEHLG) in spring 2000. Following an extensive research programme, including more than twenty separate studies undertaken by the SPU and external consultants (Walsh 2002),[103] a public consultation process was launched in September 2001, lasting about eight weeks. The NSS was finally launched by the government in November 2002. The main actors involved in drafting the strategy were government departments. 'The ministry of finance was the strongest' (interview Breathnach). Moreover, 'business organisations and trade unions and farming organisations' (interview Ó Broin), i.e. those bodies included in the partnership process, played a major role. There was no parliamentary involvement,[104] and the official consultation process was 'largely a cosmetic exercise' (interview Ó Broin): the time frame for submissions was tight, considering that groups wishing to contribute often lack resources and expertise. Moreover, the consultation constituted the final phase in the development of the NSS and groups commented on key ideas that had previously been developed. Public input was thus in no way conducive to policy formulation as such.

One of the more strongly debated aspects during the preparation of the NSS was the selection of gateways. These are defined as national engines of growth and make up the top of the urban hierarchy that is the policy focus of the NSS (O'Leary 2003a). Whereas the NDP 2000–6 had already identified Dublin, Cork, Limerick/Shannon, Galway and Waterford as gateways, the NSS designated four new ones – Dundalk, Sligo, and two linked gateways, Letterkenny/(Derry)[105] and Athlone/Tullamore/Mullingar which consists of three comparably small midland towns. The creation of this last linked gateway reflects the successful lobbying of local interests and in some way 'the classic Irish problem' (interview Ó Broin). The result of this decision-making process thus exhibits inefficient features as redistributive decisions partly arose out of clientelism (O'Leary 2003a; Rau and McDonagh 2007).[106]

---

103. The NSS has nevertheless been criticised 'for its underuse of regional economic analysis. Only one of the studies commissioned for the NSS was economic, and this was more descriptive than analytical. Data constraints have been a factor constraining analytical work. However, the lack of interest in regional issues by the economic profession based in Ireland has also played a role' (O'Leary 2003a: 28–9).

104. 'The National Spatial Strategy was never debated in parliament' (interview Breathnach).

105. Letterkenny/(Derry) is a gateway linking the Irish town of Letterkenny with the Northern Irish city Derry.

106. According to McDonagh, 'the whole kind of development of the National Spatial Strategy came down to [...] a very localized narrow kind of view of what needs to be done' (interview McDonagh).

While the NSS nevertheless constitutes a 'major, fundamental change insofar as space never really had counted in the past' (interview Bartley), its major flaw is that it does not put in place structures necessary to ensure its implementation (O'Leary 2003a; Davoudi and Wishardt 2005). '[I]t is vague enough so nobody is actually obliged to follow any of its recommendations' (interview Ó Broin) and, as such, 'it's [...] only a show somehow' (interview Breathnach).[107] Above all, the NSS does not establish the strong regional tier of government necessary for enhancing genuine regional development (O'Leary 2003a). Irish government's success in tackling the main challenge for institutional reform thus proves to be 'very poor [...] There is a great deal of fear involved to devolve any power to either the regional tier of governance or to a local tier' (interview Ó Broin). This opposition to institutional reform is caused by

'the vested interest in government departments, gatekeepers [that] could still block things, and did. Often not just for reasons of inertia but reasons of protecting [...] the policy line of their own departments [...] That really is tokenism in many respects' (interview Bartley).

In addition, politicians fear decentralisation 'because it would undermine their base' (interview Breathnach).

In sum, while the decision-making process preceding the NSS was fairly fast[108] and characterised by a comparatively low level of conflict, the document itself, though proposing a major shift in the focus of development policy, exhibits features of clientelism and, more importantly, lacks the means for successful implementation.

6.3.4   *Patterns of negotiating regional policies*

In line with our expectations, then, the processes of decision making that were initiated to tackle the perceived challenges display diverse characteristics and systematically vary between federal and unitary countries. As summarised in Table 6.5, our case studies in the field of regional development policy indicate at least two major findings.

Firstly, processes of decision making regarding regional development strategies in Denmark and Ireland coincide with our theoretically derived argumentation. As subnational actors provide no effective constraint, both national governments have considerable leeway in designing policies. However, whether such leeway results in proactive reform endeavours or entails only minor policy changes

---

107. On a wider perspective, the timing of the NSS was already notably subordinate within government policies. It 'had literally no impact on National Development Plan priorities because the National Development Plan was already two or three years into its process' (interview Ó Broin). See also O'Leary (2003).

108. The publication of the NSS was delayed slightly because of the Irish election in May 2002, 'because there was obviously going to be disappointment in certain towns when they weren't designated gateways' (interview Quinn). See also O'Leary (2003).

Table 6.5: Patterns of negotiating regional development policies in federal and unitary states

	Switzerland	Austria	Denmark	Ireland
Policy approach	New Regional Policy (NRP)	(1) Regional policy instruments in the 1990s, (2) 2000–6 and 2007–13 Programming Documents	Various regional development strategies in the 1990s	National Spatial Strategy
Main actors (subnational actors in bold)	Federal government, expert commission, **cantonal governments**	Federal government, ***Länder* governments, Conference of State Heads of Governments, Austrian Conference on Spatial Planning (ÖROK)**	Ministry of Industry and Business, subordinated agencies and councils	Department of Finance, Department of Environment, Heritage and Local Government, external experts, **local lobbyists**
Transaction costs	**High**: medium duration of negotiations (almost six years) with high level of conflict between levels	**Low**: (1) *Länder* foster own policy initiatives, (2) fast agreement due to negative coordination	**Low**: short duration of negotiations with medium level of conflict	**Low**: short duration of negotiations with low level of conflict
Access points for subnational actors	**Given**: (expert commission), consultation procedure, working group NRP, (Council of the States)	**Given**: (1) own initiatives, (2) *ÖROK*	**None**: an entirely national competence	**None**: consultation process 'largely a cosmetic exercise' (interview with Ò Broin)
Change in status quo	**Limited**: change of objectives, but partly prevalence with regard to strategies	**Considerable**: (1) correction of policy goals and establishment of many new instruments	**Considerable**: fundamental changes regarding regional policy's paradigm, its strategies, and even the distribution of competencies	**Limited**: change of policy but lack of institutional reform
Adequacy of new policy	**Controversial**: insufficient consideration of greater functional areas	(1) **Given**, (2) **controversial** due to non-binding agreement	**Controversial**: roll-back in 2003 (from cluster policies to equalising strategies) indicates programme failure	**Controversial**: lack of institutional reform, clientelistic features

	Switzerland	Austria	Denmark	Ireland
Provision for implementation	**Given**: cantons as experienced actors, funding assured	**Limited**: high number of implementing agencies, partially poor coordination, resources vary between state governments	**Highly limited**: not given by law, capability of existing structures varies, resources only through EU structural funding	**Highly limited**: no regional actors capable of implementation, no extra funding
Typical for country?	Yes	No	Yes	Yes
Theoretical expectation met?	Yes	(1) – [a], (2) **No**: negative coordination and decentralised implementation provide for fast decision making despite federal structure	Yes	Yes

[a] In our theoretical model we do not develop a hypothesis on decision-making processes in policy areas with separate competencies of the state levels.

depends upon the national governments' own preferences. Accordingly, our case studies display how the Danish government repeatedly and considerably shifted paradigms as well as strategies of regional development throughout the 1990s. At the same time, they reveal a very limited and tentative policy shift in the case of the Irish National Spatial Strategy. Though experts had concluded a far-reaching institutional reform to be highly necessary, the Irish government refrained from establishing the relevant regional tier. Such policy stability seems rational once we take into account the strong interests of government departments that aim to keep resources at the national level as well as of legislators whose career ambitions hinge upon presenting themselves as unchallenged local brokers.

Secondly, patterns of decision making in federal countries are more complex and negotiations slower than in unitary ones but they too display a high degree of within-group variance. Negotiations about regional development policies in Austria and Switzerland exhibit strong differences regarding transaction costs as well as the extent of policy shifts adopted. The case studies clearly show how actors pursuing cantonal interests caused the Swiss New Regional Policy to fall short of the *ex ante* desired degree of policy change. By contrast, Austrian regional development politics reveal greater flexibility and seem to yield an output that meets perceived challenges quite successfully. A deadlock comparable to the Swiss one was circumvented in Austria by a combination of constitutional silence on competencies and incentives set by EU structural funding. While the former enables governmental levels to act independently of each other such that both the federal level and individual *Länder* brought up new strategies to assist regional economies, the latter stimulated stronger demand for intergovernmental coordination and simultaneously facilitated it through additional resources and the possibility of negative coordination.

Comparing processes of decision making in Austria and Switzerland yields insights as to why federalism does not *deterministically* degrade policy performance. To begin with, the competences of decision making that national and subnational governments possess vary not only across federal countries but also across policy areas. And where a policy-area-specific distribution entails only a marginal need for multilevel coordination, conflicting interests do not necessarily clash in a single arena. In this case, the institutional set-up does not automatically bring about a prisoner's dilemma but may grant the various governmental levels room to manoeuvre. Mal-coordination, which hampers policy performance, may then accrue only from a poor match between the policies pursued by various regional entities, not from an institutionally induced stalemate.

Moreover, incentives set by an additional player like the EU may outweigh conflicting interests and foster coordination. This finding is in line with established research (Wachendorfer-Schmidt 1999). In this regard, the vague formulation of our *federalism hypothesis* and the tentative findings of the macro-quantitative analysis are backed by our investigation of micro-level politics. Federalism tends to induce subnational actors to deviate from cooperation and thus to restrict the latitude of national governments, but ultimately a state's capability to adequately react towards changing socioeconomic conditions arises out of incentives set by complex institutional arrangements. The next section investigates whether these micro-dynamics as observed in the typical arena of regional development also apply to the case of transport policy, an area where our statistical analyses show that both federalism and decentralisation have a deviating null-effect upon policy performance.

6.4 Decision making in the area of transport policy

Just as in the case of our investigation into regional development policies, the first step of this section on transport policy is to present country-specific information about the policy area under scrutiny (6.4.1). We can then focus more sharply on the extent to which negotiations regarding transport policies take place in the arena of national level decision making. Subsequently, an assessment of the core challenges (6.4.2) that each of the four countries faced in developing national transport policies paves the way for a focused, critical, and comparative assessment of their reform capacities (6.4.3). In each of the sections, we first shed light on the characteristics and dynamics of transport policies in federal countries, followed by an assessment of the respective patterns in unitary countries.

6.4.1 Transport as a national policy area

The overarching aim of Swiss transport policy is the enhancement of ecological, economic, and social sustainability (see http://www.uvek.admin.ch). This is pursued using a number of measures which can be roughly categorised according to their central objectives: internalising costs via vehicle taxes, optimising the use of existing road infrastructure, expanding the rail network, adopting competitive elements in public transport provision, and increasing coordination between transport and land use policies (Sager 2006: 717–8). The relevant measures thus concern the realm of both road and rail traffic, and it is important to note that the constitutional assignment of decision-making competencies differs between these areas. Responsibility for the Swiss rail network is constitutionally assigned to the federal authorities (article 87, BV) and only marginally delegated to the cantonal level via federal laws (Wälti 1996: 9–10). In the area of road traffic, federal authorities have overall responsibility for providing a network of national roads that is built by cantonal authorities (article 82 and article 83, BV).[109] However, this federal competence is partially delegated to cantonal authorities by federal laws (Wälti 1996: 9–10), while cantonal and communal roads are components of the cantonal residual powers.

Our Swiss case study will scrutinise decision-making processes within the realm of railway policies. Being a central measure for enhancing sustainability in transport and based upon popular demand, the promotion of rail traffic, both freight and passenger, earns a top position on the Swiss political agenda (Hirschi 2002). Policy on rail transport is generally influenced by the federal government; the Department of the Environment, Transport, Energy and Communications (UVEK);[110] the Federal Office for Transport (BAV), responsible for the implementation of public transport policies; cantonal governments; the national parliament; and interest groups such as the public transport union or environmental groups. Furthermore a central role is played by transport companies, most notably the Swiss Federal Railways (*Schweizerische Bundesbahnen*, SBB), which was a state-owned enterprise until 1999 and is now a special stock corporation with all its shares held by the Swiss confederation or Swiss cantons.

Turning to Austria, we find that the distribution of competencies in the area of transport policy is less fragmented than in regional development policies. Rail tracks and highways (*Autobahnen*) are in the hands of the *Bund* (article 10 B-VG). In 2002, the competence for construction and maintenance of former federal roads (*Bundesstraßen*) was shifted to the regional level (*Verländerung der Bundesstraßen*). Public transport is among the *Bund*'s duties.

Despite the fact that competences are concentrated at national level, there exist only two attempts to generate a national traffic concept (the *Gesamtverkehrskonzept 1991*, and the *Generalverkehrsplan 2002*), both non-binding and general in character (Whitelegg 2004). This is due to constant political conflicts between the traditionally 'red' (i.e. Social Democratic) Ministry of Transport (responsible for rail) and the 'black' (Christian Democratic) Ministry of Economics and Labour (*Bundesministerium für Wirtschaft und Arbeit*, BMWA) which is responsible for roads (Lindenbaum 2003). After the competencies were merged in the Federal Ministry of Transport, Innovation, and Technology (*Bundesministerium für Verkehr, Innovation und Technologie*, BMVIT) in 2000, some improvements can be observed, though the level of cooperation is still susceptible to criticism. For

---

109. The NFA recentralised the responsibility for national road construction.

110. Since 2002, the ARE, whose functions include the promotion of coordination between land use and transport policies, has also influenced transport policies.

instance, the National Traffic Concept (Generalverkehrsplan, Bundesministerium für Verkehr, Innovation und Technologie der Republik Österreich 2002) was presented in two poorly connected parts, for roads and rail respectively (interview Macoun).[111] The *Länder*'s environmental and planning competencies are another source of conflict, as they are used regularly to impede unwelcome projects.

In both federal countries, then, we are able to delineate the realm of railway policies as a purely national competence and one thus suitable for comparative assessment of both core challenges and reform capacity. In the unitary countries, decision-making competencies in each domain of the area of transport policy rest at the national level and negotiations are marked by bargaining between government ministries.

In Denmark, designing and implementing transport policy is in general the task of the National Ministry of Transport. It produces a National Transport Plan as soon as a new government takes office. The Ministry of Finance is involved in many decisions, as are the KL in decisions regarding municipal responsibilities such as local public transport, and labour unions when it comes to employment issues. The local origins of MPs and their party affiliation gain relevance in decisions on the allocation of infrastructure investments. Planning issues involve the Ministry of the Environment as well as regional and local authorities. The latter have strong autonomy over regional and local planning, but the national minister does have some instruments available to intervene in subnational planning procedures. Theoretically, conflicts between national ministries are possible, as there is no obligation to harmonise the National Transport Plan and the Planning Framework (Enemark and Jorgensen 2001). In fact, Danish planning is described as strongly sectorally divided, thereby increasing the need for coordinated strategies (Lundquist and Winther 2006).

In the Irish case, decision making in the area of transport policy is a purely national competence. Irish infrastructure planning is, however, tremendously influenced by the EU. Subsidies received by the Irish government since 1973 have in many cases covered 80 per cent of the overall costs for new infrastructure projects, especially in road construction (Rau and McDonagh 2007). Even though the influence of EU funding is in decline,[112] the process of setting up National Development Plans (NDP) has 'become a central part of public planning for infrastructural investment' (Fitz Gerald 2002: 193). The Department of Finance has responsibility for the NDP planning process and negotiates the document with the EU Commission. It has therefore emerged as the central actor in negotiation processes regarding transport policy, while outside experts as well as other government departments play an important consultative role. In this regard, it is important to note that no specific Department of Transport existed in Ireland

---

111. The *Generalverkehrsplan* mentions all existing project ideas, without clearly ranking them. It is therefore a political document reflecting several political interests rather than a statement of the priorities of Austrian transport planning.

112. As a consequence the role of PPP is increasing (Killen 2007; Reeves 2003).

until 2002. As a consequence, many other departments were and still are involved in negotiations regarding transport issues and this fragmentation entails high horizontal coordination needs. Significant input into transport decisions is also given by the National Roads Authority (NRA), an independent statutory body that is responsible for the planning and supervision of construction and maintenance works on all national roads.[113] Social partners and RAuth are additionally consulted, though the input of the latter is severely constrained (see Chapter 6.2).

The realm of railway policies constitutes a clearly delimitable national competence in both federal countries, whereas the central governments in the chosen unitary countries are solely responsible for designing both road and railway networks. Our subsequent evaluation of core challenges thus focuses on developments that provoke reform debates over railway policies in Switzerland and Austria but allows for a broader perspective in both Denmark and Ireland.

6.4.2   Core challenges in transport policies

The core challenge for both passenger traffic within Switzerland and freight transport through Switzerland is increased mobility, especially on roads (Sager 2006: 713).

Table 6.6: Motor vehicles and passenger traffic on roads in Switzerland, 1960–2000

	Motor vehicles		Passenger traffic on roads	
Year	*Total number*	*Δ previous decade in %*	*in m vehicle km*	*Δ previous decade in %*
1960	858,882		10,413	
1970	1,666,143	93.99	25,980	149.50
1980	2,702,266	62.19	35,184	35.43
1990	3,776,829	39.77	44,782	27.28
2000	4,584,718	21.39	51,649	15.33

Source: Bundesamt für Statistik. *Kosten und Finanzierung des Verkehrs – Daten, Indikatoren, Externe Kosten.*

As seen in Table 6.6, both indicators of the strain on intra-Swiss road infrastructure display a positive, but declining slope. Traffic more than tripled from 1960 to 2000. The external costs of this trend[114] were increasingly noticed, creating the need not only to optimise the use of existing road infrastructure, but also to upgrade the rail network and intensify a modal shift towards rail transport.

---

113. See http://www.nra.ie/ for details. Irish roads are divided into national roads (6 per cent) and non-national roads (94 per cent). The maintenance of the non-national roads is a function of the C/C.

114. For data on accidents, noise, health, and congestion see http://www.bfs.admin.ch/bfs/portal/de/index/themen/11/02/blank/key/externe_kosten.html.

A first step towards the last was taken with the introduction of synchronised timetables by the SBB in 1981. This brought about a massive improvement of rail service quality which led to increasing demand, but also indicated limits of capacity of both the rail infrastructure and the rolling stock. As a consequence, pressure to comprehensively modernise the rail network was further increased (interview Sager) and finally led to Rail 2000, a huge modernisation project adopted in 1987.[115] Its decision-making process constitutes the main focus of our analysis of Swiss transport policies.

Just as in Switzerland, increased mobility on roads provides the strongest pressure to expand railway capacities in Austria. Changing lifestyles and extensive use of land led to increased traffic, especially in metropolitan areas (Adelsberger 2003: 141). Between 1990 and 2000, traffic on motorways and A-roads increased by 28.8 per cent. Most of this increase occurred on motorways, whose usage increased by 55.6 per cent in this period. Alpine transit also experienced an enormous augmentation: it more than doubled from 1.2 million trucks per year in 1994 to 2.8 million in 2004 (Bundesministerium für Verkehr Innovation und Technologie der Republik Österreich 2007). The 'fall of the Iron Curtain' changed traffic flows within Austria considerably and increased traffic to Austria's eastern and northern neighbours (Czech Republic, Slovakia, Hungary, and Slovenia). Austria's transport policy had to adjust to these new settings.

Additionally, the long-lasting conflict between ministries had hampered investment in the railroad network. A cooperation initiative during the 1970s cured some of these ills, but Carinthia, Styria, and Salzburg did not agree to the cooperation conditions and were therefore not included in the federal investment programme (Lindenbaum 2003). The poor interregional connections, particularly between Vienna and southern Austria (Carinthia, Styria), were subject to increasing investment demands during the 1980s and 1990s. In the course of these debates, the Federal Minister, Matthias Reichhold, even saw the poorly connected city of Graz 'in great danger' (2002) if the pivotal Koralm and Semmering tunnel projects were not realised. Negotiations revolving around both tunnel projects thus constitute suitable cases for our in-depth analyses of reform capacity.

Turning to the unitary countries, the main challenges in designing adequate transport development lie in the interaction of country-specific characteristics (like the geographic setting of Denmark or the economic boom of Ireland) and growing economic necessities. In Denmark, the main challenge derives from the fact that the country's capital is situated on an island in the far east of the country, distant from the mainland. Additionally, the whole country was increasingly perceived as being situated at Europe's periphery, a perspective that was fostered especially by the lobby organisation *European Round Table of Industrialists* (ERT). Their 1984 report *Missing Links* (European Round Table of Industrialists 1984) sketched a scenario in which Scandinavia would not participate in the economic transnationalisation and would fall behind in comparison with its competitors

---

115. See http://www.parlament.ch/d/dokumentation/do-archiv/Seiten/do-bahn-2000.aspx.

unless it had a better connection to Central–Western European markets.[116]

Additionally, the economic crisis of the 1980s hit the Danish capital. Its industrial base crumbled, and the biggest Danish naval base, Holmen (for 200 years the largest employer in the region), was moved to Frederikshavn (Jutland) in 1988, leading to a sharp rise in unemployment. The movement to suburbia, mainly by the wealthy, severely eroded the capital's tax base (Majoor and Jørgensen 2007). At the end of the decade, a 'need to revitalise the economy' was felt in Copenhagen. Greater integration of Copenhagen and Malmö (the Øresund region) was seen as a promising strategy (Lundquist and Winther 2006). In this context, the idea of an integrated Øresund region covering Copenhagen and Southern Sweden came up. Taking up a suggestion from *Missing Links*, it was decided to construct a fixed link across Øresund to Malmö.[117] This provided the chance to develop an ambitious infrastructure project in Copenhagen, the Ørestad project, which lies at the heart of the following case study of Danish transport policies.

Instead of geographic constraints, the main challenges for contemporary Irish transport policy emanate from dramatic economic and demographic changes. As FitzGerald clearly states: 'the economy has outgrown its clothes! The infrastructure that was appropriate for a relatively poor EU economy in the 1980s is wholly inadequate to deal with the need of the present' (2002: 179). Amplified by the scattered nature of Ireland's population distribution, unplanned urban and suburban sprawl, and a massive rise in car ownership,[118] infrastructure constraints are seen as a major threat to the perpetuation of Ireland's economic success (OECD 2006; Reynolds-Feighan 2003) and, moreover, lead to traffic congestion, noise pollution, and environmental contamination (McDonald and Nix 2005; Fitz Gerald 2002). These trends are expected to continue[119] and constitute major problems for both larger urban centres, especially the Greater Dublin Area (GDA),[120] and for many rural areas that 'have undergone depopulation and decline, which has raised such issues as the cost of maintaining a relatively under-used roads infrastructure and how (if at all) public transport should be provided' (Killen 2007: 100, Fitzpatrick Associates 2006).

The Irish government's approach to tackling these problems has long focused on EU-subsidised investments in the national roads system. In recent years, however, it has launched two separate national programmes that address these

---

116. Chairman of the ERT was Pehr Gyllenhammar, chairman of Volvo, who had a natural interest in a road connection between his Swedish manufacturers and the delivery area.

117. For an extensive discussion of the project, see Figueroa 2005, Ross 1995, or Zank 1991.

118. The number of cars per 1000 persons in Ireland grew from 66.1 in 1961, through 200.8 in 1986, to 291.6 in 1996 (Killen 2007).

119. For traffic forecasts see http://www.nra.ie/Publications/RoadTraffic/.

120. The GDA is especially affected by traffic congestion; the number of trips during morning peak hours increased by nearly 65 per cent from 1991 to 1999 (Killen 2007: 107). While the available suburban rail systems (the Dublin Area Rapid Transit (DART) and the light rail transit (Luas)) have experienced an increase in use, virtually all urban bus services compete with cars for road space and are very slow.

challenges: Transport 21, a ten-year capital transport investment framework (2006–15) costing 34.4 billion euros and covering exchequer and PPP capital investments in national roads, public transport and regional airports;[121] and the 2001 Rural Transport Initiative (RTI)[122] that 'provides financial support to bodies attempting to introduce rural transport services and has given rise to a number of schemes offering both fixed-route and demand-responsive community buses' (Killen 2007). The Irish section thus offers case studies of the decision-making processes preceding both of these programme launches.

6.4.3   Negotiating transport policy reform

Building upon the preceding section, the following analyses of negotiations initiating policy reforms in the area of transport will focus on major and clearly definable infrastructural projects in Switzerland (Rail 2000), Austria (Semmering and Koralm tunnels) and Denmark (Ørestad project) but have a slightly broader focus in Ireland, where Transport 21 and the RTI both constitute major attempts to deal with the encompassing challenge of economically induced infrastructure needs. Just as the preceding analyses of regional development policies did, each of the following country-specific sections systematically touches upon a number of core characteristics: the capacity of subnational actors to influence reform processes as well as their actual involvement; the duration of negotiations as well as the intensity of their conflict; the extent to which a change of status quo was achieved as well as the adequacy of the new policy; and, finally, a prospective assessment of implementation capacities or deficits. Again, while each of the following case studies deals with these questions separately for each country, Section 6.4.4 consolidates the findings from a comparative perspective. It thereby aims, firstly, at a systematic comparison between reform processes in federal and unitary countries but is also, secondly, sensitive towards intra-group variance.

6.4.3.1 Switzerland. Negotiating Rail 2000

Negotiations accompanying the Rail 2000 project can be subdivided into three phases. The first phase ends with the initial adoption of Rail 2000 in 1987. The second phase emanates from financial constraints in the early 1990s and leads to a split of the project's realisation into two stages in 1995. While the project's first stage (B21) was completed in 2004, the realisation of those remaining, called ZEB, has been debated since 2002 and has been negotiated in parliament as part of the *Gesamtschau FinöV*.[123] These negotiations constitute the third phase of the

---

121. Transport 21 is made up of two investment programmes: a national programme and a programme for the Greater Dublin area. For further information see http://www.transport21.ie/.

122. The initiative was awarded long-term funding in 2007 and renamed the Rural Transport Programme (RTP). For further information see http://www.pobal.ie/RTP.

123. In 1998, the funds of the two largest transport infrastructure projects Bahn 2000 and NEAT were pooled into the Funds for the Financing of Public Transport (*Gesamtschau zu Bau und*

overall decision-making process. Our analysis shows that the extent of cantonal involvement as well as cooperative behaviour between cantonal governments varied throughout these stages.

The first phase began in the mid 1970s when the federal government together with the SBB promoted the construction of a New Main Transversal (*Neue Haupttransversale*, NHT) in an effort to tackle the massive deficit in intra-Swiss rail capacity. The NHT was intended to improve travel time between western and eastern Switzerland. It was subject to a consultation procedure initiated by the federal government in 1983, and predicated upon a routeing proposal of Lausanne–Berne–St Gallen. The results exhibit a wide variety of cantonal positions. Sixteen cantons generally approved the project and asked for individually supporting measures. Nine cantons opposed the proposal completely, demanding instead an overall expansion of the rail network to provide equal access for the various Swiss regions (for a detailed description of individual cantons' positions see Höschen 2007: 171–2). Faced with such opposition, the EVD significantly widened and redefined the NHT concept into Rail 2000. The latter is a railway modernisation project that builds upon a state-wide, large-scale capacity expansion and thus benefits all parts of Switzerland. It was finally adopted by parliament and passed by a subsequent facultative referendum in 1987. The high level of conflict between cantons in the first of the three phases thus led to a decision of spatially and financially expanded infrastructure investments.

However, financial constraints at the beginning of the 1990s inevitably made it necessary to renegotiate the timing of individual projects. The resulting division of the project's realisation into two stages severely disadvantaged the central, north-western and eastern parts of Switzerland (Keller *et al.* 2008: 74–5). Consequently, it is interesting to analyse how this prioritisation was rendered possible. Two factors deserve attention in this regard. First, the overall package of Rail 2000 was left untouched. The prioritisation of specific projects was thus paralleled by the federal government's credible undertaking that the second stage of the project's realisation would ensure the promised regional distribution of investments (interview Maibach). Second, the necessary decisions were delegated to the SBB, which conducted the division of the project's realisation into two stages. The 'evaluation was thus depoliticised' (interview Maibach)[124] and the Federal Council was able to build upon the technical arguments proposed by SBB in an effort to justify its report. Although cantonal critique was advanced within the parliamentary debate (Schweizerischer Bundesrat 1994), the Federal Council's

---

Finanzierung von Infrastrukturvorhaben des öffentlichen Verkehrs, FinöV). Those projects to be realised in the second stage of Bahn 2000 are known as a ZEB (*Zukünftige Entwicklung der Bahninfrastruktur*, Future Development of Railway Infrastructure) and constitute one of the modules of FinöV. The allocation of FinöV's remaining capital has been negotiated on the basis of the Federal Message on the Overall Examination of FinöV (*Botschaft vom 17. Oktober 2007 zur Gesamtschau FinöV. Bau und Finanzierung von Infrastrukturvorhaben des öffentlichen Verkehrs*, BBl 2007 7683). For details on recent negotiations see http://www.parlament.ch/D/dokumentation.

124. 'Die Evaluation war entpolitisiert', translation by authors.

report was officially taken cognisance of and not rejected.

The third phase of the decision-making process is made up of negotiations on the remaining projects of Rail 2000 (ZEB) and began in 2002. It is led by the BAV which comprehensively integrated cantonal interests into the early process of re-prioritisation but also works in strategically advantageous[125] close cooperation with the SBB. In contrast to earlier negotiations, cantonal involvement is characterised less by individualised lobbying; it is marked instead by the central role of the cantonal conference of directors of public transport (*Konferenz der öffentlichen Verkehrsdirektoren*, KÖV). Cantonal positions within the process of negotiating were thus far more coordinated than before, even though the KÖV's regional conferences[126] as well as the cantonal governments lobbied for additional individual projects during the consultation procedure of the *Gesamtschau FinöV* (Eidgenössisches Departement für Umwelt Verkehr Energie und Kommunikation, Bundesamt für Verkehr 2007). The KÖV thus presents itself as a well-established network that aims at a spatially broad allocation of funding (interview Maibach), and seeks adequate financial support for ZEB that is independent of cost developments in the realm of the New Railway Link through the Alps (*Neue Eisenbahn-Alpentransversale*, NEAT) (Konferenz der kantonalen Direktoren des öffentlichen Verkehrs 2007). So the cantons 'did not lobby individually against each other, but did impact the process directly as a regional power' (interview Maibach).[127]

In sum, patterns of decision making in the realm of transport policies as revealed by Rail 2000 display varying characteristics. On the one hand, cantons are strongly involved in the process and push for a broad and regionally balanced investment strategy.[128] Once the package of individual projects had been approved by the federal authorities (and by a popular vote), they did so in a more coordinated way (phase 3) than before (phase 1). It is plausible to assume that negotiations were perceived as being less redistributive once the overall investment had been secured. Moreover, the federal strategy of relying on SBB's technical expertise

---

125. The BAV again used the SBB's technical expertise to dampen cantonal investment expectations (interview Maibach).

126. The following regional conferences of the KÖV exist: Western Switzerland, Northern Switzerland, Inner Switzerland, Zürich, and Eastern Switzerland.

127. 'Sie [haben] nicht einzeln, [...] gegeneinander lobbyiert, sondern [...] die Kantone sind als regionale Interessensvertretung direkt in den Prozess gegangen', translation by authors.

128. A comparable pattern of actors and interests was visible in the negotiations preceding the adoption of the NEAT in 1992. They were characterised by constant debate on routeing variants. Cantonal interests were therefore bundled in regional committees (Splügen Committee, Lötschberg Committee, Gotthard Committee) that lobbied extensively for their preferred routeing. The most direct consequence of this regional lobbying is the adoption of the so-called 'net variant' (*Netzvariante*) that encompasses the construction of both the Lötschberg and the Gotthard base tunnels, as well as an additional message regarding access to the eastern region. The NEAT thus reflects the Swiss population's extensive willingness to pay for environmentally friendly transport investments and the deeply rooted acceptance of regional integration in Swiss political culture (for an extended description of the decision-making process preceding NEAT see Höschen 2007).

left less room for individual lobbying. The federal authorities are thus bound to take cantonal interests into account but the highly technical area of infrastructure investment enables the federal government to partly circumvent the 'federal mechanism' (phase 2 and, partly, phase 3).

6.4.3.2 Austria. Negotiating the Koralm and Semmering tunnels

Turning to Austria, geographic conditions dictated by the steep and curving connection between Vienna and Graz (the second largest Austrian city) posed a specific challenge for transport development. Further on, between Graz and Klagenfurt, there is no direct train connection – the necessary detour extends a trip between the two cities to three hours. To improve the situation, two large tunnels are planned. The Semmering base tunnel is located between Lower Austria and Styria and would improve the connection between Vienna and the southern region. Travelling time would be reduced by approximately 30 minutes and conditions for freight transport also much improved. The Koralmbahn project, designed to reduce travel time between Klagenfurt and Graz from three hours to one, also requires a major tunnel. Both projects are the subject of much dispute among the Austrian public and in politics and science.

Planning for the Semmering tunnel started in 1980. In 1989, project responsibility was assigned to the newly founded High Performance Railway Line Corporation *(Hochleistungsstrecken AG,* HL-AG), which fostered planning until authorisation by the railway law of 1994. In 1991, Carinthia and Styria had included the two projects in their regional traffic concepts. In contrast, Lower Austrian accordance had been rather hesitant. The *Länder*'s approval procedure after 1994 reflected that fact. While Styria gave the go-ahead to the project shortly after the federal authorisation, Lower Austrian authorities demurred on the basis of environmental and water laws. The *Umweltverträglichkeitsprüfung* (UVP), in which the *Land* and district authorities approve the environmental impact of a project, provides a useful means of delaying implementation. Subsequently, a long-drawn-out conflict arose between the government of Lower Austria, which tried to impede the project using environmental law, and the HL-AG, which managed to have the Lower Austrian decisions declared illegal and unconstitutional by federal courts. At the same time test drilling of the Styrian part of the tunnel began. After several years of conflict, the Semmering negotiations experienced a breakthrough in April 2008: the Lower Austrian *Landeshauptmann*, Erwin Pröll, signalled his approval of a different route for the Semmeringbahn. The new plans were finished in 2010, and submitted to the *Umweltverträglichkeitsprüfung* with an estimated completion date of 2020 – about thirty years after the debate started. Lower Austria's opposition to the plans may indeed have been exclusively issue oriented and motivated by environmental concerns. It is plausible, however, that the *Landeshauptmann* used this project, which was highly debated in public but low on his state's priority list, to demonstrate his influence on federal politics and to please his local electorate, even in opposition to his own party, the ÖVP.[129]

The Koralm tunnel highlights another aspect of decision making on transport issues. While the two projects are geographically close and highly interrelated, the Koralm tunnel is to connect Styria and Carinthia, whose *Länder* governments have both always supported the project. Accordingly, obstruction from the *Länder* side was not expected. Additionally, between 2000 and 2007, the BMVIT was headed by fellow party members[130] of the late Carinthian *Landeshauptmann* Jörg Haider, who had always fostered the Koralm project. Indeed, the tunnel construction was authorised by Federal Minister of Transport Monika Forstinger shortly after she had taken office. In 2004, a treaty between the federal government and the respective *Länder* was signed. Despite this fact, Koralm is still subject to political conflicts. Financing is – partly due to the non-binding character of the National Traffic Concept – still unsettled (Lindenbaum 2003; Bundesministerium für Verkehr Innovation und Technologie der Republik Österreich 2002). The former ÖVP–BZÖ government tried to increase sunk costs by starting extensive test drillings. When Haider's BZÖ lost office in 2007, he feared the new government would cancel the project and threatened to sue the federal government for non-compliance with the treaty (APA 2007b, February 5). After the Styrian (SPÖ-led) government intervened (APA 2007c, February 7), the Social Democratic Chancellor Gusenbauer offered assurance that both tunnel projects would be a 'top priority' (APA 2007a, February 9) for his government.

Our study shows, then, that both projects are highly dependent on political factors. Construction depends on party affiliation (Koralm) or the willingness of individual *Länder* politicians to divorce themselves from federal politics (Semmering). Efficiency criteria seem to play a minor role. About 500 million euros have been spent to date. The total cost is computed as 4 billion euros for the Koralm and 1.25 billion for the Semmering tunnel. Recent estimates indicate twice this amount (interview Macoun).

Moreover, the general value of the Koralm project is doubted. Austrian Federal Railways (*Österreichische Bundesbahnen*, ÖBB) managers have been quoted as asserting that to be economically viable it would be necessary to evacuate Klagenfurt and Graz completely once a day and to transfer the population of each city to the other (APA 2007a). This is not even disputed by the Ministry of Transport, one of whose representatives writes that the Koralm tunnel would 'radically change the Austrian rail structure like no other project', but at the same time confesses that 'the cost-effectiveness of the project is low' (Adelsberger 2003: 144).[131] The Institute for Transport Planning and Traffic Engineering at

---

129. Pröll is known for such actions. As John and Weissensteiner (2002) write: 'the *Landeshauptmann* does not care about party discipline when it is about scoring votes' ('schwarzes Kaderdenken schert den Landeshauptmann wenig, wenn es gilt, beim Wähler zu punkten', translation by authors).

130. Monika Forstinger (FPÖ) was Minister of Transport 2000–2, followed by Hubert Gorbach 2003–7 (FPÖ, from 2005 BZÖ).

131. 'Kein anderes Projekt verändert die Struktur des österreichischen Eisenbahnnetzes so grundlegend

the University of Technology, Vienna, criticises existing project studies on the Koralm project as unrealistic, and forecasts cost overruns as well as little impact on traffic flows (Institut für Verkehrsplanung und Verkehrstechnik (TUW-IVV) 2007). Others bemoan the fact that other highly desirable projects are protracted because of the high political priority of the two tunnel projects (Paulick 2006).

So the politics of Austrian railway planning encompasses strong regional interests which rely on informal party channels as well as formal (*Umweltverträglichkeitsprüfung*) measures to influence negotiations and decisions. While transaction costs are consequently high, it remains a matter of debate whether such hampering of central government's actions ultimately improves or damages performance.

6.4.3.3 Denmark. Negotiating Ørestad

During the 1980s, the Copenhagen government demanded additional funding from the national level, justifying this demand by the structural problems the capital faced. The national government, formed by Conservative and Liberal parties, however, was not eager to comply.[132] To find a solution, a commission was formed. Its so-called Stallknecht report of November 1989 highlighted the importance of infrastructure improvement to fully benefit from the Øresund region's potential. A core factor, as argued in the report, would be the construction of a fixed link over the Øresund. Although other goals were also outlined in the report, the national government prioritised the fixed link, leaving the question of regional development to a Capital Development Council (*Hovedstadens Udliklingsråd*, HUR). Simultaneously, another commission, the Würtzen committee, was established to find solutions to the capital's traffic problems. After the HUR had failed, a small faction of the Würtzen committee, sometimes called the 'three musketeers' (Andersen 2003: 101),[133] decided to focus on the development issue and created the Ørestad/Metro project (Hansen and Jamison 2004). The western strip of the island of Amager, situated south of Copenhagen city centre and close to the airport and the future Øresund Fixed Link, which had been unpopulated until then, was to be developed into a high technology park and connected to the city by a new metro line.

The initiative of the 'musketeer' committee members was advanced in a political environment characterised by disparate priorities (this paragraph and the following description of the decision-making process is mainly based on

---

wie die Koralmbahn, kein anderes Projekt hat daher eine so ausgeprägte Raumwirksamkeit. Zugleich ist die betriebswirtschaftliche Rentabilität dieses Projekts vergleichsweise gering, so dass die österreichische Verkehrspolitik gefordert sein wird, ein angemessenes Finanzierungsmodell zu entwickeln', translation by authors.

132. The problem of the shrinking tax base had already been solved through a special fiscal equalisation scheme for the capital region (see Section 7.1).

133. The three were Anne-Grethe Foss, head of the planning department of Danish National Railways (DSB), Dan Christensen, architect in the Copenhagen municipality, and Erik Jacobsen, head of department in the Ministry of Finance.

Hansen and Jamison 2004; Majoor and Jørgensen 2007). The Conservative Party was eager to keep its reputation as a pro-business party and wanted to establish Denmark as a region for high technology investments. Additionally, the Conservative government had abolished the Greater Copenhagen Council, which had been responsible for intermunicipal planning issues. This action had been widely criticised, challenging the party to prove that innovation was possible using private companies without intermunicipal planning. The Social Democratic Party was in favour of the project as well, mainly because of the opportunity for infrastructure investments and subsequent positive effects on employment. The local government of Copenhagen and its mayor Jens Kramer Mikkelsen (also a Social Democrat) were interested in improving the city's local transport network – and a metro crossing the city from east to west was the missing link in the system.

The Liberal Party and many MPs from the mainland were sceptical about the project, regarding the Copenhagen government as mismanaged and inefficient. For many MPs from Jutland, a large investment in the capital region was reason to suspect the national government of privileging the Zealand region. These positions reflect the major cleavage between Jutland and the capital region in Danish politics.[134] Copenhagen County, all minor opposition parties,[135] several non-governmental environmental organisations, and some citizens' action committees from the island of Amager opposed the project.

The actual decision-making process was quite rapid. Shortly after the publication of the Würtzen report in March 1991, bills on the Ørestad, the fixed link across the Øresund, and the development of the former naval base in Copenhagen harbour were jointly introduced in parliament by the Finance Minister. The bill on the Øresund fixed link passed in August 1991. Ørestad required more time and passed in June 1992. However, the interesting part of the process had already taken place under the table before the Würtzen report had been published. In February 1991, only four weeks before the official publication date, the details of the Ørestad project were publicly revealed by an article in the newspaper *Politiken*.

At that time, the outlines of the project had already been drawn up by a small group of politicians contacted by the three 'musketeer' members: the National Transport Minister, Kaj Ikast of the Conservative Party, the Liberal MP Svend Heiselberg, and the Social Democratic Party Leader, Svend Auken.

> This was the main result from this commission, which was originally established to solve all traffic problems in public transport in the greater Copenhagen area. So, instead of making more bus routes, or improving transportation facilities to the suburbs around Copenhagen, they came out with this one proposal and in the meantime, they cleared it with these three parties (interview Dahlin).

It was expected that building the new metro line to West Amager would boost

---

134. Also because the Liberal party (*Venstre*) mostly represents the rural population of Jutland.

135. The Radical Liberals, the Progress Party, the Christian Democrats, the Socialist Party, and the Unity Party opposed the project.

prices for the land to be sold to the expected investors at Ørestad. The outsourcing of the Ørestad development to a privately managed corporation had the advantage of keeping the costs out of the national budget.[136] Additionally, two highways in the north of Jutland were planned.[137] This was publicly perceived as a success for the 'Jutland mafia' (Majoor and Jørgensen 2007: 196).

By these means, the difficulty of getting approval in national parliament for a large infrastructure project in the Copenhagen area was reduced (Majoor and Jørgensen 2007). The proposal, as it stood, benefited all three parties involved: the Conservatives got their high technology project; the Social Democratic mayor got a new metro; the Liberal party was appeased by the financial design of the project. And the Jutland MPs were compensated with two new motorways. This 'forced marriage' of the three major parties prevented strong opposition to the project: 'From this point, nothing can be changed. When the political deal is made, it is beyond the point of no return' (interview with Per Henriksen, quoted by Hansen and Jamison 2004: 58–9). However, it was not at first certain that the law would be passed. One reason was an internal conflict within the Social Democratic Party. The party leader, Auken, was actually in favour of the project, but faced opposition in his party due to bad personal relations with the traditional socialist coalition partner. When Auken was replaced in April 1992, the new party leader (Poul Nyrup Rasmussen) positioned himself as pro-Ørestad. The second problem was the status of the construction site as a nature reserve which had been requested by environmentalists and approved in June 1992. However, it was overridden by the Ørestad law (Folketing 1992) eighteen hours later, which dismissed all pending cases of nature reserve establishment.

The municipality of Copenhagen was quite content with this decision-making style. It was a short-circuiting of existing municipal planning procedures which would have included extensive public hearings. This political deal benefited the three largest political factions as well as the initiators.[138] The whole decision-making process was criticised for being exclusive, nontransparent, and not publicly debated. The results are diverse: Ørestad development is difficult and investments drip rather than flow. Lundquist and Winther (2006) demonstrate that Copenhagen has actually seen a decreasing number of jobs in high-tech industries: 'The pace of changes in the industrial structure and creation of new jobs were slower in Greater Copenhagen than in the rest of Denmark' (Lundquist and Winther 2006: 126). Thus despite its free hand, the government failed in its aim of strengthening high-tech economy in the capital region.

---

136. For the effects of this outsourcing on implementation efficiency, see Section 7.4.2.

137. The E45 from Aalborg to Frederikshavn (constructed 1996–2000) and the E39 from Aalborg to Hirtshals (constructed 2000–2).

138. The former transport minister Flemming Hansen and former Copenhagen mayor Jens Kramer Mikkelsen are on the managing board of the Ørestad Development Corporation, as is Anne-Grethe Foss, co-initiator of the project, who has been chairperson of the Copenhagen Metro since 2007.

6.4.3.4 Ireland. Negotiating Transport 21 and the Rural Transport Initiative

The Irish government announced Transport 21 in November 2005 after a preparation phase that lasted eleven months.[139] According to McDonagh, Transport 21 'appeared quite suddenly in a fanfare as opposed to something that had a long [...] process of engagement' (interview McDonagh). The preparation of the programme was mainly led by the Department of Transport and the Department of Finance. Since the respective ministers 'jointly presented it [to the Cabinet] and got agreement' (interview Callanan), the role of other departments, like the Department of the Environment, was limited to pure consultation. Even though Callanan states that 'the local and regional involvement in decisions [...] on Transport 21 is very limited' (interview Callanan), there is reason to assume that the degree of input varies significantly between C/C. Transport 21 has been criticised for its urban bias towards the GDA and, moreover, for including a number of prestigious projects for political rather than efficiency reasons (Barrett 2006: 50–1).[140] It thus seems that some local or regional interests have been more successful than others in pushing for specific projects to be included in the Transport 21 package.[141]

The investments specified in Transport 21 also suggest strong influence from the NRA and the Railway Procurement Agency (RPA)[142]; Transport 21 is criticised for being 'very much a traditional type of approach in the sense that it is about building more roads' (interview McDonagh) and, moreover, focused on railways rather than buses (Barrett 2006). Nevertheless, the share of investment earmarked for public transport has increased in comparison with the NDP 2000–6 (see Table 6.7).[143]

Another criticism frequently raised is that the cost-benefit analysis underlying individual projects of Transport 21 is 'very wanting' (interview McDonagh) and that 'bundling projects in a €34.4 billion package [...] exposes the taxpayer to megaproject risk' (Barrett 2006: 54).[144] While the non-disclosure of detailed

139. See the speech by Martin Cullen T.D., minister for transport, at the launch of Transport 21, 1 Nov. 2005, accessible at http://www.transport21.ie/MEDIA/Launch_Material/Speech_by_Martin_Cullen_TD.html.

140. Examples include the Claregalway Bypass as well as the Metro North in Dublin (interview Rau).

141. Whereas the bias towards Dublin clearly reflects its exceptional position as a commercial and industrial center as well as its magnitude in population numbers, the strength of GDA's transport lobby can be explained in terms of the existence of the Dublin Transportation Office (DTO), a government agency formed in 1996 which provides transport and land use advice to organisations operating in the Greater Dublin Area. The DTO's long-term strategy A Platform for Change (Dublin Transport Office 2001) has informed Transport 21 to a large extent. See http://www.dto.ie.

142. The RPA is a government agency, responsible for ensuring the provision of light rail and metro infrastructure as well as passenger services. For further information see http://www.rpa.ie.

143. The perception of insufficient investment in public transport is justified with respect to the money actually spent during the implementation of Transport 21 in 2007: only 29 per cent of the money allocated went into delivery of public transport projects (Transport 21 Division - Department of Transport 2008).

144. For more on megaprojects and risk, see Flyvbjerg *et al.* 2003.

Table 6.7: Investment in Irish national roads and public transport

Programme	Investments specified for national roads in million (NDP) and billion (Transport 21) euros	Investments specified for public transport projects in million (NDP) and billion (Transport 21) euros	Per cent of investment in public transport
NDP 2000–2006	5.9	2.8	32
Transport 21	18.0	15.9	47
NDP 2007–2013	13.3	Greater Dublin Area: 12.9 RTI: 0.09	49

Sources: Government of Ireland 1999, 2007; Transport 21 Division – Department of Transport, own calculations.

economic analyses is explained by government representatives as part of a strategy aiming at a 'generally competitive tendering process' (interview Callanan), it also reflects a general lack of data and systematic analysis regarding transport issues in Ireland (van der Kamp 2001).

So while Transport 21 was prepared fast and with a relatively low level of conflict, it reflects features of a reactive rather than a proactive policy approach (Rau and McDonagh 2007). In addition, though it provides a detailed list of projects, the inadequacy of the underlying cost-benefit analysis entails major challenges for its implementation.

Irish government was initially very slow to tackle the challenge of rural transport provision. The absence of any top-down strategy (Rau and McDonagh 2007) to limit social exclusion deriving from unmet transport needs gave rise to 'repeated calls by rural-based community and voluntary organisations for improved transport infrastructure and non-conventional demand-based transport solutions' (Rau and Hennessy 2009: 362). This demand was finally answered by the government's commitment to finance 'pilot measures for rural public transport' (Government of Ireland 1999) that led to the launch of the RTI in 2001. Small-scale funding (4 million euros) was provided for 34 pilot rural transport groups. In 2007, the Rural Transport Programme (RTP) put the funding on permanent grounds and raised it to 9 million euros.[145] Both the RTI and the RTP were prepared at central level by an Interdepartmental Group on Rural Transport. Local involvement was limited to local transport audits and needs assessments conducted by County Development Boards.[146]

While the RTI/RTP clearly constitutes a change in policy direction insofar as it is especially targeted at public transport in rural areas, the change achieved in the status quo can only be seen as an 'initial step' (Rau and Hennessy 2009:

---

145. The Minister for Transport has subsequently decided to gradually increase funding to about 18 million euros (Fitzpatrick Associates 2006: i).

146. A more strategic involvement of those groups providing services under the RTI/RTP is prohibited by their limited resources and technical expertise.

364). Firstly, it has not been accompanied by the necessary policy reform in the area of bus licensing which is still highly regulated (Barrett 2001; Rau and Hennessy 2009: 362). This protects the state-owned company *Córas Iompair Éireann* (CIÉ)[147] and 'involves excess costs for users, creates economic rents for producers and signifies regulatory capture of the government' (Barrett 2001: 16). Secondly, the funding provided by the RTI/RTP is marginal in relative terms and as such the government is accused of 'hand[ing] over to community groups the responsibility of actually delivering a [...] national service [...] on the cheap' (interview McDonagh). Thirdly, 'the project still presents itself as a project-based solution to a systemic problem' (Rau and Hennessy 2009: 364). In sum, the RTI/ RTP constitutes a comparatively late step in the right direction, but one that needs further adjustment.

6.4.4 Patterns of negotiating transport policies

Approaches in both unitary countries, then, involve considerable policy shifts which were decided upon without regional involvement. Negotiations were fast and non-transparent, hence transaction costs were low. In Denmark, environmentalists' objections were overridden by the Ørestad Act (Folketing 1992), which dismissed all pending cases of the establishment of nature reserves. Even so, the major investment decision, Ørestad, is highly controversial with regard to its economic efficiency, and is subject to accusations of pork-barrel politics. Comparable inefficiencies plague the quickly achieved Transport 21 programme in Ireland, as experts criticise its bias towards private transport and the GDA as well as the inclusion of prestigious projects for political rather than efficiency reasons.

Negotiations in both federal countries reveal, in contrast, a high level of intergovernmental conflict. Austrian *Länder* politicians use party political channels (Koralm and Semmering tunnels) to further their interests but also rely on their competences in an adjacent policy area (environmental policy) to delay unwanted projects (Semmering tunnel). Whether this detracts from efficiency in practice is, however, questionable, as the general worth of the Koralm project has been doubted (Institut für Verkehrsplanung und Verkehrstechnik (TUW-IVV) 2007). In Switzerland, negotiations attached to the Rail 2000 project reveal varying levels of transaction costs. Once federal authorities (and popular vote) had approved the highly cost-intensive package of individual projects, cantons influenced a necessary reprioritisation in a more coordinated way because negotiations appeared less redistributive. Moreover, there was less room for individual lobbying as the federal strategy was to rely on Swiss Federal Railway's technical expertise.

In a nutshell and as depicted in Table 6.8, processes of decision making again differ markedly between federal and unitary countries. While negotiations in

---

147. Since the Transport (reorganisation of *Córas Iompair Èireann*) Act (Department of the Environment Heritage and Local Government 1986), CIÉ has created three wholly owned subsidiary limited liability companies: Irish Bus (*Bus Éireann*), Dublin Bus (*Bus Átha Cliath*) and Irish Railway (*Iarnród Éireann*).

federal countries frequently reveal conflicts between governmental levels which in general delay negotiations as well as shape their output, the Irish and Danish governments are barely influenced by subnational interests. However, our analyses also detect that federal slowness does not necessarily hamper efficiency in a policy area which is characterised by highly cost-intensive decisions pertaining to large-scale projects.

6.5 Patterns of policy reform in unitary and federal states

We are now able to summarise our findings regarding the first institutional logic and to take on various perspectives of comparison in order to, firstly, assess the extent to which our theoretical arguments referring to a causal connection between federalism (and unitarism) and political performance are corroborated; and, secondly, specify whether we gain new theoretical insights from comparing across policy areas. Finally, we turn to the question of whether the within-group variance on the decentralisation dimension that our case selection entails (with Switzerland being a federal–decentralised and Austria a federal–centralised country) has an additional impact upon those dynamics we witness at the stage of decision making.

Turning to the first endeavour, we find that qualitative evidence on processes of decision making by and large corroborates the theoretical expectations which arise from the first institutional logic. Given a strong move towards reform, negotiations entail higher transaction costs in federal than in unitary countries, as subnational actors are well integrated and frequently pursue diverse strategies to foster their interests. In Switzerland, cantons rarely act in a coordinated way, but take up divergent positions. As a consequence, negotiations are either protracted (NRP) or lead to cost-intensive policies (Rail 2000). The Swiss case studies clearly show that cantonal governments are systematically integrated into the stages of policy formulation and decision making in both our policy areas. Cantonal governments argue for individually or regionally developed modifying proposals during the consultation procedure and significantly impact policy output. Patterns of decision making in the area of regional policy most clearly fit the theoretical expectation as they reflect the federal government's inability to unilaterally push for a comprehensive reform, even if it is perceived to be highly necessary. The NRP was preceded by extensive bargaining and changes the status quo only to an extent that is acceptable to the vast majority of cantons. Negotiations regarding the expansion of the rail network are subject to a slightly different logic. While cantons, and especially regions, again lobby for specific projects, the outcome of the respective decision-making processes clearly constitutes a change of status quo as considerable, regionally balanced investments are agreed upon. Based on popular support for costly developments, infrastructure investments are in this respect perceived as (literally) fostering integration.

Turning to the second federal country, Austria, patterns of policy reform are more heterogeneous. *De jure*, institutions of Austrian federalism are irrelevant within national decision making. Subnational actors in most cases have no formal veto power over national law proposals. Nevertheless, the influence of regional

Table 6.8: Patterns of negotiating transport policies in federal and unitary states

	Switzerland	Austria	Denmark	Ireland
Policy approach	Rail 2000	(1) Koralm tunnel (2) Semmering tunnel	Ørestad	Transport 21
Main actors (regional actors in bold)	Federal government, Federal Office of Transport (*BAV*), Swiss Federal Railways (*SBB*), **cantonal governments, cantonal conference of directors of public transport (*KÖV*), regional committees**	Federal Ministry of Transport, Innovation and Technology, High-Performance Railway Line Corporation (*HL-AG*), **governments of Lower Austria, Styria, and Carinthia**	Würtzen committee (responsible for finding solutions to the capital's traffic problems), representatives of major political parties, **Copenhagen mayor**	Department of Finance, Department of Transport, National Roads Authority (NRA), **local lobbyists**
Transaction costs	Level of transaction costs varies depending on coordination between cantons and role of SBB (**high** in the beginning, **medium** later on)	(1) **Medium**: fast negotiations but conflicts regarding realization and financing, (2) **high**: long duration of negotiations with high level of conflict; delays and planning changes	**Low**: short negotiations in a back room deal, circumvention of public hearings	**Low**: short negotiations (11 months) with low level of conflict
Access points for subnational actors	**Given**: consultation procedure on routing proposals, (parliamentary debate), negotiations between *KÖV* and *BAV*	**Given**: party channels, (1) ruling party part of federal government (2) competences in the area of environmental policies used to delay project and exert influence	**None**: exclusive and non-transparent decision making	**None**: except for the Dublin Transport Office

	Switzerland	Austria	Denmark	Ireland
Change in status quo	**Considerable**: comprehensive though very expensive modernization of rail network	**Considerable**: far-reaching construction decision passed	**Considerable**: far-reaching construction decision passed	**Limited**: major investments for roads but less for public transport
Adequacy of new policy	**Given**	(1) **Controversial** cost-effect relation, (2) **given**	**Controversial**: no job creation in high-tech industries detectable; pork-barrel	**Controversial**: focus on roads inhibits sustainability; pork-barrel
Provision for implementation	**Given:** *SBB* as experienced actor, funding assured though reprioritization necessary	**Highly limited**: *HL-AG* responsible for implementation, financing unclear, Semmering tunnel blocked by Lower Austrian government, cost-intensive solution at hand	**Given**: state-owned private company with implementation rights, government guarantees	**Limited**: NRA and Railway Procurement Agency as experienced actors, weak economic analysis stresses funding
Typical for country?	Yes	Yes	No	Yes
Theoretical expectation met?	Partly	Yes	Yes	Partly

interests on national policy is high because of internal party structures and the strong position of the *Landeshauptleutekonferenz*. The *Landeshauptleute* derive their influence from their role both within their parties and within their administration. Just as in Switzerland, the *Länder* thus pursue individual policy strategies in both our case studies. However, their impact varies. On the one hand, deadlock in regional policy is circumvented by both constitutional silence on competences and incentives set by EU structural funding. Negotiations in transport policies, on the other hand, exhibit prolonged decision-making processes as *Länder* governments use channels of informal influence in an, at least partially electorally motivated, effort to block central government's policy proposals.

Turning to the unitary countries, the most straightforward and theory-corroborating finding is the largely unconstrained room for manoeuvre that unitary governments possess. Our case studies did not detect a single instance where regional or local associations in Denmark or Ireland had a lasting impact upon processes of national level decision making beyond mere consultation. This is most visible in the Danish case. The Danish government changed its regional development strategy radically in a relatively short time period and very early in comparison to other countries. From the point in time the Porter study was published to the development of a new strategy, less than three years passed. In 2003, the framework for regional policy changed again while the administrative organisation at subnational level persisted. The decision-making process for the Ørestad/Metro project was fast but non-transparent, its legitimacy questionable and its results not necessarily efficient. The process was characterised by deals behind closed doors between individuals from three major parties and single-issue lobbyists. Regional interests were taken into account only in the shape of pork-barrel demands from Jutland politicians who were compensated with package deals. However, it seems that this finding cannot be identified as the general pattern in transport policy, but is rather related to large infrastructure projects in Denmark.[148]

Similarly, patterns of decision making in Ireland seem to corroborate our theoretical model. There is no systematic involvement of subnational actors in negotiations at the national level and the government's capacity to tackle policy challenges seems considerable. As a consequence, decision-making processes in the areas of regional policy and transport policy are swift and exhibit a low level of conflict. Thus far they match our theoretical expectation. However, two features of the output of Irish decision-making processes deserve critical attention. Firstly, in both policy areas necessary changes to the underlying policy framework are delayed. In the case of development policies an encompassing change in the status quo is inhibited by both government ministries and politicians who stymie decentralisation in an effort to protect both their financial and political bases. Policy change in transport is mainly constrained by government agencies, such as the

---

148. This finding holds not only for other policy areas, but also for other Scandinavian countries. In Sweden, for instance, the related Øresund fixed link provoked an intensive debate. The government decided to give the people a voice and local demands were registered (Ross 1995).

NRA and RPA, and by the regulatory capture of the government that protects the CIÉ group. It thus turns out that those actors centrally positioned within processes of decision making have no or little interest in pressing ahead with reforms that outside experts consider necessary. Secondly, inefficiencies of policy output partly arise from extensive lobbying of locally oriented politicians. In the absence of an effective local government structure, lobbyists frequently turn towards nationally elected politicians in an effort to increase their C/C's share of funding. Both the NSS and Transport 21 have been found to exhibit, at least partially, features of local pork-barreling.

Viewed as a whole – from a perspective that compares federal to unitary countries – subnational interest representation increases transaction costs a great deal in federal but little in unitary countries facing strong reform initiatives. In the latter, processes of decision making in both policy areas are fast and characterised by a low degree of conflict between levels.

With regard to the second comparative perspective, that is, policy areas, two findings stand out. Firstly, it seems highly consequential that transport policy is characterised by projects that are especially cost-intensive. Consequently, individual decisions entail a need to be scrutinised intensively beforehand. This might mean federalism has a positive effect, as the strong integration of subnational actors into processes of decision making not only protracts negotiations but also increases actors' accountability by lowering information asymmetries and fostering public attention. In cases of potentially ineffective projects, subnational governments in federal states may then use their decision-making competences in adjacent policy areas to put the project's implementation in doubt and thereby inhibit the respective decision. Thus cost-intensive and presumably inadequate transport projects were delayed and scrutinised intensively in Austria (Semmering tunnel), but agreed without genuine questioning in Denmark (Ørestad projekt) and Ireland (Transport 21 as a package of projects). These dynamics – which were not visible in the area of regional development policy – may be one reason underlying our statistical non-findings with regard to performance effects in infrastructure policy.

Secondly, pork-barrel politics seems to be more easily integrated into decisions regarding transport policies than those on regional development. While in Ireland both policy areas are affected, there is anecdotal (Denmark: road construction is a centralised policy area here) and systematic (Austria) evidence of transport pork-barrelling in two of our other sample countries.

With such policy-area-specific findings at hand, our case studies, finally, allow us to speculate about interaction effects between federalism and decentralisation. Within the group of federal countries, the degree of subnational discretion in implementation processes seems to have a repercussive effect on patterns of decision making. In both Switzerland and Austria, subnational entities are responsible for implementing federal law in many policy areas. However, in Austria, the *Länder* have neither political nor financial discretion at hand during the implementation of concrete laws, but make use of specific state competences to delay or impede federal projects. Despite their lack of own resources and exclusive competences, they manage to influence national policies this way through the *Landeshauptleutekonferenz*. This board of influential party officials, though not formally vested with veto power, is extensively engaged in shaping federal legislation. Our analysis shows that this integration partly accounts for the protraction of reform processes. In Switzerland, on the other hand, cantons have *de jure* as well as *de facto* extensive discretion to prioritise during policy implementation. As a consequence, their set of options is enlarged. Next to extensively using their 'voice' in the pre-parliamentary process, they may opt for 'exit' during policy implementation instead of completely blocking federal negotiations. In cases of incongruent preferences between the federal level and individual cantons, policy implementation varies significantly across cantons; individual cantons may even completely refuse to comply (Braun 2003: 76–7). Based upon the precondition that regional distinctions in policy output are generally accepted, this 'loose coupling' of the Swiss federal system (Armingeon 2000: 121–2) allows for more flexibility in national decision making as federal laws are less detailed and rest upon incentive measures.[149] From this perspective, the fact that the revised NRP grants almost full discretion to cantonal implementation may be another reason why consensus was finally reached.

In a within-group comparison of unitary countries, our studies show that the amount of information needed for an adequate reaction to core challenges is potentially insufficient in unitary and highly centralised countries as these may lack local and/or regional expertise. This is especially visible in the case of Ireland, where a lack of regional economic indicators and analyses may further impede the will to opt for institutional reform as it increases uncertainties regarding the potential outcome of such a reform. In contrast, the powerful Danish Local Government Association provides expertise for local competence areas.

Our detailed case studies, making use of within-group and inter-group comparisons of divergent multilevel set-ups, thus (1) find systematic differences between federal and unitary reform dynamics on a general level; (2) yield new insights into the peculiarities of bargaining over large-scale cost-intensive infrastructure projects such as in transport; and, finally, (3) identify interaction effects between the federalism–unitarism and the decentralisation–centralisation dimensions of territorial state activity which opens up new research perspectives that should in the future stimulate more dialogue between political science research on federalism and public finance research on fiscal federalism.

---

149. However, it is also responsible for huge uncertainties regarding the governing capacity of the federal government (Braun 2003; Linder and Vatter 2001).The same holds for policy areas with concurrent competences in Austria, e.g. regional development strategies.

chapter seven | the logic of policy implementation in centralised and decentralised countries

In this chapter, we turn to the comparison of patterns of policy implementation. We focus on the micro-level mechanisms deriving from the degree of decentralisation our country cases are subject to. We thus evaluate in detail the cogency and institutional logic underlying our *decentralisation hypothesis*. To start with, Section 7.1 provides a general description of the cases' implementation schemes. It shows that the theoretical preconditions for efficiency gains from decentralisation are present in the cases of Switzerland and Denmark, in contrast to Ireland and Austria. Section 7.2 then compares fiscal behaviour and discipline of subnational actors in our four cases. It shows that the dynamics of subnational borrowing are indeed affected by the underlying institutional structure, as postulated in the *HBC* and *interaction hypotheses*. In Austria and Denmark, however, we find additional mechanisms in place. In the former, regional governments make strategic use of the soft character of budget constraints, triggering generous federal transfers and shifting debt burdens to the federal level. In the latter, subnational fiscal discipline is additionally reinforced by mutual control between the municipalities. Sections 7.3 and 7.4 compare processes of implementation in regional development and transport policy, respectively. Finally, Section 7.5 draws conclusions on the general patterns of policy implementation in the different country cases and policy areas.

7.1   Multilevel country profiles

We start with a brief overview of tasks and resources of subnational entities in Switzerland and Denmark, as opposed to Austria and Ireland. In particular, we are interested in the extent to which the theoretical preconditions for efficiency gains from decentralisation (see Chapter Two and Chapter Five) hold. These comprise sufficient staff and financial resources, a fiscal balance between expenditures and own revenues or unconditional grants, and substantial policy discretion at the subnational level. Furthermore, patterns of horizontal cooperation can also affect the implementation capabilities of subnational units. The specific modes of budget constraints, which according to our theory affect decentralised resource allocation contingent upon the type of federalism, are dealt with separately in Section 7.2.

Let us discuss first the decentralised countries in our sample, Switzerland and Denmark. Subnational levels in Switzerland play an extremely important role. They own numerous competencies (e.g. health, welfare, education, public order, regional planning and infrastructure, among others), and, given the 'cooperative' character of the Swiss federal system, 'most federal programmes and central government functions are carried out by the cantons and the municipalities; no parallel federal administration with its own regional services and agencies has been put in place' (Vatter 2005: 8). Policy discretion as well as fiscal compensation for cantonal implementation tasks are constitutionally guaranteed (article 46, BV). In fact, cantonal policy implementation is rarely subject to detailed regulation and the central level rarely uses its instruments of surveillance in order to monitor compliance (Wälti 1996: 22). In 2005, 54 per cent of all public expenditure in Switzerland was allocated by cantons and municipalities and 52 per cent of the subnational expenditure was covered by own tax revenue (International Monetary Fund 2008, authors' own calculations). Patterns of policy implementation in Switzerland are thus strongly influenced by the role that subnational units play.

The cornerstone of autonomy in implementation matters is financial means. Generally speaking, the Swiss tax system allows for large revenue discretion on the part of the cantons and municipalities (Spahn 1997b: 327–8; Dafflon 1999). Taxation powers are constitutionally ascribed to all three levels of government and the cantons are authorised to levy any type of tax that does not belong to the exclusive authority of the confederation (like the value added tax, see article 42, BV). The 'main progressive taxes on personal and corporate income are state and local taxes, whose rates differ from canton to canton and – within cantons – from municipality to municipality' (Kirchgässner and Pommerehne 1996: 353). The small size of many cantons and municipalities and differences in the tax base mean that the financial and administrative resources that cantons and municipalities have at their disposal to engage in innovative policy implementation vary considerably.[150] Two issues deserve attention in this regard. First, to what extent does horizontal coordination between cantons and/or municipalities compensate for their respective weaknesses? Second, which incentives arise from the Swiss system of financial equalisation? We will deal with these aspects in turn.

Firstly, structurally weak cantons have three options for the effective implementation of complex federal policies: to cooperate with other cantons, to outsource the provision of public goods to larger cantons, or to privatise them (Linder and Vatter 2001: 112–3). Cross-jurisdictional coordination is often sought by concordats,[151] and thus contractual agreements for cooperation in legal, administrative or judicial matters (Bolleyer 2006a). These can be interpreted as a functional equivalent of territorial reform, diminishing spill-over effects and taking advantage of economies of scale. However, their effectiveness is often limited by the small number of cantons entering,[152] the wide variety of cantonal administrative structures and interests that complicate collaboration (see Bochsler

---

150. An invaluable database on cantonal administration and finance is provided by the Project 'Banque de données sur les structures des administrations cantonales (BADAC)', initiated by the Swiss Graduate School of Public Administration (IDHEAP) in 1990. See http://www.badac.ch.

151. Implementation deficits may also be softened by secondary harmonisation, that is, via mechanisms of informal coordination and information exchange. However, only cantons that have strong interests as well as sufficient resources available seem to engage in secondary harmonisation (Sager 2003).

152. It remains to be seen whether this will change with the application of the two new instruments of obligatory cantonal cooperation put into effect with the new financial equalisation system.

et al. 2004), and the fact that they 'suffer from a severe lack of democratic legitimacy due to their bureaucratic character' (Vatter 2005: 9).

Second, the tremendous differences between cantonal financial capacities have led to the evolution of a complex system of financial equalisation (Commission on Fiscal Imbalance 2001; Spahn 1997a; Spahn 1997b; Dafflon 1999; Bird and Tarasov 2004). Before the far-reaching reform of the *Neugestaltung des Finanzausgleichs und der Aufgabenteilung zwischen Bund und Kantonen* (NFA),[153] financial equalisation was to a large extent channelled through specific grants,[154] revenue sharing and cantonal contributions to the social security system (Dafflon 1999). The first two were allocated partly on the basis of a 'fiscal capacity' index that considers cantonal income per capita and tax revenues as well as the cantons' tax burden and expenditure requirements, as indicated by a factor for mountainous regions. The equalisation allowed for a moderate horizontal redistribution, with the remaining disparities accepted as there 'is no claim to obtain identical economic and fiscal conditions across cantonal and communal jurisdictions' (Dafflon 1999: 290). The NFA that finally came into effect in January 2008 pursues two main objectives. First, an encompassing reassignment of functions, based upon the principle of subsidiarity, which decouples federal and cantonal tasks.[155] Second, a reform of the financial equalisation mechanisms that increases the cantons' own resources. The new system thus rests upon four pillars: *resource equalisation* that is both vertical and horizontal (a minimum two thirds and a maximum 80 per cent are provided by the cantons) and based upon tax potential rather than the fiscal capacity index outlined above; a *guaranteed minimum* of 85 per cent of the average tax potential for all cantons; *cost equalisation* accounting for structural disadvantages; and a *cohesion fund* that provides compensatory, closed-financed payments (Fischer *et al.* 2003; Schaltegger and Frey 2003; Braun 2010; Biaggini 2006).

In Denmark, the local government tier in particular performs many and quite demanding tasks. This high level of decentralisation was further strengthened during the 1970s. The Local Government Reform of 1973, when 1,098 municipalities were reduced to 275, transferred to the municipalities all administrative tasks relating to the welfare state or to citizens, like schools, social security (e.g. care for the elderly and day care) and public infrastructure (local roads, supply of water and gas, waste management) (Kjellberg 1988). At the same time, the national government changed much of its legislation to broader, general guidelines, giving the executing agencies more leeway to implement policies their own way (Bogason 1987; Hansen 1997). In order to improve the central government's monitoring capacity, administrative procedures and accounting rules were standardised and

---

153. For detailed information see http://www.efv.admin.ch/d/themen/finanzausgleich/.

154. Data on central government grants can be accessed at http://www.efv.admin.ch/d/themen/bundes-finanzen/subventionen/subventionsdb8.php.

155. The remaining cooperative areas are now subject to contracts inspired by New Public Management ideas.

control measures were tightened (Hansen 1997).[156] During the 1980s, a strong trend towards extensive user participation led to the introduction of powerful user boards at schools, nurseries, and similar institutions (Lidström 2001). With the Local Government Reform 2007,[157] the municipalities have also taken on more responsibilities devolved from the regional level, such as areas of health care, special education, labour market policy, planning and roads, business services and cultural activities (Indenrigs- og Sundhedsministeriet Danmark 2004). In addition to their assigned tasks, Danish municipalities are allowed to develop their own initiatives, as long as they do not deviate from principles of the free market and non-discrimination and the goals of national policies (Dosenrode and Halkier 2004). The amount of discretion in practice depends on the policy area. Whilst in some areas local governments act independently, in other fields (foremost social welfare) subnational levels have to implement state tasks, acting solely as local administrative agencies of the central state. As Tonboe (1991: 32) puts it: 'Initiatives and implementation are decentralised, but decisions and control are highly centralised. This centralisation is almost exclusively at the ministerial level'. Danish local governments thus play 'a dual role as units of local self-government and units of local state administration' (Hansen 1997: 47).

The regional level's job is of a 'primarily administrative nature' (Dosenrode and Halkier 2004: 13). After 1973, the institutions on the regional level, the counties, were only allowed to execute tasks requiring a high level of coordination between municipalities (Hansen 1997). The counties' main tasks were planning,[158] road infrastructure, high schools, and hospitals. After the 2007 reform, the regions have additionally become responsible for the coordination of regional development through newly established Regional Development Forums and for regional public transport.

The major role of subnational entities, in particular the municipal tier, is reflected by their high share of general government expenditures (50.55 per cent in 2007, International Monetary Fund 2008, own calculations) and also by the large number of subnational public servants. Subnational levels have autonomy over their administrative organisation (Christensen and Pallesen 2001). In 2006, 56 per cent of public employees worked for local governments; another 23.5 per cent were employed by the regional level. Only 20.5 per cent of the total of 765,000 public servants were paid by central government. Local governments thus employ 15.2 per cent of the total Danish labour force (Statistics Denmark, www.dst.dk).

Regarding local government finance, Denmark is one of the most decentralised countries in the world. Most local government revenue comes from a 'piggyback tax' on income taxation, a flat tax supplement fixed by individual

---

156. The reforms were sometimes criticised as an unintentional recentralisation of Denmark (Picard 1983).

157. For details on the path to reform and the reform itself, see Bundgaard and Vrangbaek (2007).

158. The 1970s were called the 'golden age of planning' (Bogason 1991: 279) for the counties, because of the high levels of resources and discretion they held.

Table 7.1: Revenue sources of Danish local governments, 2006

Revenue source	Amount in million Danish Kroner	Percentage
Taxes and social contributions	282,003	51.87
Income tax	254,239	46.76
Grants	209,601	38.55
Loans	7,213	1.33
Other	44,895	8.26
Total	**543,712**	**100.00**

Source: International Monetary Fund 2008.

municipalities.[159] From this source local governments generate up to 50 per cent of their total income (see Table 7.1). Minor income sources are a property tax and a share of the corporate tax. In a 1970 reform, several conditional grants were replaced by a large block grant, leaving substantial discretion to the municipal units. Specific grants are another large revenue source for local governments: central government reimburses the lion's share of the social expenses for which the municipalities are responsible. The percentage varies depending on the expenditure function.[160] During the 1990s Social Democratic governments reintroduced several specific grants in order to create incentives for local governments; this measure, partly considered an act of 'recentralisation' (Hansen 1997: 62), in effect enlarged the scope for local government's action. In 2004, the share that specific grants contributed to local and regional governments' revenues was slightly higher (15 per cent) than the amount gained from the general grant schemes (11 per cent) (Lotz 2005). Counties are financed largely through tax revenues and a block grant, their particular responsibilities not qualifying for reimbursements. The regions lost their tax powers in the 2007 reform and are currently financed through grants from the central (80 per cent) and local levels (20 per cent; www.regioner.dk).

Fiscal equalisation of municipalities is accomplished through two mechanisms. First of all, the central government block grant has a redistributive impact.[161] Additionally, a horizontal equalisation scheme between all municipalities adjusts 62 per cent of the differences in the tax bases and 'objective expenditure needs' calculated by the national government. Prior to the 2007 reform, two parallel schemes were in force: municipalities in Greater Copenhagen were equalised over

159. In 2007, tax rates varied between 21.9 per cent (Holmsland) and 27.8 per cent (Langeland) (Danish Ministry of Finance, www.skm.dk).

160. Pensions are reimbursed up to 100 per cent, illness to 75 per cent, social welfare to 50 per cent and housing to 40 per cent (Hansen and Jensen-Butler 1996).

161. The aim is to empower poor municipalities and counties to provide a supply level in accordance with the national mean. The amount for individual municipalities is calculated by a sophisticated system based on the local tax base (Lotz 2005). The system has a redistributive impact and includes three different grant schemes: for municipalities of Greater Copenhagen, for other municipalities, and for counties (Pedersen 2002b).

85 per cent of tax base differences, the rest of Denmark over only 45 per cent. Greater Copenhagen's high equalisation rate caused incentive problems which the new scheme has resolved (interview Mouritzen).[162] Counties were equalised across 80 per cent of the difference from the national mean in tax base and expenditure needs (Indenrigs- og Sundhedsministeriet Danmark 2002).

Municipalities cooperate frequently in the area of public services, like waste management or purification plants. The relationship between municipalities and counties is more problematic. Counties cooperate with each other, but they do not work together with big cities within their own borders. All attempts to establish cooperation schemes between local and regional governments have so far failed (Dosenrode and Halkier 2004). The new organisational structure requires some cooperation at the regional level, as during the set-up of a regional development plan, but competencies promote more rivalry than incentives to cooperate.[163]

There is a broad consensus in Danish society and in the political arena that a decentralised allocation of resources is efficient and target-oriented. Reforms are regularly aimed at increasing this efficiency further which eventually leads to some recentralisation or mergers of local or regional entities. The 2007 reform was explicitly justified by the existence of economies of scale (Indenrigs-og Sundhedsministeriet Danmark. The Commission on Administrative Structure 2004; Christoffersen 2005; Christoffersen and Larsen 2007). High societal homogeneity and converging preferences (Pedersen 2002a) make adequate regional provision of public goods a lower-ranked reason for decentralisation.

In summary, the institutional set-up that defines subnational entities' leeway in Denmark and Switzerland matches the quantitatively based categorisation of both countries as decentralised ones. Moreover, the preconditions for efficiency gains are largely present in both countries. Implementation in Denmark is very decentralised in both fiscal and functional terms (Blom-Hansen and Pallesen 2001). Danish local governments perform a wide variety of tasks and in general there is more discretion during implementation than in most other countries (Lidström 2001). In this, Denmark greatly resembles other Scandinavian countries (Petersson 1994), sometimes in the most unambiguous way (Hansen 1997; Kjellberg 1988; Jorgensen 2002). The outlines of a policy are generally drawn by laws, leaving room for action by both national ministries and subnational entities. Following the principle of 'general competence', local governments are allowed to execute tasks that are not fulfilled by already existing agencies and that do not infringe upon legal and administrative rules. Local jurisdictions are in charge of more than 60 per cent of total government expenditure. Municipalities have substantial

---

162. Experts underline different aspects of the financing scheme: some detect inherent incentive problems due to high equalisation rates removing incentives for efficient management (interview Christoffersen), while others stress the political utility of reimbursements and fiscal equalisation (interview Mouritzen).

163. In addition to the elected regional councils, new Regional Development Forums with municipal (and other) representatives have been established. Both institutions have veto powers in relation to the Regional Development Plan.

tax-raising competencies in addition to a large, non-earmarked block grant. Thus, fiscal imbalance is low and responsibilities and financing are in almost all cases located at the same level, assuring a high level of fiscal equivalence.

Switzerland is without doubt one of the most decentralised countries in the world (Adamovich and Hosp 2003; Feld *et al.* 2005). Cantons hold the lion's share of competencies, have autonomous tax-raising power and enjoy substantial room for manoeuvre generally granted by federal laws. The old system of financial equalisation, based mainly on categorical grants, has been subject to profound criticism for inducing overprovision, reducing regional distinctiveness (Schaltegger 2001: 13), and promoting rent-seeking (Braun 2010). The dominant perception that the negative effects of extensive central co-financing outweighed the positive ones (Fischer *et al.* 2003) led to the NFA reform. Though it is too early for comprehensive empirical studies on the effects of the NFA, recent evaluations point towards potential improvements that ameliorate the inefficiencies depicted above by increasing cantons' own resources (Biaggini 2006: 69; Braun 2010: 18) and thereby enhancing allocative efficiency and accountability (Fischer *et al.* 2003: 419) as well as transparency (Schaltegger and Frey 2003). A weak point of the decentralised Swiss state, however, is the limited size of subnational entities. It is thus generally hard to judge whether variance in implementation processes signals efficiency as predicted by the decentralisation theorem and/or detects that weak cantons/municipalities simply lack the resources, expertise and technical competence to adequately implement complex federal laws (Wälti 1996; Linder and Vatter 2001: 107–8). Despite these weaknesses, both Denmark and Switzerland meet the theoretical preconditions to benefit from the positive effects of their decentralised state structure.

We now examine the two centralised countries in our sample, Austria and Ireland. Austrian subnational governments receive 18 per cent of general government revenue and are responsible for 29 per cent of total expenditures (International Monetary Fund 2008, own calculations). In the public debate, regional differentiation and efficiency gains through decentralised provision of public goods play no role – uniformity of living conditions is the predominant concept (Erk 2004). Hence, subnational variance in most policy areas is negligible (Obinger 2002) and unwanted (interview Fallend). The country can thus be described as an extraordinarily centralised political system financially, even compared to unitary countries (Bußjäger 2002). In many policy areas, decision making is situated at the federal level, but the national government depends on the *Länder* administrations during the implementation stage of policy making. Within this Indirect Federal Administration, *Länder* governments are subordinated to the national ministries.[164] Law formulation is generally detailed, implementation is organised hierarchically and leaves little discretion to the executing bodies (Erk 2004). In practice, identical implementation by the *Länder* is assured by federal

---

164. Below the *Länder* level, the districts and municipalities also implement higher-level decisions, of both the federal and the *Länder* level (*mittelbare Landesverwaltung*).

decrees (*Ausführungsbestimmungen*) and the legality principle (*Legalitätsprinzip*, article 18.1 B-VG), which requires a formal authorisation by law for every administrative act (Fallend 2005). The *Landeshauptmann* and his administration act in these policy areas as implementing bodies without much discretion. In general, strong links between state and federal administrations (Fallend 2005) provide for an administrative coordination between state levels that works 'like clockwork'. And in practice intergovernmental conflicts regarding questions of implementation are uncommon.[165]

The Austrian finance system is quite centralised, especially compared with other federal states (Fallend 2005). The lion's share of tax income is earned by the federal level. 86 per cent of the tax revenue are shared taxes raised by the central government (*gemeinschaftliche Bundesabgaben*). Another 9 per cent are federal taxes; the subnational own tax share is only 5 per cent of all revenue.[166] Subnational entities are financed mainly through central government grants, assigned by complex formulas.[167] In 2007, the *Bund* received 73.4 per cent of all tax revenues, the *Länder* 9.4, Vienna 6.2, and the other municipalities 11.0 per cent. In 2006, 52 per cent of the *Länder*'s expenditures were financed by grants (see Table 7.2). The municipalities have a stronger financial basis through fees and taxes, but the absolute revenue level is quite low as municipalities account for only 16.8 per cent of general government revenues (International Monetary Fund 2008, own calculations).

The amount and distribution of central government transfers are negotiated every four to five years[168] and fixed in the fiscal equalisation scheme (*Finanzausgleichsverhandlungen*) (Bundesministerium für Finanzen der Republik Österreich 2005; Obinger 2002). These negotiations include not only fiscal equalisation and transfers, but also the apportioning of shared taxes and joint

165. In recent years, there have been only two conflicts, where *Landeshauptleute* did not accomplish federal orders. The first is shop closing times (Pelinka 2008) and the second the conflict over bilingual road signs in Carinthian towns with a Slovenian minority (*Kärntner Ortstafelstreit*, Pallaver 2008; Karpf and Adamovich 2006; Pelinka 2008; Institut für Föderalismus 2005). However, the sanctioning power of the federal level in the case of non-compliance is unclear. Legally, disciplinary measures are possible (as with any subordinate public servant) but in reality difficult to enforce (because of the *Landeshauptmann*'s strong political power). Additionally, as the *Landeshauptmann* as executive of federal orders (*Träger der mittelbaren Bundesverwaltung*) may only be monitored and sanctioned by the federal government and not the *Land*'s parliament, accountability is quite low and leaves him some discretion.

166. By law, the *Länder* are allowed to raise new taxes in previously untaxed areas (*Steuerfindungsrecht*). *De facto* this right has been hampered by the federal state several times, for example when Lower Austria tried to introduce a tax on mobile phone transmitter masts (Institut für Föderalismus 2005: 48–9).

167. The distribution among the levels differs between tax types. In the period 2005–2008, for most shared taxes, the ratios were: *Bund* 73.20 per cent, *Länder* 15.19 per cent, municipalities 11.61 per cent (Statistik Austria).

168. The present agreement (Bundesministerium für Finanzen der Republik Österreich 2005) is valid for the period 2008–2013.

Table 7.2: Subnational revenues in Austria, percentage by source, 2006

	Taxes and social contributions	Grants	Borrowing	Other revenue	Total
State level	35.69	51.94	–0.01	12.27	100.00
Local level	60.67	14.06	2.82	26.47	100.00

Source: International Monetary Fund 2008, own calculations.

financing schemes.[169] However, the arrangements show remarkable stability over the last decades (OECD 1997). The fiscal equalisation system is complex and commonly separated into a primary, a secondary, and a tertiary (or 'grey') equalisation scheme. The primary scheme comprises the apportioning of shared taxes *between* levels (vertical equalisation) and *within* levels to entities (horizontal equalisation). The secondary scheme comprehends additional grants between levels of governments which are allocated according to expenditure needs and mostly for specific tasks (*Bedarfszuweisungen*).[170] In the third step of fiscal equalisation, the distribution of resources in areas co-financed by the federal level is arranged.[171] Ultimately, the redistributional effect favours mostly municipalities with only low own revenues (Bröthaler *et al.* 2002).

Despite the lack of financial resources and policy discretion, subnational entities employ a large share of public servants. In 2004, 47 per cent of public servants were employed by the *Länder* (see Table 7.3). This high personnel decentralisation is due to the many implementation tasks that are located at state level. With regard to their internal administrative organisation, *Länder* have a substantial amount of autonomy (Weber 1992). This accounts for significant institutional variation on the subnational level, e.g. in the implementation of regional development programmes (see Section 7.3.3). Cooperation between the *Länder* occurs (mainly through formal agreements), but is not very frequent.[172] There are several examples of horizontal cooperation on the municipal level (sewerage, purification plants, public transport) (Bauer 1991), but few arrangements between two or more *Länder*.

169. These schemes have become more common since the 1970s, when the *Bund* began to attach investment decisions to the respective *Land*'s co-financing (Pelinka 2008).

170. The substantial *Gemeindebedarfszuweisungen*, for example, consist of a share of the municipalities' revenue handed over to the state government, which is entitled to assign the resources to the municipalities according to its own criteria.

171. For more information on the fiscal equalisation scheme, see e.g. Lehner (2002, 2006), Schönbäck and Bröthaler (2005), Bröthaler and Bauer (2006), or Bußjäger, Bär, and Willi (2005).

172. Examples are the *Planungsgemeinschaft Ost* (Association Regional Planning of Vienna, Lower Austria, and the Burgenland) or the *Österreichisches Institut für Bautechnik* (Austrian Institute for Technical Approvals).

Table 7.3: Number of Austrian public employees (full-time equivalents) by state level, 2004

	Central govt	Regional govt	Local govt	Total
Number of public employees	132,756	180,498[a]	70,400	383,654
Percentage	34.6	47.0	18.3	99.9

Source: Österreichisches Bundeskanzleramt, based on data provided by federal, state, and local governments; own calculations.

[a] Approximately 75,000 of the *Länder* civil servants (about 42 per cent) are teachers paid by central government (Grossmann and Hauth 2004).

The Irish state ranks among the most centralised systems in Europe. However, the network of public, semi-public and private actors as well as the degree of national, regional or local participation involved in implementation processes varies depending on the policy area. The main responsibility for policy implementation in Ireland rests with fifteen government departments. Traditionally, the minister dominates their internal hierarchy and '[i]n essence, the minister *is* the department' (Chubb 1992b: 69, emphasis in original), whereas the role of senior civil servants like secretaries, deputy secretaries, and assistant secretaries has been officially recognised only since the Public Service Management Act (Oireachtas 1997; O'Halpin and Connolly 1999; Connolly 2005). A major criticism is also a lack of coordination between departments (Verheijen and Millar 1998; Taylor 2005; OECD 2008). Irish public administration is characterised by the delegation of authority to, on the one hand, state agencies which are subordinate and accountable to the respective department (Saalfeld 2008: 209) and, on the other hand, to state-sponsored or semi-state bodies (Chubb 1992b: 245). This spatial dispersion began in the 1960s and in the mean time has resulted in a mosaic of non-overlapping state or state-sponsored agencies at sub-county, county or quasi-regional level. These form an extremely complex subnational governance structure that involves nearly 500 agencies (see O'Broin and Waters 2007, Appendix I, for a detailed overview). The measures of ministerial control over state-sponsored bodies range from appointing all members of the relevant governing board to monitoring devices. Parliament's control, however, is weak (Collins and Quinlivan 2005: 394–5; Chubb 1992b: 253–4).

Local authorities provide public services in eight policy areas: housing (Norris 2003), water supply and sewerage (Gleeson 2003), non-national roads (Howell 2003), development incentives and control (Grist 2003), environmental protection (O'Riordain 2003), and recreation and amenity (MacGrath 2003). They are thereby subordinate to the Department of Environment, Heritage and Local Government (DoEHLG) and the amount of their discretion is affected by legal constraints, their internal management structure, and their financial scope. Until 1991 the 'doctrine of ultra vires' banned them from undertaking action in any areas other than those listed. This was modified by the Local Government Act 1991 (Oireachtas 1991) which assigns any local authority a general competence and entitles it to engage in activities 'to promote the interests of the local community' (Section 6.1.*a*).

The internal structure of C/Cs, however, is characterised by a managerial system 'designed to facilitate the control by national political leaders over local authorities' (Almy 1980: 477) and hence severely restricts the scope of action for local governments. The key to the relationship between elected councillors and the appointed manager is the difference between 'reserved' and 'executive' functions. '"Reserved" functions are the responsibility of the elected councillors and cover important matters of policy and principle: financial affairs, development plans, passing of by-laws. All other functions are executive and automatically come under the authority of the manager' (Loughlin 2001: 69). The C/C manager is thus responsible for the day-to-day running of the local authorities: he 'organises, controls and if necessary disciplines the staff; enters into contracts; gives or withholds planning permissions' (Sheehy 2003: 137). Given their position as full-time salaried officials appointed by a Local Appointment Commission,[173] managers are said to be dominant in their relationship with the council (Laffan 1996; Collins 1985; Loughlin 2001). The *de facto* capability of councillors to engage in innovative policy making is therefore small.[174]

A spatially comprehensive regional layer was only established with the RAuth and RAss in 1994 and 1999, respectively. Their main function is to monitor the delivery of EU Structural Fund assistance as well as 'to promote co-ordination of the provision of public services in the authority's region' (Government of Ireland 1993, article III.14(1)). Their capability to do so is, however, severely constrained as neither has tax-raising powers.[175] The daily work of the RAuth is typically done by one secretary and one or two additional staff members (McDonagh 2001: 169), so they are 'in practice […] quite modest organisations' (interview Callanan). A similar assessment can be made of the two RAss. They are financed through the national government, have a full-time director as well as 15 to 18 staff members and 'have no real powers, they simply have very little function. Their function was really to inform planning and help co-ordinate, they haven't achieved much even on that' (interview Bartley). Even the establishment of regional structures in Ireland is closely linked to a policy of raising financial means from the European Structural Funds and this is especially obvious with regard to the RAss (Boyle 2000; Bannon and Russell 2001). Referring to their severely limited competencies, McDonagh speaks of 'a cosmetic exercise in regionalisation that would net the Irish government some extra 590 million Euros' (2001: 171). Even though the

---

173. His (or her) power is derived from statutory provisions and not delegated by the council. Councillors may only suspend him for incompetence or misconduct on the basis of a two-thirds majority vote and ask the Minister of Environment, Heritage and Local Government for dismissal.

174. Following the 1996 government initiative *Better Local Government*, Strategic Policy Committees were created in an effort to enhance the role of local councillors as well as to allow for an integration of sectoral interests in local policy making. Whereas achievements in the latter area have been assessed quite positively, the involvement of elected councillors in strategic policy making rather than operational work is still perceived as weak. See Callanan (2005), and Forde (2005).

175. Most of the expenses of RAuth are refunded by the local authorities within the region, which themselves have quite limited funding.

Table 7.4: Sources of revenue of Irish local authorities, 2007

Revenue provided by	in million €	in %
Government grants and subsidies (specific purpose grants)	1,055.9	22.0
Local Government Fund (general purpose grant)	942.7	20.0
Goods/services	1,475.5	31.0
Commercial rates	1,244.8	26.0
Provision for debit/credit balances	3.2	0.1
County demand	−2.2	−0.1
Total receipts	4,719.9	100.0

Source: Department of the Environment Heritage and Local Government, *Local Authority Budgets 2007*.

administrative system is thus spatially dispersed to a certain extent, it is in effect highly centralised.[176]

Next to these legal and organisational features, the strongest constraint on local governments' discretion is their financial capacity. Total budgeted expenditure of the local government sector (C/C Councils, Borough Councils and Town Councils, as well as miscellaneous bodies like Joint Drainage Boards and non-rating Town Councils) accounted for only 10.5 billion euros in 2007: that is, 5.6 per cent of Irish Gross Domestic Product (Department of the Environment Heritage and Local Government). Their main sources of income in 2007 can be seen in Table 7.4.[177]

The largest share (42 per cent) is provided by government grants and subsidies. 53 per cent of these are specific grants[178] and the remaining 47 per cent emerge from the Local Government Fund (LGF) that was established in 1999 in order to provide C/C with a sound financial basis. It is at most funded by the full proceeds of the motor tax[179] supplemented by a central contribution, and its allocation is provided by means of a statistics-based Needs and Resources Model.[180] Grants

---

176. The programme for decentralisation launched by the government in 2003 is a case in point as it is no more ambitious than the (electorally promising) relocation of offices from Dublin to certain designated areas. For a critical assessment see Kirby (2007).

177. The fiscal system described is the current one. For an overview of the former system as well as of the local authorities' processes of budgetary decision making, see Ridge (1992).

178. The largest grants paid by the state to local authorities are those for road works, for water supply and sewerage schemes and for housing.

179. In 2007, the Local Government Fund provided 1532 million euros, and the full proceeds of the motor tax accounted for 955 million euros. See *Local Authority Budgets 2007* (Department of the Environment Heritage and Local Government, appendix II).

180. The Needs and Resources Model takes into account how much each local authority should spend on each service/activity and the income each authority should generate (e.g. from rates, charges, fees, rent etc.). It has been used to help determine the distribution of general-purpose allocations since 2000. The idea behind its introduction was to have 'an objective approach to making allocations [since] the representative bodies [...] at a political level, cannot agree on what is the best way to give a weighting for [...] roads − lengths of roads, miles in your area or kilometres − [...]

from the LGF are, at least in theory, general purpose and thus discretionary. Those parts of the LGF grants deriving from the motor tax (62 per cent in 2007) are, however, to be spent on roads, and local authorities' expenditure discretion is generally very limited. Moreover, central government exerts significant control over the LGF, as the minister determines on a yearly basis what the exchequer contribution will be. Local authorities thus face limited security (Forde 2005). The remaining share of local authorities' income is provided by (commercial) rates on valuation (26 per cent) that are levied annually on immovable property,[181] and by income from goods and services (31 per cent).[182]

The total income provides the basis for local authorities' current expenditure and thus funds the day-to-day running of the authority (including staff salaries, housing maintenance, pensions etc.). The 2007 expenditure breakdown was: road transportation and safety 27 per cent, environmental protection 19 per cent, housing and building 15 per cent, water supply and sewerage 14 per cent, recreation and amenity 9 per cent, agriculture, education, health and welfare 6 per cent, development incentives and control 5 per cent, and miscellaneous 6 per cent.[183] Subnational expenditure accounted only for 13 per cent of total public expenditure in 2006 and 80 per cent of this is not covered by own tax revenue (International Monetary Fund 2008, own calculations). The amount of fiscal imbalance is thus extremely high.

To sum up the Irish case, it is obvious, given their characteristics of internal organisation, policy and financial discretion, that local and regional entities can hardly engage in innovative service delivery. Regarding the RAuth, Breathnach quite frankly states

Regional Authorities is the most misnomer. They have absolutely no authority [...] They have absolutely no powers *de facto*. They are just talk-shops, they don't have any function' (interview Breathnach).

In addition, they – as well as the RAss – lack direct democratic legitimacy as their members are nominated from among the elected members of the C/C councils. Local governments are no better off. Budgeting processes leave very little room for their own prioritisation: 'Effectively 90 per cent of the budget' (interview Callanan) is non-discretionary and is determined by either central legislation or regulations. The general competence assigned to local entities by the Local Government Act 1991 is thus 'in the main hypothetical, as most local governments don't have the financial resources to fund new initiatives' (O'Broin and Waters

---

because that would obviously favour some areas more than others' (interview Callanan).

181. Examples include buildings, factories, shops, railways, canals, mines, woods, rights of fishery and rights of easement over land.

182. The most important include rents for local authority housing, home loan repayments, charges for water supplies, waste collection and sewerage facilities.

183. Capital expenditure, on the other hand, is financed largely by state grants as well as from development levies and borrowings.

2007: 31).[184] In effect, almost all public expenditure decisions are taken at national level and most

> services delivered at local level are managed or planned by national organisations with little or no local or regional autonomy (O'Broin and Waters 2007: 21).

High fiscal imbalance and regulatory measures embodied in the Irish system entail a number of negative effects. First and foremost, fiscal imbalance sets incentives for over-provision by creating fiscal illusion and thus a systematic possibility of externalising costs (Olson 1969). These effects are far less visible in centralised than in decentralised countries because subnational units' expenditure accounts for less. Nonetheless, the fact that there is

> an assumption amongst the public that local services will come through this magical pot of central money [...] leads to a demand led system' (interview Callanan).

Moreover, the Needs and Resources Model

> is not very efficient [...] from [...] a fiscal point of view. [...] It's not a formal rule, but if you don't spend your allocation within the year, you can expect a reduction in your allocation in the following year (interview Callanan).

Another case in point is that central government's caps on commercial rate increases do not necessarily depress local government expenditure. They may rather constitute

> an invitation to go to the three per cent. [...] Because if they cap [...] this year, they might do the same next year and it will be [...] again a percentage increase. [...] It can have a perverse effect (interview Callanan).

This might explain why in recent years political pressure rather than a formal limit has been applied. The Irish system thus sets both continuous and periodical incentives to overinvest money, albeit on a comparatively limited scale.

These negative effects have been widely noticed by both academics (Forde 2004, 2005; Barrington 1991; Callanan 2003) and policy makers, as the recently published Green Paper *Stronger Local Democracy: Options for Change* (Department of the Environment Heritage and Local Government 2008) shows. Callanan concludes:

> the story of local government finance in Ireland is quite depressing in terms of the changes. [...] There have been studies and research reports on local government finance since the 1970s [...] And they all say more or less the same thing, that there is [...] an over-centralisation in the financial system, there is a lack of discretionary resources [...] There is also an unhealthy disconnect between what service people get and what they pay for (interview Callanan).

---

184. We will evaluate more closely the developmental role of C/C in Section 7.3.4.

Nevertheless, there have been no significant changes to the system to date.

In Austria, due to major implementation competencies, the *Länder* have extensive administrative capacities. However, this does not mean that they have discretion during implementation. In most cases, they operate on behalf of the federal government following detailed federal decrees. The federal government also executes many operational tasks and operates redundant administrative structures in some areas like railways, which is considered inefficient (Bußjäger 2002). The fiscal system does not grant substantial fiscal autonomy to the *Länder* and municipalities who particularly lack resources.[185] Both levels depend primarily on transfers whose binding character varies. At the least, the sums flowing from the secondary and tertiary equalisation schemes are earmarked for specific purposes by the higher level. This results in inefficiencies in various policy areas.[186] Analyses show that effective local development that would lead to a wider tax base may result in net losses for the local government concerned, because of reduced resources from fiscal equalisation. In extreme cases, up to 144 per cent of tax gains would be compensated for by equalisation schemes (Schneider 2002).

In sum, both countries show clear patterns of centralisation. While in the Irish case the lack of resources and competencies is the limiting factor, Austrian *Länder* are mainly constrained by limited policy discretion. Complex fiscal arrangements and limited own-revenue resources produce additional inefficiencies. Overall, the subnational units of both decentralised countries display a much more comfortable financial situation, more policy discretion, and better fiscal balance than their centralised counterparts. However, federal Austria, due to the mere existence of capable subnational institutions with large personnel resources, differs markedly from the Irish, unitary–centralised case. Our case studies on regional development and transport policies assess to what extent such difference matters for efficient policy implementation. The countries show the patterns we theorise are relevant to the potential benefits of decentralised policy implementation. However, we derived an additional qualification for such benefits to take effect, namely hard budget constraints and subnational fiscal discipline. This is the topic of the following section.

7.2   The bail-out game: territorial organisation and fiscal discipline

In this section, we test our *HBC* and *interaction hypotheses*. As outlined above, we expect that competition between widely unrestricted subnational entities might cause them to overspend to the cost of other regional or local authorities or future generations (Goodspeed 2002). In theory, rules that effectively ensure

---

185. For reasons discussed at length below, the *Länder*'s situation is better.

186. This is true especially in the areas of education and health. In the former, the *Länder* employ teachers, while their salaries are covered by the *Bund*. In the latter, the *Länder* as operators of hospitals regularly cut costs, thereby aggravating the financing problems of the social security system. Due to the complicated equalisation system and the *Länder*'s fear of ending up disadvantaged, moves towards more fiscal equivalence have failed.

subnational fiscal discipline are essential for a country's performance. These rules can be established either by market pressures or hierarchical oversight (Inman 2003; Rodden *et al.* 2003), a notion that we linked to specific territorial state organisations in the *interaction hypothesis*. Accordingly, we expect subnational entities in the unitary countries, Denmark and Ireland, to be effectively constrained by central government oversight. The same holds for Swiss cantons due to the market pressures they are subject to. For Austria, theory would expect softer budget constraints and hence a diminished performance with regard to subnational fiscal discipline. We deal with each of the three cases subsequently.

Budget constraints, together with the arguments formulated above, can thus be utilised to formulate an expectation of the countries' performance ranking: First, we expect decentralised countries to perform better than centralised ones – Switzerland and Denmark should thus do better than Austria and Ireland. Second, federal countries tend to perform worse, and third, soft budget constraints diminish performance further. Hence, Denmark should be the best-performing country, followed by Switzerland, then Ireland. Austria brings up the rear.

7.2.1   Ireland and Denmark. Fiscal discipline in unitary countries

Let us first turn to the unitary countries. In Ireland the Local Government Act 2001 tightly regulates the budgeting process of local authorities (Davis 2003; Dollard 2003). Each year, a draft budget is prepared under the direction of the manager and in consultation with the corporate policy group.[187] This draft budget estimates expenditure as well as revenues from state grants and the local authority's own resources from goods and services. The full council then considers and sometimes amends the draft budget. It has to approve the (amended) budget within twenty-one days. Afterwards, the annual rate on valuation (commercial rate) is determined so as to finance any remaining deficit.[188] Irish C/C are thus not allowed to adopt unbalanced annual budgets. Moreover, the Minister for the Environment, Heritage and Local Government has the power to cap rate increases and to constrain local authorities' discretion over revenue. Limitations of this kind were applied in 1983, 1984, 1985, 2000, 2001, and 2002 (Davis 2003). Even though there has been no formal cap subsequently, there was 'political pressure put by the minister to keep increases in rates […] within certain limits' (interview Callanan). The strongest constraint on local current budgeting, however, is set by law. Should a C/C council be unable to adopt a balanced budget within twenty-one days, the minister may remove the members of the local authority from office and appoint a commissioner to carry out their functions for the remainder of the legislative period. This last

---

187. The corporate policy group is a committee which consists of the chair of the local authority and the chairpersons of the strategic policy committees that mirror the major functions of local authorities. They are thus joint committees bringing together expertise from all service areas.

188. Rates differ significantly between C/C. In 2008, the annual rate on valuation was 51.75 in Westmeath and 78.93 in Kerry. See Local Authority Key Financial Data under http://www.environ.ie/en/LocalGovernment/LocalGovernmentAdministration/LocalGovernmentFinance/.

happened in 1985 but the threat remains a strong incentive to fiscal discipline.

Separately from the rules for the current budget, a local authority may 'borrow money in any manner which it considers suitable' (Local Government Act 2001, Section 106) for capital investments, given the sanction of the appropriate minister who may set up specific regulations. Prior to 1990 the money was mostly provided by a local loans fund that was wholly or partly subsidised by the department. Since then, capital investments have largely been funded by a scheme of grants from different government departments (Davis 2003). Whilst local authorities are thus generally allowed to opt for loan finance they have to include any repayments in subsequent budgets as part of their current expenditure. Repayments thus become part of their 'inescapable demands' and severely constrain an authority's financial leeway in subsequent years. Local authority accounts are, moreover, audited annually by an external Local Government Audit Service.

Quantitative as well as qualitative data show that the highly regulatory budget constraints determined by central legislation serve as a very effective instrument for enhancing subnational fiscal discipline. There has been no case of a central government bail-out and C/C make little use of loan financing for capital investments. For more than twenty years local authorities have balanced their current budgets. Expert assessments attribute this to strongly anticipatory behaviour on the part of the local authorities. Local governments fear their own dissolution and 'when it comes to the threat, the local government will back down' (interview Breathnach). The central government's power to abolish C/C councils is

> the nuclear option [that] has been threatened a number of times to individual authorities. Usually every year, there is some authority [...] that has a problem agreeing a budget [...] Usually the Department of the Environment would say 'Well, if you don't get on with it now, we will just remove you from office'. So it's quite an effective way of getting them to make a decision (interview Callanan).

The high level of subnational discipline in Ireland thus emerges out of the interaction between strategically behaving actors in a highly regulatory environment, just as the interactive logic of the bail-out model predicts.

In Denmark, different restrictions are in place for regional and local authorities. The rules for the regional level are quite simple: Counties are not allowed to finance more than 25 per cent of their investments through loans (Pedersen 2002b); the newly established regions are not allowed to borrow at all. The constraints local governments face are more numerous and more complex. They include hierarchical oversight, but also elements of mutual control by municipalities, and local electoral accountability. Hierarchical rules for local governments on raising new loans were severely restricted after an increase of local debts in the 1970s. Short-term borrowing is allowed on condition of a surplus in the municipalities' financial account in the preceding 365 days. Permission for long-term borrowing depends on the purpose of borrowing. Permission is automatically granted for infrastructure investments in priority areas.[189] The extent to which borrowing for other purposes is allowed is regulated by the finance ministry, allotting a loan bracket to each municipality according to expenditure needs. Within their loan bracket, municipalities are allowed to raise loans without the permission of higher authorities. The Finance Ministry and the County Prefects monitor subnational budgeting (Bjorna and Jenssen 2006). If municipalities want to borrow more than their bracket allows, they need approval by the Ministry of Interior and Health. An annual financing pool has been established for these exemptions (Council of Europe 1998). These features of hierarchical monitoring are not absolute, but the total of all loans and hence the sizes of the individual loan brackets are subject to the annual budget negotiations between the finance ministry and the KL. It is therefore possible to increase public spending by relaxing the borrowing constraints, an option in fact used from time to time.[190]

Apart from borrowing, there is a particular system of mutual control that regulates local government expenditures. As Danish local governments spend approximately 60 per cent of the general government budget, managing local expenditures is particularly important for keeping general government expenditure under control (Blom-Hansen and Pallesen 2001).[191] This is organised through an institutionalised bargaining scheme between the national finance ministry and the local government association, KL. In annual negotiations, outlines of local governments' budgets are drawn and the total amount of permissible expenditure is fixed. Within this arrangement, local governments plan their own budget which is afterwards scrutinised by the central government. Distribution between municipalities and compliance with the negotiated agreement has to be guaranteed by the local governments themselves or by their association. In the case of non-compliance, i.e. overspending, sanctions can be imposed on all local governments by the central government. The sanctions that are legally possible include individual and collective grant cuts and fines payable to the central government (Blom-Hansen and Pallesen 2001). The option of collective grant cuts leads to a prisoner's dilemma: all municipalities face collective sanctions, but for individual local governments there is an incentive to overspend.

After severe conflicts over central government grant cuts in the 1980s,[192] KL

---

189. This right is sometimes misused for creative budgeting: Local governments raise loans for investments in infrastructure, which then become subject to a sell-and-lease-back system. This way, municipalities generate unconditional resources (Lotz 2005). This practice led to severe consequences in the case of Farum (see below) and has therefore been made subject to ministerial authorisation.

190. 'The reason why they [the municipalities] are allowed to borrow for certain purposes is that government wants them to spend. So it's difficult to say they overspend' (interview Mouritzen).

191. This holds especially if central government adopts a demand-oriented macroeconomic strategy.

192. On several occasions the local level disregarded the budget ceilings, which was countered by the national government through severe grant cuts and fines. For a more detailed description of these negotiations, see Blom-Hansen (2001), Bogason (1991), Owens and Panella (1991), and Tonboe (1991).

and the government have come to an agreement in every year since 1988. The local level agreed to zero growth of local expenditures whilst the national level granted more autonomy to the local level (interview Pallesen) and renounced further grant cuts (Blom-Hansen 1999b). However, the credibility of the threat of sanctions is judged differently. On the one hand, Danish local governments are labelled 'remarkably law-abiding and careful spenders' (Bjorna and Jenssen 2006: 316). On the other hand, the agreements on 'these spending limits [...] have been complied with less than one out of three times' (interview Mouritzen), presumably varying along with the power of the Local Government Association to ensure adherence to the negotiated agreement (Daugaard 2002). As for future developments, there are two positions among the experts. The first assumes reciprocity – actors reflect fair behaviour by others in their own actions, so it may be the case that increasing refusal to obey will cause the system to erode over time: 'to maintain a system that is not complied with [...] weakens the central government's credibility and [...] raises moral hazard problems' (Daugaard 2002: 25). The practice of sanctioning virtually all municipalities irrespective of their prior behaviour creates resentment in the compliant municipalities and might lead to further overspending in the future.[193] The second strand of literature stresses risk aversion and iterated interaction of the relevant actors, and expects increasing cooperation and hence compliance over time (Blom-Hansen and Pallesen 2001; Christensen 2000).

Local electoral accountability is a third means by which subnational fiscal behaviour is restrained. Since local governments are restricted in their ability to borrow and central government decides unilaterally on the level of the block grants, the only way to generate additional resources is to raise the municipality's share of income tax, which is an unpopular measure (interviews Christensen, Blom-Hansen). Raising taxes may result in a declining population (as residents move to neighbouring municipalities with lower tax rates) or losing the next election.[194] Local accountability and tax competition seem thus to be a relevant constraint shaping local governments' spending discipline.[195] Central government also tried to reduce local expenditure by the introduction of tax ceilings. Experts consider these as a disincentive to responsible behaviour because they prevent local governments from lowering taxes.[196]

---

193. Mouritzen reports from a city manager: 'He was so mad because they have done so much to keep their part of the agreement [...] and then he suddenly realised that all the other municipalities did not do that. They were not punished. He was mad as hell. So it is not a success story' (interview Mouritzen).

194. Central government seemingly mistrusts this mechanism. As a reaction to municipal behaviour, at various times tax ceilings have been introduced. These ceilings impose sanctions if tax rates are raised by the local governments, regardless of their previous levels. Tax competition is thus weakened, albeit considerable variance in local tax levels remains.

195. Concerns that larger municipalities would reduce local government 'proximity' and thus accountability did not materialize (Larsen 2002).

196. '[N]ext year you may be forced to raise taxes again [...] So you are punished next year if you are a good guy this year' (interview Mouritzen). This holds especially for large cities due to economies

Empirically, there are not many cases of severe fiscal difficulties in the Danish case, which points to the reasonable effectiveness of existing constraints. There are two exceptions. First, the Faroe Islands suffered from financial difficulties after an economic and financial crisis and were bailed out by the Danish government in the early 1990s. Experts argue that this happened solely for political reasons and was not a precedent for Danish local governments to rely on a bail-out by central government should they become bankrupt. The second example is the famous case of 'Farumgate' (2002). Farum, a small municipality on the outskirts of Copenhagen, became famous in the 1990s because of the radical privatisation strategy of its charismatic mayor, Peter Brixtofte.[197] His administration implemented several ambitious projects between 1986 and 2002.[198] These projects were primarily financed by sale and lease-back and other public–private partnership (PPP) arrangements (von Maravic 2007).[199] It was a way of taking out loans that routine state supervision long overlooked. When Brixtofte's excessive spending habits hit the headlines, the system collapsed.[200] In the end, Farum was put under the control of the national government and had to raise taxes from 19.6 to 22.8 per cent. The national government granted a special subsidy of two billion Danish crowns. It has been the only example of a bail-out for Danish local governments and it was highly controversial among the public. The Farum case was mostly the result of criminal conduct and not of disincentives in the Danish local finance system. However, neither local accountability nor national control measures prevented Brixtofte's excessive use of opaque PPP arrangements (Flyvbjerg *et al.* 2004; Flyvbjerg 2007).[201] But the consequent publicity means that municipalities are unlikely to regard overspending and bail-out as a viable option in the future (Greve and Ejersbo 2002; Jorgensen 2002).

In 2006, Danish local governments were 131.8 billion Danish Kroner or 17.7 billion euros in debt. This equates to about 2.5 per cent of the Gross Domestic

---

of scale: 'It's impossible for them [the large municipalities] to lower their costs. [...] They have to spend money, because otherwise we have a tax level below the national average' (interview Christoffersen).

197. This strategy caused Farum to be named one of the 'Cities of Tomorrow' by the Bertelsmann Stiftung (Greve and Ejersbo 2002).

198. Among other projects, a football ground for 12,000 spectators (Farum has 19,000 inhabitants), a large mall, a handball arena and a marina. Free trips to the Canary Islands were offered to every pensioner in Farum.

199. The municipality provided the ground for the football stadium and left construction and operation to a finance company, FIH. FIH financed the construction by loans which were secured by the municipality using fees for 20 years.

200. The Farum scandal became public when journalists published a restaurant bill showing that Brixtofte had charged several hundred Euros' worth of red wine to the city's account. It turned out that the mayor had raised loans up to one billion Danish Kroner (134 million euros) without consulting either local parliament or the national government. Brixtofte was sentenced to two years' imprisonment.

201. As a result, sale and lease-back arrangements are now subject to authorisation by the Ministry of the Interior and Health.

Table 7.5: Denmark's EMU debt and EMU deficit as a percentage of GDP, 1992–2007

	1992	1993	1994	1995	1996	1997	1998	1999	2000	2001	2002	2003	2004	2005	2006	2007
Account balance	−2.6	−3.8	−3.3	−2.9	−1.9	−0.5	0.1	1.5	2.4	1.5	0.3	0.1	2.0	5.2	5.1	4.9
Debt	68.0	80.1	76.5	72.5	69.2	65.2	60.8	57.4	51.5	48.7	48.3	45.8	43.8	36.4	30.5	26.2

Source: Statistics Danmark.

Product. Denmark's total debt is – at 26.2 per cent of GDP – comparatively low. However, as can be seen in Table 7.5, this is the result of several years of fiscal discipline and surpluses. In sum, existing measures to hold state levels back from irresponsible fiscal behaviour are effective.

The Danish finance system meets our theoretical expectations. Alongside strict hierarchical budget constraints which limit local borrowing, we find additional mechanisms that build upon local governments' mutual self-control and local accountability and restrict local expenditure quite effectively. Local politicians face political costs in the local (and maybe also the national) arena if they exceed their budget significantly. This explains why Danish local governments comply relatively strictly with the spending ceilings agreed in the budget negotiations despite the weak threat of sanctions. In this regard, Denmark resembles the Swiss case. According to our theory, strong decentralisation, low fiscal imbalance, and hard budget constraints keep the level of public debt low and the fiscal discipline of local governments regarding borrowing high, which in turn should enable Danish implementation to be highly efficient.

7.2.2 Switzerland. Fiscal discipline in a federal–decentralised country

Our theoretical proposition expects responsible fiscal behaviour by subnational governments in Switzerland, because limited interdependencies strongly reduce the costs of the 'no bail-out' option and cantons therefore face a credible constraint. Their fiscal behaviour is thus subject to market pressure by both financial markets (via interest rates) and inhabitants (via tax competition and inter-cantonal migration).

Both budgetary decision-making processes and fiscal performance vary extensively across Swiss cantons (Bochsler *et al*. 2004: 147–8). There are, nevertheless, certain external as well as internal constraints that systematically reduce the danger of unsound financing by the cantons. Swiss cantons are not subject to regulatory budget constraints set up by federal authorities,[202] except for a prohibition on borrowing from the central bank. The 'main *external* limitation on budgetary sovereignty of the cantons is intrinsically *competition* with other cantons' (Dafflon 1999: 276, emphasis in original). Tax competition entails that

---

202. Nor does horizontal coordination play a strong role. Though a conference of cantonal finance directors exists, it does not regulate debt issues in a coordinated way (Braun 2007: 247).

unsound financing practices bring the risk of losing financial capacity as businesses and individuals may choose to 'exit' (Adamovich and Hosp 2003: 9). Moreover, cantonal deficits are financed on the capital market, so that unsound financing increases interest rates (Braun 2007: 247) and negatively affects future loan options. The Swiss system is characterised by a high level of tax competition and its positive as well as potentially negative consequences[203] have been subject to thorough analysis. Quantitative studies show that although tax competition to some extent induces high-income earners to reside in low-tax cantons and municipalities (Kirchgässner and Pommerehne 1996), intercantonal migration is generally low (Feld 1997). Tax competition has neither resulted in significant capitalisation of tax savings (Kirchgässner and Pommerehne 1996: 359–60) nor in a 'race to the bottom' that would induce an undersupply of public goods (Pommerehne et al. 1996). In sum, the revenue leeway given has largely contributed to a competitive and efficient provision of public goods (Adamovich and Hosp 2003: 7–8; Feld et al. 2005).

Inefficient financing is further constrained first, by the 'voice' of direct democracy (Dafflon 1999: 276), which also serves, it is argued, as an important mechanism for preventing the detrimental effects of tax competition (Feld 1997), and, second, by instruments of budgetary self-regulation fixed in financial laws or cantonal constitutions. Almost all cantons require a more or less balanced budget and have adopted the 'golden rule' that restricts deficit spending to capital expenditures on a pay-as-you-use basis (Dafflon 1999). Notwithstanding this, cantonal debt increased in the 1990s (see the following subsection) and eight cantons reacted by introducing new fiscal instruments, e.g. an automatic revenue adoption in St Gallen, Solothurn, Appenzell-Ausserrhoden, Graubünden and Fribourg (for details see Stauffer 2001; Kirchgässner 2005: 29–30; Schaltegger and Frey 2004). To date, no canton has ever been bailed out by the federal government or has even asked for its support in dealing with indebtedness.[204] Cantonal actors thus do not anticipate interventionist behaviour by the federal government and the 'no bail-out' option is a credible threat.

In the case of the Swiss communes, budgeting processes are subject to cantonal supervision and often constitutionally regulated by at least two instruments: the requirement of a more or less balanced current budget, and the demand that local revenues be sufficient to cover current expenditure, debt interest and the running costs of investments (Dafflon 2002: 215; Dafflon 1996: 231). Though cantons sometimes lack effective sanctions were communes not to respect the requirements (Dafflon 2002: 228), one common response is a restriction of communal autonomy (Dafflon 1996: 231). Local communities generally try to prevent such intervention (Feld and Kirchgässner 2006: 20) and are further constrained by direct democracy.

---

203. For a summary of the main theoretical arguments see Pommerehne et al. (1996: 293–4), Ter-Minassian (1997), Norregaard (1997), and Feld (2005).

204. In one instance a commune (Leukerbad) went bankrupt and tried to file a suit for a bail-out by its canton. However, the Supreme Court in Lausanne absolved Valais of responsiblity and no bail-out occurred (Feld and Kirchgässner 2006: 28).

Table 7.6: Increase in net debt by state level in Switzerland, 1990–2000

	Net debt in 1990 in million SFR	Net debt in 2000 in million SFR	Increase in per cent, 1990–2000	Share of total net debt in 2000	In per cent of GDP
Federation	25,030	83,027	231.71	61.94	20.0
Cantons	12,098	38,348	216.98	28.61	9.2
Communes	9,667	12,667	31.03	9.45	3.1
Total	46,795	134,042	186.45	100.00	32.3

Source: Schweizerischer Bundesrat 2006: Anhang B.6.

Despite these institutional arrangements, Switzerland has witnessed a significant increase in public debt in the 1990s. As Table 7.6 shows, this increase is attributable to the confederation[205] as well as the cantons. Economic analyses show that the major cause of rising indebtedness at both levels is deficits in current budgets. Increasing needs, especially in the area of social and health policies, interact with slower economic growth and cause systematic deficits (Schweizerischer Bundesrat 2006: 12f.; Kirchgässner 2004; Feld and Kirchgässner 2006: 4). Rising debts thus have cyclical rather than structural origins.

In fact, patterns of cantonal debt vary extensively. Between 1990 and 2004, deficits increased especially in Geneva, Vaud, Berne and Zurich, but less so in the small rural cantons of Appenzell-Innerrhoden, Appenzell-Ausserrhoden, Obwalden, and Uri (Schweizerischer Bundesrat 2006: 13f.). Table 7.7 displays the variance in cantonal debt per capita in 2005.

These differences in the borrowing behaviour of cantons can be explained by variance in the fiscal instruments (Feld and Kirchgässner 2006: 7–8; Krogstrup and Wälti 2008: 134–5; Braun 2010), intracantonal (fiscal as well as administrative) decentralisation (Freitag and Vatter 2004; Schaltegger 2001: 13; Freitag and Vatter 2008), the degree of urbanisation (Dafflon and Pujol 2001), and the existence as well as the use of direct democratic instruments[206] (Spahn 1997b: 334; Feld and Kirchgässner 2006; Schaltegger 2001: 13; Feld and Schaltegger 2005). The restrictive character of the latter might derive from the fact that the 'idea of "sound financing" is firmly entrenched in people's mind' (Spahn 1997b: 334). Additionally, the fiscal preferences of cantonal populations exhibit an independent effect on the extent of cantonal borrowing requirements (Dafflon and Pujol 2001:

205. The federal government's capacity to adequately respond to these developments proved to be severely constrained because there is no fiscal referendum at the federal level that would limit expenditure, only popular votes on new taxes as well as tax rates that inhibit revenue adaption. One reaction was the introduction of a 'debt brake' at the federal level, requiring the adjustment of expenditures to revenue which is smoothed over the business cycle. Its long-term effects remain to be seen (Kirchgässner 2005: 33–4).

206. All cantons, except for Vaud, have financial referenda, which are mandatory and optional in 13 cantons, only optional in seven cantons, and mandatory for new spending projects but not optional in five cantons. For details see pages 185–6 in Feld (2005).

Table 7.7: Cantonal debt in thousand SFR per capita (resident population), 2005

Canton	Debt per capita	Canton	Debt per capita	Canton	Debt per capita	Canton	Debt per capita
ZH	6,931.17	GL	6,778.06	AR	2,502.96	VD	13,816.55
BE	7,504.22	ZG	4,227.33	AI	2,228.76	VS	5,958.47
LU	5,992.92	FR	3,426.92	SG	3,319.09	NE	11,351.67
UR	6,590.36	SO	5,414.16	GR	5,083.19	GE	50,943.25
SZ	2,991.21	BS	26,553.41	AG	3,657.70	JU	7,296.53
OW	5,405.42	BL	11,881.02	TG	4,162.76	-	-
NW	6,830.39	SH	4,517.24	TI	5,972.33	-	-
Overall Mean:		8,512.97	Stddev.:	9,947.83			

Source: BADAC.

Abbreviations of cantons: AG Aargau; AI Appenzell Innerrhoden; AR Appenzell Ausserrhoden; BS Basel-City; BL Basel-Country; BE Berne; FR Fribourg; GE Geneva; GL Glarus; GR Graubünden; JU Jura; LU Lucerne; NE Neuchâtel; NW Nidwalden; OW Obwalden; SH Schaffhausen; SZ Schwyz; SO Solothurn; SG St. Gallen; TG Thurgau; TI Ticino; UR Uri; VS Valais; VD Vaud; ZG Zug; ZH Zurich.

65). As they are significantly determined by cultural patterns (Pujol and Weber 2003), this might partially explain why 'French and Italian speaking Swiss cantons exhibit a lesser degree of fiscal discipline' (Freitag and Vatter 2008: 12).

In sum, revenue discretion, competition, direct democracy, and the credibility of the 'no bail-out' option interact to bring about comparatively sound financing by both Swiss cantons and communes (Braun 2007: 247–8). The prevalence of fiscal self-regulation by the cantons can then be interpreted as a reflection of the strong perception of accountability, and the remaining variance in fiscal performance is explained by intercantonal differences in the hardness of their respective budget constraints.

> [The] Swiss example shows […] that with appropriate institutional rules the bailout problem can be solved in a federal country in a satisfactory way, it does not have to lead to irresponsible behaviour of lower level communities (Kirchgässner 2005: 41).

7.2.3 Austria. Fiscal discipline in a federal–centralised country

Finally, we turn to the case of Austria. As a federal–centralised country, characterised by a high level of fiscal interrelations, theory predicts a weak fiscal performance by subnational entities. As expected for a federal country, state borrowing is not constitutionally restricted. Thus, there is no hierarchical control by the federal level. Despite the fact that state and local representatives are democratically elected, the constraining effect of electoral accountability also seems to be limited. Executive dominance of the state legislatures (Bußjäger 2007), insufficient legal provisions

(Pelinka 2008) and, in the case of proportional governments, a bias against open conflict and lack of an institutionalised opposition (Fallend 1997) diminish the monitoring function of the *Länder* parliaments and hence the regional electorate. At the same time, subnational governments are highly dependent on transfers and fiscal relationships are interdependent. It is thus questionable whether the federal government can credibly threaten subnational entities with a 'no bail-out' strategy.

This limited ability of central government to restrict borrowing by subnational levels effectively became a major problem in the context of the EMU.[207] The Austrian national government tried to handle it by negotiating a national stability pact (*Stabilitätspakt*) with the state governments and the local government associations in 2001.[208] For each year, a fixed deficit ceiling is assigned to the tiers of government. If subnational entities break the ceiling, sanctions can be imposed by a board in which the national Ministry of Finance and the *Länder* governments are equally represented and have to decide unanimously. Table 7.8 shows the stipulated and actual deficit ceilings for the years 2003 to 2007.

It is obvious that the *Länder* governments exceeded their maximum borrowing level every single year in this period. Nonetheless, no sanctions have so far been imposed. The stability pact, hence, is a toothless tiger. A semi-effective sanction, however, is that the federal government links the allocation of funds in the secondary fiscal equalisation scheme to past adherence to the pact by the states (interview Bröthaler).

Local borrowing is permitted for 'necessary' expenditures if it is the only financing option for these purposes and does not endanger fiscal sustainability and other local functions and commitments. However, these restrictions are vague and flexible and therefore subject to administrative discretion by the supervising authority, the *Länder* (Thöni *et al.* 2002). The individual *Länder*'s interpretation of these general rules varies greatly:[209]

> The authorisation process described is not an efficient instrument for limiting local debts. [...] In principle, local self-government and restrictive local supervision by higher government tiers seems incompatible (Thöni *et al.* 2002: 62).

Overall, budget constraints applying to state and municipal governments in Austria have to be classified as soft. Without effective internal sanctioning mechanisms,

---

207. The Stability and Growth Pact limits annual borrowing to 3 per cent of GDP and total indebtedness to 60 per cent of GDP. The EU ultimately sanctions breaches of the limits by high fines. Breaking the rules therefore incurs macroeconomic costs.

208. Legally, it is an agreement according to article 15a B-VG, limiting borrowing by the tiers of government. The pact was renewed in 2004 and 2007.

209. Tyrol requires approval of each loan application exceeding 10 per cent of the prior fiscal year's expenditures. Other *Länder* reserve a right to approval when total local indebtedness exceeds 33 per cent (Upper Austria) or 100 per cent (Salzburg) of the municipality's current revenues. The Burgenland government requires approval for any local borrowing. There has been no research on the effects of these different practices on municipalities' debt levels (interview Bröthaler).

Table 7.8: Budget balance in Austria by state level as percentage of GDP, 2003–2007

	Actual balance					Prescribed balance in the stability pacts 2001 and 2005					Actual – prescribed balance[a]				
	2003	2004	2005	2006	2007	2003	2004	2005	2006	2007	2003	2004	2005	2006	2007
General government	-1.33	-4.41	-1.54	-1.6	-0.42	0	0	-1.8	-1.6	-0.7	-1.33	-4.41	0.26	0	0.28
Central government	-1.53	-4.61	-1.73	-1.55	-0.62	-0.75	-0.75	-2.4	-2.2	-1.4	-0.78	-3.86	0.67	0.65	0.78
Länder (incl. Vienna)	0.16	0.19	0.11	-0.13	0.1	0.75	0.75	0.6	0.6	0.7	-0.59	-0.56	-0.49	-0.73	-0.6
Municipalities (not incl. Vienna)	0.04	0.01	0.08	0.08	0.1	0	0	0	0	0	0.04	0.01	0.08	0.08	0.1

Source: Österreichischer Städtebund 2008, Österreichischer Nationalrat 2001; 2006, own calculations.

[a] Negative numbers indicate breaches of the prescribed deficit ceiling.

subnational governments have an incentive to free ride: 'If only one government unit (one local or even one state government) extends its deficit financing, it will benefit from both the positive effects of the national fiscal stability and its own expanded financial scope' (Thöni *et al.* 2002: 63).

Interestingly, it is not the *Länder* but the federal level that is responsible for most public debt: Austrian public debt amounts to 59 per cent of GDP (2007) and for most of it (53.8 per cent of GDP), the federal level is responsible. Subnational debt is low in absolute numbers, but can be not inconsiderable in percentage terms, given the small budgets of states and local governments.[210] Nevertheless, the high level of federal debt runs counter to our theoretical expectation. It can be explained by the dynamics of Austrian fiscal equalisation schemes. Given the extensive fiscal interrelations between levels (see previous subsection), the Austrian finance system is 'a matter of give and take' (interview Bröthaler).[211] Formally, the federal government is required to negotiate finance issues with the states, but it is in a strong position within the regular *Finanzausgleichsverhandlungen*, as the fiscal equalisation law can be passed by simple majority in the *Nationalrat* and the *Länder* have no veto power.[212] However, it seems that *Länder* governments use the fact that effectively they cannot be prevented from excessive borrowing as a trump card in fiscal negotiations. This way, they obtain high federal transfers in compensation for limited borrowing, which forces the *Bund* either to borrow or to cut costs in other areas – e.g. grants to municipalities (Thöni *et al.* 2002). This explanation is supported by several facts. Firstly, since 1945 the federal level has never taken a unilateral decision on fiscal equalisation. Secondly, most public debt is taken on by the federal level even though a government that has a realistic option of allocating tax revenue unilaterally would be expected to keep more resources to itself. Thirdly, the *Länder* overall seem far more comfortably resourced than the *Bund* (e.g. interview Fallend). Whereas national public servants have suffered various cuts, e.g. in their pension system, state bureaucrats still work under generous terms and conditions, and the same is true for conditions in the areas of education (teachers), health (hospitals) and infrastructure (extensive road paving in rural areas).

To sum up the Austrian case, regional governments face soft budget constraints, as our theory predicts. Countermeasures such as the *Stabilitätspakt* are partially effective at best. Due to the peculiarities of the Austrian fiscal equalisation system

---

210. All *Länder* together are indebted by 7.9 billion euros. This represents 32.5 per cent of their annual budget. The municipalities have borrowed 5.52 billion euros (27 per cent of their annual budget). An alternative calculation estimates the municipalities' debt (artificially reduced by accounting tricks) to more than 15 billion euros (Grossmann and Hauth 2004). The *Bund*'s debt amounts to 1.51 times its annual budget (International Monetary Fund 2008, authors' own calculations). These data refer to 'official' debt according to the Maastricht accounting rules established in the context of the European Economic and Monetary Union (EMU). The debts of several state-owned but privatised companies are legally excluded from that account.

211. 'ein gegenseitiges Geben und Nehmen', translation by authors.

212. According to the fiscal constitutional law (*Finanz-Verfassungsgesetz*, F-VG).

and high external pressure on the national government from the European Stability pact, regional governments manage frequently to externalise costs to both national and local governments and – especially through national level borrowing – to future generations (Wachendorfer-Schmidt 2000; Goodspeed 2002). In terms of our game theoretical model, the *Bund* prevents anticipated subnational borrowings and shoulders most of the burden itself.[213] The *Länder*, in contrast, benefit from generous transfer agreements and high *Bedarfszuweisungen*.[214]

According to expert assessments, reforms are difficult to achieve, partly because it is feared that small changes to the complicated system may have unintended consequences. Often, the *Länder* prefer leaving a task with central government, implementing it in the framework of Indirect Federal Administration (combined with federal grants for this purpose), to the alternative of more competencies of their own which would lead to more tax competencies and more responsibility *vis-à-vis* the voter.

7.2.4 Patterns of subnational fiscal discipline

In line with our theoretical predictions we conclude that both unitary and federal–decentralised countries are able to maintain comparatively high subnational fiscal discipline, though by varying means. While the Irish and Danish governments tend to use hierarchical oversight and hard borrowing rules to keep subnational entities financially disciplined, Swiss cantons are subject to tax competition and market pressures as their high degree of fiscal independence from the federal level makes the no bail-out option highly credible. The Austrian system, in contrast, shows evidence of less disciplined behaviour. Neither electoral accountability nor additional mechanisms (*Stabilitätspakt*) seem to be reasonably effective. Additionally, our study highlights several interesting details. First, an underestimated factor is accountability through subnational elections. In both Switzerland and Denmark, this is of major importance. Thus, there is pressure not only from the financial market and tax competition with neighbouring regions, but also from the threat of not being re-elected. This pressure is in the Swiss case further reinforced by the strong role of direct democracy and evident voter preferences for sustainable financing. Second, Danish central government has introduced a local expenditure ceiling which is administered by the local governments themselves. They thereby mutually reinforce fiscal discipline since they otherwise, at least in theory, face collective sanctions. A third insight is an unexpected result in the Austrian case: the soft budget constraints are apparently used by the *Länder* not to borrow excessively themselves, but instead as a strategic instrument in fiscal negotiations with the federal government. This way, they are able to maintain a

---

213. Plans to introduce a formal 'debt brake' as in Switzerland failed (Brandner *et al.* 2005). The debt brake is basically a formal expenditure limit depending on the revenues and the economic situation. In contrast to common borrowing restrictions, it allows for anticyclical measures.

214. These are resources assigned to the municipalities, but kept by the *Länder* to be redistributed according to special programmes or 'individual specific needs'.

relatively comfortable level of resources situation, while the lion's share of public debt is shouldered by the national level.

In sum, subnational fiscal discipline can be ensured by both market and hierarchical measures, as well as by a peer group and electoral accountability. Additionally, soft budget constraints in a federal–centralised country apparently induce subnational actors to shift the burden of their own fiscal behaviour away from themselves. Our findings thus suggest worse fiscal performance by Austria compared to the other countries. However, it is unclear whether and to what extent this affects subnational *policy* performance.

7.3 Implementation in the area of regional development policy

As we have shown in Section 7.1, the countries selected for our in-depth analyses of policy implementation processes satisfy the criteria our theory requires for decentralisation to have a positive impact. In the next step we disaggregate the patterns and focus on different policy areas. We thus check for the existence and relevance of the causal mechanisms developed in Chapter 5.2. In this section, we analyse regional development policy. Transport policy will be dealt with in Section 7.4. Since the quantitative analysis showed robust positive effects for decentralisation on performance in regional development policy, the analysis in this section is of a theory-testing character.

We start with Switzerland and Denmark as decentralised countries, followed by Austria and, finally, Ireland. In line with our theoretical interest, we chose regional development projects, following expert advice in each country. Specifically, we look at the infrastructure programme for mountainous areas (IHG) in Switzerland and the National Spatial Strategy (NSS) in Ireland. In the cases of Denmark and Austria project selection was much more difficult. The mazelike competence structures in Austrian regional development policy, along with the atypically strong decision-making role of *Länder* governments (see Chapter 6.3.1), generate a multitude of parallel programmes on the national, regional, and local level and make it impossible to single out a specific scheme. We analyse the national COMET programme and the implementation of EU structural funds which is influenced by the *Länder* in order to illustrate this plurality. In the Danish case, there has simply been no national programme since the early 1990s. However, because the national government plays a role in the allocation of EU structural funding, we select this programme for scrutiny.

The country sections are structured as follows. We first briefly describe the programme under investigation with a special focus on the preconditions for efficient decentralised implementation. Secondly, we scrutinise the amount of subnational variation, vertical as well as horizontal coordination and present expert assessments of the programmes' overall efficiency. Our analysis of implementation processes is thus guided by the following questions: Is the programme adequately funded? Does the allocation of resources occur according to regional and local needs and preferences? Does the dissemination of tasks as well as the size of funded regions make up for lost economies of scale? Are potential difficulties with small-scale service provision compensated for by an adequate degree of horizontal coordination? And is the provision of public services considered efficient? We sum up our findings in Section 7.3.5.

7.3.1 Switzerland. Implementing IHG and NRP

As outlined in Chapter 6.3.3.1, Swiss regional development policy has undergone a far-reaching reform (NRP) that came into effect at the beginning of 2008. Since it is thus too early to comprehensively evaluate its effects, we shed light on the efficiency of strategies for regional development with a focus on the instruments of the first generation of Swiss regional development policy (especially the IHG). With regard to the NRP, we restrict ourselves to a tentative assessment of the instruments and possible effects.

The first generation of Swiss regional development policy mainly subsidises costs for capital appropriations and is directed at helping mountainous regions in financing infrastructure (IHG) or supporting individual enterprises, either within the IHG regions (BGB), in monostructural regions (BWE) or within the tourist industry (HKG).[215] Given that the IHG is endowed with the largest financial contribution[216] and has been quite extensively evaluated (Bieger *et al.* 2004; Thierstein and Behrendt 2001; Frey 1985), we will scrutinise the efficiency of its implementation as an example of the first generation's instruments. Its major characteristics are depicted in Table 7.9.

The implementation of the IHG is based upon 54 IHG regions in mountainous areas that have been defined as such by the federal government in agreement with the cantons and make up about 66 per cent of Swiss total area. These IHG regions are composed of 1,222 communes (in 2000) and are classified as eligible to receive interest-free loans for investments in basic infrastructure or contributions to interest expenses. In an effort to channel support, regional associations and offices have been created that put together development concepts. In practice, these regions thus

> accumulated important tasks: They not only represent and promote their region, but are also responsible for the co-ordination and the implementation of the regional development concept and serve as advisory body to the communes, the local economy and the population (Wälti and Bullinger 2000: 89).

---

215. The respective laws are the *Bundesgesetz über Investitionshilfe im Berggebiet* (IHG), in effect since 1974 (Bundesversammlung der Schweizerischen Eidgenossenschaft 1997c), the *Bundesgesetz über die Gewährung von Bürgschaften und Zinskostenbeiträge in Berggebieten* (BGB) of 1976 (Bundesversammlung der Schweizerischen Eidgenossenschaft 1976), the *Bundesbeschluss zugunsten wirtschaftlich bedrohter Regionen* of 1978 (BWE since 1994) (Bundesversammlung der Schweizerischen Eidgenossenschaft 1978), and the *Bundesgesetz über die Förderung des Hotel- und Kurortkredits* (HKG) of 1967 (Bundesversammlung der Schweizerischen Eidgenossenschaft 1967).

216. The programmes' costs in 2002 were 100 million SFR loans and 5 million SFR financial contributions for the IHG, 3 million SFR for the BGB, 8 million SFR for the BWE, and 13 million SFR for the HKG (Buser 2005).

Table 7.9: Characteristics of the IHG in Switzerland

Objective	Compensation for locational disadvantages
Beneficiaries[a]	Public investors in 54 IHG regions
Instruments	Interest-free loans for investments in basic infrastructure Contributions to interest expenses
Finance	Capital income of IHG fund Cantonal co-financing 50%
Costs per year (federation)	100 m SFR loans (2002) 5 m SFR financial contributions (2002)
Actors in policy implementation	54 IHG regions with regional associations and offices, Cantons, Seco
Advantages	Reduction of locational disadvantages; preservation of decentralised settlement; regions as functional areas; operating experience in inter-communal coordination; regional associations compile adequate development plans that integrate regional and land use policies (Interview Boesch)
Disadvantages	Windfall gains[b]; small-scale infrastructure hardly attracts business; increased mobility induces movement of labour; insufficient assistance for greater infrastructural projects

Sources: Buser 2005, Eidgenössisches Volkswirtschaftsdepartement 2004b, von Stokar, Vettori, Steinemann *et al*. 2004, and Thierstein and Behrendt 2001.

[a] For maps of the respective eligible areas, see Bundesamt für Statistik, *Karte. Die wirtschaftlichen Erneuerungsgebiete (WEG 01) der Schweiz*; [b] The existence of windfall gains was clearly called into question by one interviewee (interview Boesch).

The IHG regions possess considerable discretion as to the inclusion of specific investments within their development plans. Though they support mostly public sector investments in basic infrastructure, the IHG has been interpreted as a 'programme for all purposes' (Bieger *et al*. 2004: III).[217]

The allocation of subsidies to the various IHG regions is largely determined by the subventions the respective cantons provide, as these trigger federal contributions. The size of subventions granted by cantons varies widely (Bieger *et al*. 2004: IV) and so does the style of collaboration between the cantons and the respective regions (interview Boesch; Bieger *et al*. 2004: VI). Cantonal co-financing thus implies 'that the cantons may keep considerable powers over the allocation of the financial aid' (Wälti and Bullinger 2000: 90).[218] Given the high level of policy discretion enjoyed by the IHG regions and the financial discretion of the cantons, the 'cantons and communes thus remained the masters of regional economic development' (Wälti and Bullinger 2000: 90).

---

217. 'Allzweckprogramm', translation by authors.

218. Cantonal influence on the flow of investments is additionally strengthened as they decide about the degree of interest reduction granted as well as its duration.

As the theory predicts, the IHG's implementation is characterised by a high level of subnational policy discretion that allows for regionally varying patterns of resource allocation. Moreover, since over 60 per cent of the country is eligible for the programme, it is not very selective. Actual resource use varies widely due to cantonal decisions on co-financing. This is in line with our theoretical expectation. However, while its design as an instrument of co-finance enhances subnational policy discretion and intercantonal variation, on the other hand it reduces the degree of fiscal balance. One unintended, negative consequence is co-financed investments in infrastructure that would have taken place even without federal financial involvement (windfall gains). Moreover, given sufficient resources for investments in small-scale infrastructure but limited capacity for enhancing larger developmental projects, the overall assessment of the IHG's effects is mixed. While it significantly mitigates the locational disadvantages of mountainous regions and enhances inter-communal cooperation within the regions, the programme reaches its limits with regional competitiveness, mainly because of the limited capabilities of small cantons (see Table 7.9). This constraint, the comparative weakness of the BWE and HKG,[219] and limited coordination between these instruments (Eidgenössisches Volkswirtschaftsdepartement 2004b: 14; Wälti and Bullinger 2000: 98) led to the perceived necessity for reform as described in Section 6.2.1.

Second-generation instruments, initiated after the reorientation of Swiss regional development policy in 1996, shifted the focus towards actor-centred support of developmental projects and networks. They were designed to foster innovation, entrepreneurship and endogenous potential (like Regio plus), as well as inter-cantonal cooperation (like INTERREG). The entire responsibility for implementation was therefore delegated to the cantons so that they became even 'more autonomous in administrating the regional development programmes' (Wälti and Bullinger 2000: 91). These instruments, and especially Regio plus, were tentatively evaluated as being efficient (Buser 2005: 24) and partly foreshadow characteristics of the intended policy shift initiated with the NFA and the NRP, particularly the cantons' anticipated increase in financial as well as political discretion. On the one hand, the cantons are the sole partners of the State Secretariat for Economic Affairs (SECO) in negotiating their implementation programmes for the NRP. On the other hand, cantonal responsibility and discretion is increased by the NFA. Investments in maintenance and development of basic infrastructure are henceforth the job of cantonal services financed by the global budget. Boesch thus speaks of a 'cantonalisation of regional policy' (interview Boesch).[220] However, whether or not this increased political and financial discretion enhances or reduces efficiency remains to be seen. Though pilot projects reflect a wide variety of

---

219. Nevertheless, the first generation of regional development policy yielded a number of examples of 'best practice' which exhibit great diversity in content. See http://www.seco.admin.ch/themen/00476/00496/00498/00503/index.html?lang=de.

220. 'Kantonalisierung der Regionalpolitik', translation by authors.

initiatives supported,[221] it is far too early to assess whether structurally weak cantons will be able to carry out their new tasks effectively and whether reducing the IHG regions' importance leads to a loss of valuable expertise.

7.3.2   Denmark. Implementing EU structural funds

After the abolition of all nationally financed programmes in 1991 (see Chapter 6.3.3.3), both counties and municipalities were allowed to develop promotional activities between 1993 and 2006. In 2007, the implementation structure changed. The newly established national programmes are now coordinated at the regional level by Regional Growth Forums (RGF) and implemented by municipalities or external agencies.[222] We focus here on the earlier period, because evaluation of the new programmes is not yet possible. In the 1993–2006 period, the regional policy framework was provided by the national government and the European Union (Ahedo Santisteban 2006), while implementation was in the hands of the subnational entities. National influence was exerted mainly through setting up the criteria of regional resource distribution.[223] Moreover, the government made sure that the subnational initiatives stayed within the legal boundaries of the EU programme (interview Halkier). Apart from that, administration and supervision were executed by the Danish Enterprise and Construction Authority (DEACA). The Ministry of Economic and Business Affairs was usually not involved in day-to-day work (Bogason 1987).

In practice, the level of discretion was very high. While officially the programmes were coordinated at the national level by DATI[224] (Bachtler and Yuill 2001), at least in the early 1990s, 'the regions could essentially do whatever they wanted to do' (interview Halkier). However, later the government attempted to gain influence by setting the main focuses and agendas (interview Halkier). Regional governments have no revenue of their own but depend on national and EU grants, which results in an above-average fiscal imbalance. Moreover, despite the regions formally being allowed to develop own regional strategies, the unequal allocation of resources was a limiting factor. Because the EU was until 2007 the only source of finance for regional development measures, except for the obligatory national co-funding (Halkier 2006), the degree to which legal discretion could be used by the subnational entities varied (Ahedo Santisteban 2006). Only the regions which obtained EU structural funding were capable of developing a profiled promotional strategy.[225] As Table 7.10 suggests, North

---

221. See http://www.seco.admin.ch/themen/00476/00496/00498/00504/index.html?lang=de.

222. Regions are by law not allowed to implement (interview Halkier).

223. In the 2007–13 period these criteria are: the region's share of the population of Danish peripheries (45 per cent), the region's share of the total Danish population (40 per cent), the region's share of unemployed (10 per cent) and less educated people (5 per cent) (Neubauer et al. 2007).

224. This agency is today known as the Danish Enterprise and Construction Authority.

225. These were mainly municipalities in North Jutland and some of the Baltic Islands.

Jutland and Bornholm benefit disproportionately from ERDF resources. In the 2007–13 period, North Jutland receives nearly three times the amount per capita than Central Jutland (21 compared to 8 euros) (Neubauer *et al.* 2007).

Table 7.10: Regional distribution (percentage) of EU Objective 2 funding in Denmark

Period	North Jutland	Central Jutland	South Denmark	Zealand	Capital region	Bornholm	Total
2000–06	26.2	14.4	21.3	16.8	17.8	3.3	100.0
2007–13	25.3	16.2	23.1	16.2	15.9	3.3	100.0
Population share	10.6	22.5	21.8	15.0	29.3	0.8	100.0

Source: Halkier 2006.

The effectiveness of these individual strategies differed. North Jutland experienced high growth rates and there are several examples of successful and innovative developments (Villadsen 2002).[226] The Aalborg region had been phased out of the ERDF programme in 2000. Meanwhile, the Baltic Islands did not experience any substantial development (interview Halkier). One of the main criticisms of the programme was its small scale: promotional activities before 2006 were criticised for having been uncoordinated and ineffective. This holds not only for the municipal level but also for cooperation between local and regional governments and for coordination between the national ministries (interview Halkier). Municipalities were perceived as too small for effective regional coordination and counties lacked resources for it. The 2007 local government reform aimed to strengthen institutional capacities and regional coordination by merging municipalities and setting up five new regions, mainly for coordination purposes (see Section 7.1).

At first glance, the new structure reduces some problems: the regional level is now in charge of coordination and national funding has increased. In terms of efficiency, however, some doubts remain. The Regional Growth Forums are additional to the elected Regional Councils. This division of labour exacerbates rivalry between the regional and local levels:

All these interests are brought together in regional development boards. And then you have a competition between the regional development board and the regional, politically elected council (interview Christoffersen).[227]

However, because both institutions, the RGF and Regional Council, possess veto powers over the Regional Development Plan, there is a hypothetical danger of

---

226. The Aalborg telecommunications cluster, for instance.

227. This weakening of the regional level might have been an intended effect of the reform – the original hope of the Conservative Party was to abolish the regional level completely.

institutional deadlock. The regions depend on transfers and the interests of local politicians who are members of the RGF. Furthermore, the regional boundaries are accused of dampening efficiency because they cut through economically homogeneous regions in Eastern Jutland (interview Halkier). Whether the Forums are able to coordinate promotional measures effectively cannot be evaluated yet. The potential for institutional or instrumental innovation is limited by compulsory adherence to the national framework (Damborg and Halkier 1998).

The evidence from regional development policy during the 1990s is mixed. On the one hand, it was criticised as underfunded and poorly coordinated. Despite a general absence of detailed national regulation, its innovation potential had thus been low. On the other hand, North Jutland at least (as one of the two regions that received substantial EU funding in that period) effectively promoted regional growth. The highly selective allocation of resources and large amount of discretion hence enabled the region to react to local weaknesses and needs in an efficient manner. The new scheme is designed to foster regional cooperation, but also aggravates rivalries between governmental levels. Additionally, regional boundaries are drawn according to political criteria not efficiency reasons.

7.3.3   Austria. Implementing COMET and STRAT.AT

The area of regional development policy, in contrast to many other policy areas, is characterised by dual competencies and a major role played by the *Länder* (see Chapter 6.3.1). Downes (2000) counted 60 federal and 130 state programmes in 1994. The number has decreased only marginally since then (interview Mayerhofer). This reflects the will of subnational entities to include the highest possible number of actors:

> The overall result is a complex and opaque structure which, in reality, often works principally on the basis of informal links between individuals (Downes 2000: 249).

At the federal level, at least three ministries[228] and the chancellery are active in regional development. Policy in this area is mostly implemented through national agencies. Examples are TIP (Technology, Information, and Policy consulting), the Austrian Economic Service (*Austria Wirtschaftsservice GmbH*, AWSG) or programmes like COMET.[229] TIP has been established jointly by all three ministries and is administered by the Austrian Institute for Economic Research (*Österreichisches Wirtschaftsforschungsinstitut*, WIFO) and the Austrian Research Centre Seibersdorf (ARCS). TIP's main goal is to facilitate innovation

---

228. The BMVIT, the Ministry of Science and Research (*Bundesministerium für Wissenschaft und Forschung*, BMWF), and the BMWA.

229. Other agencies enumerated by Huber (2002) are promotional banks like *Kommunalkredit AG*, *BÜRGES_Förderbank*, *Investkredit AG* and many semi-public and private bodies like development corporations, consultancies and technology centres. Prior to a concentration process in 2000, several additional federal agencies and programmes had existed (interview Mayerhofer).

and interaction between academic research and industry. The AWSG is a federal promotional bank. Its purpose is to provide low-interest loans to individual projects. COMET, finally, is the current name of the Austrian competence centre programme, operated by the Austrian Research Promotion Agency (*Forschungsförderungsgesellschaft*, FFG), aiming to foster regional technology clusters. Both AWSG and FFG operate under the joint control of BMVIT and BMWA. The federal chancellery is active foremost in the area of EU structural funds. The associated ÖROK coordinates the Regional Strategic Reference Frameworks required for EU funding. The chancellery also coordinates other regional and national development strategies as well as the regional managements.

The *Länder* devised plenty of regional promotional activities. Due to the wide variety, it is not possible to give a full overview here. Heintel (2004) lists for Lower Austria one Regional Development Agency (ECOplus), managing 12 industrial parks and several start-up centres, 12 Regional Innovation Centres (*Regionale Innovationszentren*, RIZ), 5 regional managements, 6 LEADER+ groups, one EUREGIO, several cross-border cooperation centres and local tourism cooperatives, and 71 micro-regions (*Kleinregionen*). The administration of the promotional programmes differs between states. While in Lower Austria all these activities are administered by the relevant government department, several other state governments established a Regional Development Agency, such as the Carinthian Economic Promotion Fund (*Kärntner Wirtschaftsförderungs Fonds*, KWF), to support local Small and Medium Enterprises (SME).

Since EU accession 31 regional management agencies have been founded in order to develop 'bottom-up' projects for regional coordination below the state level and across state borders (Fallend 2007). Members are local, district, and *Länder* representatives, and the social partners. Their task is mainly to act as a platform for negotiation and informational exchange between the participants (Draxl *et al.* 2004). Other cooperation structures exist in the ÖROK (see Section 7.2) and in several regional agencies such as the *Planungsgemeinschaft Ost* (PGO) founded by Vienna, Lower Austria, and Burgenland to 'adjust, coordinate, and prepare questions of regional planning in eastern Austria'.[230]

Bund, Länder and EU are all deeply involved in regional development financing (see Table 7.11). Regional management boards and state agencies also receive resources from other European structural funds, namely ERDF and ESF. These resources are divided between the regional managements and the states' promotional agencies like the KWF.

---

230. 'Abstimmung, Koordination und Vorbereitung raumplanerischer Fragen in der österreichischen "Länderregion Ost"' (www.pgo.wien.at), translation by authors.

Table 7.11: Volume of regional development funds in million euros in Austria, 2000–2006

European funds			National funds			
ERDF	ESF	EAGGF	Federal level	State level	Other	Total
1,076.0	760.7	120.8	349.8	409.7	183.7	2,900.7

Source: Österreichische Raumordnungskonferenz (ÖROK).

Abbreviations: ERDF European Regional Development Fund; ESF European Social Fund; EAGGL European Agricultural Guidance and Guarantee Fund.

Table 7.12: Number of projects funded by the Austrian COMET programme (first call), 2006

Programme line	BL	CA	LA	SB	ST	TY	UA	VA	VI	Total
K2	-	-	-	-	2	-	1	-	-	3
K1	-	1	1	-	4	1	3	-	1	11
K	-	-	-	1	4	-	-	-	1	6

Source: Österreichische Forschungsförderungsgesellschaft (FFG).

Abbreviations of Austrian Länder: BL Burgenland; CA Carinthia; LA Lower Austria; SB Salzburg; ST Styria; TY Tyrol; UA Upper Austria; VA Vorarlberg; VI Vienna.

Among so many programmes and actors, it is impossible to find one that reflects all the characteristics of Austrian regional development policy. In the following, we analyse the implementation processes of the federal COMET programme and of STRAT.AT. The former is an example of a selective approach at the federal level. The latter is a financially highly relevant area with a particularly pronounced need for coordination between regional governments and between the regional and federal levels.

COMET (known in Austria as *Kompetenzzentrenprogramm*) was announced in 1997 by the federal ministries BMVIT and BMWA, as a result of the finding that technology transfers between scientific research institutes and business did not work effectively (interview Mayerhofer). Today the programme is executed by the *Forschungsförderungsgemeinschaft* (FFG), an agency established in 2004 jointly by the two ministries, and financed by the participating enterprises (between 40 and 60 per cent) (Peneder 1999) and the government. A third of the public finance stems from the *Länder*'s budgets. The COMET programme is organised competitively: the *Länder* are invited to apply for funding in open competition. Their applications are examined by the FFG and external experts. The final decision is taken by the Federal Minister.[231] The programme design and the funding decision are the main elements by which the federal government maintains its influence, apart from that

---

231. As of 2008, this was the Minister of Women, Media, and Regional Development. The 2009 government reallocated regional development to the Ministry of Economy, Family and Youth.

Table 7.13: Approved development funds by Austrian Länder in million euros

	BL	CA	LA	SB	ST	TY	UA	VA	VI	Total
EFRE	175.3	82.8	177.7	18.0	196.3	44.9	123.4	22.4	12.7	853.5
Federal level	42.3	28.3	51.2	9.6	124.6	25.6	59.2	6.7	2.4	349.8
Land level	36.6	21.9	118.4	5.7	124.4	17.2	60.6	11.5	13.2	409.7
Other national	6.8	0.8	51.5	3.1	79.2	9.4	19.4	13.4	0.1	183.7

Source: Österreichische Raumordnungskonferenz (ÖROK).

Abbreviations of Austrian *Länder*: BL Burgenland; CA Carinthia; LA Lower Austria; SB Salzburg; ST Styria; TY Tyrol; UA Upper Austria; VA Vorarlberg; VI Vienna.

the applicants are free to take their own decisions (interview Mayerhofer).

Effectively, two of three K2-centres, four of eleven K1-centres, and four of six K-projects[232] are located in Styria (see Table 7.12). While one cannot verify whether the chosen projects were really the best ones, regional concentration is a clear indicator that proportional distribution was not the decisive criterion in the allocation decision (interview Seidl). Contrary to our theoretical expectation, the central state in this case is not politically required to compensate disadvantaged regions, but can operate a selective strategy. However, the clear competitive framework of this programme is uncommon in Austrian development policy. In most programmes consensual solutions are still preferred (interview Seidl).

The most prominent example of the consensual approach is our second example, the implementation of EU structural funding under a common national framework. EU accession led to profound changes in the orientation of Austrian regional development policy (see Chapter 6.3.3.2). The traditionally high autonomy of subnational actors was reduced by the demand for Single Programming Documents that required national coordination. Complex administrative requirements reduced the scope of activity especially for small and local programmes (Huber 2002). Since the first funding period in which Austria participated (1995–9), the EU has increased flexibility to some degree. For the 2007–13 period, the EU demanded the presentation of a National Strategic Reference Framework (NSRF), in Austria called STRAT.AT (Österreichische Raumordnungskonferenz (ÖROK) 2006). The *Bund* and *Länder* decided to leave the coordination of this common framework to the ÖROK. In 'short and intense' (interview Seidl) negotiations, considerable differences in the resources granted to individual *Länder* were fixed (see Table 7.13).

Despite the common framework of the NSRF, there is much discretionary leeway for the *Länder* (see Chapter 6.3.3.2). Both the NSRF and the operational programmes allow for much interpretation by the *Land*'s administration (Kanonier

---

232. These are the three lines of the COMET programme. The K2-programme is the most lucrative (maximum of 5 million euros annually over ten years), followed by the K1- (1.5 million annually over seven years) and K-projects (0.45 million annually over three to five years).

2003, interview Mayerhofer).[233] The administrative structure also varies in form and number of agencies (Steiner and Jud 1998). Carinthia, focusing exclusively on enterprises and research areas, implements all of its activities through the KWF, while Lower Austria uses a much wider variety of agencies.

The performance of individual programmes varies greatly. A positive example is the Regional Managements established in the 1990s. These are mainly founded on intermunicipal cooperation and financed by the EU LEADER initiative (Draxl *et al.* 2004). They are described as efficient network supporters (Heintel 2005) employing capable, entrepreneurially oriented personnel (interview Boesch). On the other hand, the consensual agreements at the ÖROK level are contrasted with much more competitive thinking at the agencies' level. Here, backyard policies are common and only partly coordinated by higher levels. Solutions across *Länder* are rare (Kanonier 2003). The widely applied partial funding by the federal level results in a prisoner's dilemma. Competition on appropriations dominates the relationships among the *Länder*, because the allocation of promotional agencies affects the fiscal equalisation funds a *Land* gets (interview Mayerhofer). This is illustrated by the Austrian cluster initiative. Neighbouring states have frequently founded cluster initiatives in the same sectors, like wood or automotive industries, making it unlikely to reach a 'critical mass' and achieve positive externalities. Moreover, the *Länder* are strongly centralised internally and incapable of a selective approach: for example, 'it comes to fifteen technological centres [in one state], just because there are fifteen districts' (interview Mayerhofer).[234] At the local level, we find a similar picture. Municipalities extensively designate construction areas, because the *Bund*, through its housing programme (*Wohnbauförderung*), is required indiscriminately to subsidise all infrastructure investments in these areas (interview Mayerhofer).

In sum, Austrian regional development policy is multi-faceted. Contrary to our theoretical expectation and the general characteristics of Austria's territorial structure, regional development policy allows for substantial discretion within the common reference framework. This does not necessarily result in subnational variation, as *Länder* governments and their promoting agencies compete for the same federal resources and business investments (interview Mayerhofer). Competition for federal funding thus reduces efficiency gains substantially and hampers coordination between regional governments. Below *Länder* level, there are examples of both centralised 'sprinkler' policies (one technological centre per district) and of efficient cooperative network structures (Regional Managements).

---

233. While Vienna uses most of its ERDF resources for restoration measures, Carinthia and Burgenland use roughly two thirds of these funds for promotion of enterprises. Styria and Upper Austria have a clear focus on research and development, while Vorarlberg, Salzburg and Lower Austria invest foremost into tourism programmes. Tyrol balanced its budget more or less between all these purposes (Österreichische Raumordnungskonferenz (ÖROK)).

234. 'Es gibt z. B. Technologiezentrenprogramme und es ist dann halt so, dass zwei oder drei [...] vielleicht funktionieren könnten, [...] und dann gibt es auf einmal 15, weil es 15 Bezirke gibt', translation by authors.

7.3.4   Ireland. Implementing the National Spatial Strategy

Current development policies in Ireland are mainly delivered through two different channels. On the one hand, development has traditionally been carried out by central administration and agencies,[235] like Enterprise Ireland or the Industrial Development Agency (IDA),[236] supplemented since the 1990s by different Local Development Initiatives (LDI). On the other hand, the NSS promises a new, regionalised approach to development by focusing on an urban hierarchy of gateways and hubs and a hierarchical integration of development plans. The current chapter evaluates both the achievements of LDI and the implementation of the NSS.

Facing high levels of unemployment and poverty in rural areas and fuelled by bottom-up pressures as well as EU policy, Irish governments in the 1990s perceived an increasing necessity to tackle these problems at a local level (Walsh 1998; Carroll and Byrne 1999; Turok 2000). C/C were, however, found to be too weak to undertake a wider role in community development (Loughlin 2001). Instead of enhancing their financial resources different government departments set up a completely parallel structure of Local Development Initiatives (LDI), including Area Based Partnerships (ABP) and County Enterprise Boards (CEB). Ireland moreover participated in the EU LEADER programme.[237] The main characteristics of these initiatives regarding funding, accountability and functions are depicted in Table 7.14.

The achievements of individual initiatives have been subject to thorough analyses (Taylor 2005; Sabel 1996; Loughlin 2001; Moseley *et al.* 2001; Storey 1999; Walsh 1998). These studies show that LDI's practical problem-solving approach enables it to provide services and facilities that are of 'direct assistance to many poor and unemployed people' (Turok 2000: 23, see also Sabel 1996; Moseley *et al.* 2001; Varley and Curtin 2002). However, their capacity to pursue an innovative and integrated approach to local economic development is constrained by lacking their own resources and their limited discretion (Loughlin 2001; Walsh 1998; Moseley *et al.* 2001). Broadly speaking, 'the operational programmes are reasonably specific. Availability of finance plus the various bureaucratic requirements either from central government in Dublin or from Brussels would

---

235. Two regional development companies exist: Shannon Development, a government-owned regional development company dedicated to promoting and developing the Shannon Region, and www.udaras.ie, the regional authority responsible for the economic, social and cultural development of the Irish speaking regions (*Gaeltacht*). Given their exceptional role they will not be assessed in more detail in this book.

236. Enterprise Ireland is responsible for the development and promotion of the indigenous business sector and IDA for securing new investment from overseas in manufacturing and internationally traded services sectors. Both have contributed significantly to Ireland's economic success.

237. As described at the outset of this chapter, the governance structure at subnational level includes up to 500 actors. The current case study, however, concentrates on those local development initiatives that were specifically targeted at fostering business development and tackling unemployment in disadvantaged areas.

Table 7.14: Characteristics of Irish local development initiatives

	Established in	Financed by	Accountable to	Composition of board	Main functions
38 area-based partnerships	Pilot programme (12 ABPs), established in 1991, streamlined and extended to 38 in 1994	Until 1999 partly by EU Structural Funds, since 2000 wholly by exchequer. Funding allocated by Area Development Management (ADM) Ltd	Dept. of Community, Rural and Gaeltacht Affairs[a] Evaluation by ADM Ltd	State agencies, social partners, local elected members, community and voluntary sector	Prepare and implement a local development plan to counter disadvantage, coordinate the activities of state agencies
35 LEADER groups	1992–1994: LEADER 1 1994–1996: LEADER 2 2000– : LEADER+	Initially funded by the EU, since 2000 publicly funded by Dept. of Agriculture and Food	Dept. of Community, Rural and Gaeltacht Affairs[b]	Representatives of local communities, state agencies, local authorities, and social partners	Local business plans are agreed between local action groups and the Dept. (oversight)
35 county enterprise boards	Established in 1993, statutory status since 1995 (Industrial Development Act)	Exchequer and EU Structural Funds	Dept. of Enterprise, Trade and Employment	Independent chairperson, 4 local elected members; nominees of state agencies, social partners, small businesses	Promote microenterprise, job creation objectives (for areas not covered by IDAs)

Source: Ó Broin and Waters 2007: Appendix I, modified by authors.

[a] **Until 2002:** Dept. of Tourism, Sport and Recreation; [b] **Until 2002:** Dept. of Agriculture and Food.

have limited the autonomy of local development bodies' (interview Quinn). The 38 ABP are, for example, accountable to the semi-public company Area Development Management Limited (ADM, now Pobal) and some government departments or agencies have representatives on the partnership and development boards (Turok 2000). In addition, and irrespective of individual achievements, the efficiency of LDI is seriously affected by the lack of a coordinated approach. The limited integration of local development initiatives and local government, on the one hand, and insufficient coordination within the group of LDI, on the other hand, have significantly constrained their potential (Jacobsen and Kirby 2000; Walsh 1998). As can be seen in Table 7.14, until 2002 initiatives fell under the remit of three different government departments and 'that was creating uncertainty and tensions' (interview Bartley). Moreover, the different initiatives did not overlap geographically. As a result, services were duplicated (O'Leary 2003a).

In 2002, the Irish government finally launched a cohesion process aimed at 'amalgamating agencies and reducing the number [...] making them [...] operate within local government boundaries' (interview Ó Broin). One central device was the establishment of thirty-five County Development Boards (CDB) that comprise members drawn from councillors, the social partners, and representatives of the LDI. Each board was required to draw up a three–five-year strategy for local development which other statutory bodies are to sign up for to execute. However,

> CDBs are overly reliant on influence as opposed to statutory sanctions [...], have been unable to commit their agencies to CDB strategies and [...] to influence the planning process of major public agencies (O'Broin and Waters 2007: 46).

A more general criticism is that CDBs just add another player to the already unmanageable network of actors rather than addressing the issue of decentralisation. The functions and resources of C/C are thus still severely limited, and their level of involvement and activity is up to 'individual local authorities, it is not a statutory responsibility' (interview Callanan).[238] The cohesion process moreover implies reducing the discretion of ABP.

> Pobal [...] has increasingly involved itself in the day-to-day management [...]. They have laid down increasingly [...] bureaucratic and administrative frameworks for the partnerships to operate within [...]. The staff is from now on nationally set pay scales. So they have been brought more and more into the central public process (interview Ó Broin).

Let us now turn to the National Spatial Strategy (NSS) as an alternative approach. The implementation of the NSS also exhibits serious defects (Keane 2002: 219; Davoudi and Wishardt 2005).[239] Firstly, the Regional Planning

---

238. Waterford and Meath, for example, have developed 'their own marketing campaigns in terms of [...] inward investment but also domestic investment in their area' (interview Callanan).

239. 'The National Spatial Strategy has been informally written off. It's ignored. The series of objectives laid down by the National Spatial Strategy have been ignored again and again and again'

Guidelines (RPG) that were set up by 2004 are low quality. Secondly, and even more important, local development plans hardly take the RPGs into account. The hierarchy of plans desired has thus not been put into practice.

Even though all RAuth set up RPG by 2004,[240] these rarely exhibit a genuine regional profile. In drawing up the RPG 'local authorities were more involved than the regional authorities' (interview Callanan) and as a consequence the RPG often reflect 'a composite of County views that is expressed at regional level' (interview Ó Broin). Even though a number of regions try to cope with their lack of expertise by bringing in outside consultants, this has in turn caused 'a huge varying in quality of strategies depending on the region' (interview Ó Broin).

More significantly, however, the RPG 'are ignored by all the County development plan processes' (interview Ó Broin). Though local authorities are urged to take the RPG into consideration, there are no sanctions if they fail to do so. A comparison of the RPG and existing gateway studies illustrates the difficulties. Some RPG take into account earlier transport studies of existing gateways, e.g. the South West RPG builds upon the *Cork Area Strategic Plan of 2001*, and the South East RPG takes the *Waterford Planning Land Use and Transportation Study of 2002* into account. However, this reverses the desired hierarchy of planning. Moreover, the allocation of funds is still channelled on a sector-specific and not a spatial basis. Furthermore, major deficiencies are apparent in those regions that contain the newly established gateways. Despite the fact that the respective RAuth have set up RPG, there are to date no joint studies for the linked gateways Tullamore/Athlone/Mullingar or Letterkenny/(Derry). And even the Strategic Planning Guidelines for Dublin 'are being widely disregarded' (Morgenroth 2000: 12).

The implementation processes of the NSS are badly flawed. While this can largely be ascribed to the weakness of devices put in place earlier, on a wider perspective it reflects that 'the NSS requires the government to be geographically selective [...]. [The Irish] political system can't handle that' (interview Breathnach). Individual LDI have surely generated positive impulses for community advancement, but the overall system exhibits tremendous inefficiencies due to insufficient cooperation between actors. The resulting duplication of services and restricted accountability reflect the lack of coordination between different central government departments and agencies on a local level as well as the inability of local government to fill this gap. The experience of LDI thus, again, points to the fact that

the Irish are very bad at reforming the system [...] Rather than getting rid of it, we're setting up a new structure and keep the old structure as well (interview Ó Broin).

(interview Ó Broin).

240. The DoEHLG supervises the preparation of RPGs as well as that of County, City and Local Area Development Plans.

7.3.5 *Patterns of implementation in regional development policy*

Both decentralised countries show, as expected, a high amount of subnational variance; funding is selective and allocation strategies differ between subnational entities. In general this effectively remedies local weaknesses and supports the catch-up of poorer regions to the national average, as can be clearly seen in the Danish case of North Jutland and in Swiss mountainous regions. The findings corroborate our expectations about the positive effect of decentralised resource allocation in the area of regional development policy. Swiss cantons trigger federal contributions by their own co-financing and thus decide on the amount and use of resources. The Danish state left the funding of subnational development entirely to the EU and eligible regions were only marginally restricted by law in the use of these resources. Moreover, many municipalities developed small-scale strategies in the course of the 1990s. However, the degree of fiscal imbalance is in both cases higher than a national average, which at least in the Swiss case led to some, albeit minor, inefficiencies. Financial capabilities of decentralised entities are often limited and coordination is sometimes difficult. Both countries reformed their regional development policy approaches for these reasons, but in opposite directions. The Swiss NRP granted more financial as well as policy discretion to the cantons. Although the efficiency of these recent reforms cannot be fully evaluated yet, there is a clear tendency towards further decentralisation. Denmark, in contrast, chose to focus on the coordinating issue by establishing a new regional tier in 2007. The Danish approach thus entails a gradual re-centralisation, using the option to redraw local and regional boundaries – an option mostly ineligible for federal countries.

In both centralised countries, the provision of structural funding brings about quite a high number of regional or local development agencies which militates against an effective coordination of efforts. Inefficiencies thus arise from high administrative costs and a partial duplication of services. Although the Austrian *Länder* hold exceptionally high discretion in the area of regional development policy, they are not necessarily able to use it in an efficiency-enhancing way. More often, policy discretion is diminished by the *Länder*'s strong internal centralisation, as well as by joint-financing schemes. Allocation decisions are thus frequently driven not by local needs, but by federal funding criteria. The resulting competition for federal resources moreover hampers regional cooperation. On the subregional level, the 'sprinkler principle' predominates. However, sometimes the Austrian system produces substantial policy innovation, such as the Regional Managements. The Irish case is characterised by a multitude of sector-specific agencies, which mostly suffer from low discretion and high dependence on national ministries. The LDI show substantial variance, but their impact is very limited due to severe underfunding, lack of their own resources and limited discretion. Perceived deficits in regional coordination were tackled by establishing new institutional layers, which in both cases under investigation remained ineffective. Overall, while there are individual positive examples, regional as well as inter-sectoral coordination is inefficient in both Austria and Ireland. The findings of our case studies are summarised in Table 7.15.

Table 7.15: Patterns of implementation in regional development policy

	Switzerland	Denmark	Austria	Ireland
Policy approach	Investitionshilfegesetz (IHG)	EU Structural Funds	STRAT.AT	Local development initiatives (LDI)
Actors (regional actors in bold)	**IHG regions, cantons and local governments**	National Government, Danish Agency for the Development of Trade and Industry (DATI, now DEACA), since 2007: **regional governments, regional development forums, local governments**	Federal Ministries of Transport (BMVIT), Economics (BMWA), and Science (BMWF), chancellery, several national agencies (TIP, AWSG), **nine Länder governments with numerous outsourced agencies, 31 regional managements,** Austrian Conference on Spatial Planning (ÖROK) as coordinating body	Government departments, Area Development Management (ADM, now Pobal), **parallel structures of LDIs, established by different departments, such as Area Based Partnerships (ABP) and County Enterprise Boards (CEB), LEADER groups, counties and cities**
Financial and personnel resources	**Varying**: given for investments in small-scale infrastructure but constrained beyond it, resources provided by cantons vary	**Insufficient**: EU funds only accessible for certain areas	Personnel: **adequate**, financial conditions **varying** between *Länder*	**Adequate** for ABP, LEADER and CEBs, **insufficient** for counties and cities
Vertical fiscal imbalance	**Medium**: cantonal investments in regions trigger federal contributions (50%), leads to windfall gains	**High**: exclusively grant financed	**Medium**: mainly joint funding by EU, federal, and *Länder* levels	**High** in case of ABP, LEADER, CEBs, and counties and cities

Contd

	Switzerland	Denmark	Austria	Ireland
Policy discretion	**High**: given for IHG regions (investments are based on regionally compiled development concepts), resource allocation by cantons	**High**: within national framework, varying over time: stronger influence on policy goals by end of 1990s	**High**: *Länder* have leeway for interpretation of Strategic Reference Framework, negative coordination, central level has no monitoring competences	**Medium** for ABP, LEADER, CEB, but decreasing due to cohesion process, **Low** for counties and cities
Degree of subnational variance	**High**: with regard to provision and allocation of resources	**High**: only specific areas (North Jutland, Baltic Islands) gain EU funding	**High**: selective distribution of EU funding, organizational variation; no selective approaches at the sub-*Länder* level	**High** policy variance, but only marginal impact due to small scale and limited funding of LDIs
Horizontal cooperation	**Limited**: strong need for coordination has led to reform (*Neue Regionalpolitik*, NRP)	**Insufficient**: pre-2007 uncoordinated and ineffective, remedied through establishment of Regional Development Forums in 2007	**Insufficient**: competition on funding between *Länder* and municipalities prevails, coordination only on broad terms	**Insufficient** between national departments and agencies and between individual LDIs, no improvement through CEBs
Efficiency of Implementation	**High** with regard to regional disadvantages, small-scale infrastructure, **limited** with regard to innovation, large-scale problems and competitiveness	**Medium**: varying results, several positive examples, restricted resources	**Low**: Incentive problems through fiscal system, small scale and high administrative costs, intransparent structures let the system depend strongly on personal relationships	**Medium**: innovative approaches of individual LDIs, but insufficient cooperation and duplication of services, deficient integration of local initiatives
Typical for country?	**Yes**	**Partly**	**Yes**	**Yes**
Theoretical expectation met?	**Partly**: effects of fiscal imbalance visible	**Yes**	**Yes**	**Partly**

The behaviour of subnational and national agencies in charge of implementing regional development policy meets our theoretical expectations; the theory-testing purpose of our case studies is thus fulfilled. While selective resource allocation leads to effective development, lower discretion and increasing dependence on national funding typically tends to hamper policy performance. This is clearly visible in Ireland and subregional Austria. It can also be shown, although to a lesser extent, for the Austrian and Swiss regional level. Moreover, both centralised countries show evidence of administrative inefficiency. The most important aspect for efficient subnational variation appears to be fiscal balance. The Austrian example shows that policy discretion may produce some innovation, but the extent to which these policies meet local needs depends strongly on their autonomy from federal co-financing. The Swiss NRP seems to rest upon this insight. We can further conclude that regional coordination is an issue in all countries. It was dealt with most efficiently in Denmark by redrawing regional boundaries. However, a counter-example is the ineffective institutional layer established in Ireland. Hence, both unitary countries in principle have an institutional flexibility at their disposition that is typically inexistent in federal countries. But this does not necessarily mean that unitary countries make efficient use of it. Apparently needs for regional coordination do not fully outweigh decentralisation gains in regional development policy. Nevertheless, in policy areas with higher coordination needs, this might be different. In these policy areas, the greater flexibility of regional boundaries in unitary and decentralised countries might provide an additional advantage compared to their federal–decentralised counterparts. Federalism might thus have an additional effect on the efficiency of decentralised allocation. The analysis of the area of transport policy in the next section will provide indications.

7.4 Implementation in the area of transport policy

Our second policy area under study, transport policy, has a different purpose in the context of our research design. It was chosen because of the lack of robust quantitative findings for both federalism and decentralisation. Within our research design, it thus represents a theory-modifying case (see Chapter Five). The following section hence aims to seek explanations for the null effect and to either falsify our expected causal mechanisms or to find additional ones that convince us to modify our theoretical argument. We start with the causal mechanisms as expressed in Chapter 5.2 and the analysis follows the criteria established in Section 7.3 on regional development policy. Again, we contrast our decentralised countries with the centralised ones in our sample. We focus on public transport strategies in capital regions, which, with the exception of Switzerland, are the main economic centre of each country, resulting in large numbers of commuters from nearby areas. In Switzerland, due to its multi-centredness and high variation between regions, we analyse the policies of several large agglomerations. As a particular Irish problem and a contrasting example, rural transport is included as well.

7.4.1 Switzerland. Implementing urban transport strategies

In Switzerland, federal authorities, especially the UVEK, BAV and the Federal Roads Office (*Bundesamt für Strassen*, ASTRA), are highly involved in implementing transport policies. In 2006, the federal government spent 14 per cent of its total outlay on public transport and private road traffic (Schweizerischer Bundesrat 2007b: 58–9).[241] Cantonal involvement in transport policies varies widely, as to both the number of public personnel (Bochsler *et al.* 2004: 124–5) and the financial commitment measured by spending on transport as a proportion of total cantonal outlay. This is especially high in peripheral cantons like Uri, Graubünden, and Jura (Bochsler *et al.* 2004: 143–4). Table 7.16 compares transport outlay at each level of government.

Table 7.16: Transport outlay by state level in million SFR, 2005

	Outlays for transport 2005	Share of total
Central government	7,334	43.09
State government	6,402	37.61
Local government	3,284	19.29
Total	17,020	100.00

Source: International Monetary Fund 2008.

Federal authorities have overall responsibility for the national road network, but before the NFA the cantons were responsible for road construction. As a consequence, national road traffic as a policy area was well integrated into the system of intergovernmental financial equalisation. Federal payments were to a large extent channelled as matching grants and allocated according to the financial capacity and political will of the cantons concerned. As this system was perceived to be highly inefficient, the NFA recentralised responsibility for national road construction. Cantonal and communal roads were and still are part of cantons' residual powers. Within the area of public transport provision,[242] both federal and cantonal authorities are engaged in policy implementation and, besides monitoring and steering tasks, they greatly subsidise the SBB or other private transport companies that deliver services on the basis of performance agreements. Provision for long-distance rail traffic is thereby solely subsidised by

---

241. 72 per cent of it were subsidies paid to either cantons or transport companies.

242. Public transport provision has witnessed a number of reforms since the 1990s: most importantly the revision of the Railway Act in 1996 that introduced the commissioner's principle in regional traffic and established legal equality for all transport companies; the *Bahnreform 1* in 1999 that increased cantonal financial responsibility for regional traffic and mainly entails changes to freight transport and the SBB's role; and the *Bahnreform 2*, currently under negotiation, which is supposed to further improve the status of private transport companies as well as increase rail traffic security. The current subsection captures the status quo in 2008 but refers to earlier arrangements where appropriate. For further details see Sager (2006), and LITRA (2000).

the federation, provision for regional traffic by both the federation and the cantons, while local rail is completely ineligible for federal compensation payments.[243]

The following section turns to the analysis of urban transport strategies and focuses on public transport provision in Swiss agglomerations (on the process of urbanisation and its challenges see Kübler and Scheuss 2005; Schwab and Kübler 2001). Given the allocation of implementation competencies described, as well as non-overlapping territorial boundaries of agglomerations and political entities, the effective development of urban transport strategies is to a large extent dependent upon vertical as well as horizontal cooperation. Moreover, sectoral coordination is paramount, as planning policies are highly decentralised. Urban transport thus poses a huge challenge for many agglomerations, and the federal government has recently sought to help by providing extensive financial support for integrated projects of agglomeration transport (Eidgenössisches Volkswirtschaftsdepartement 2006; Schenkel 2001; LITRA 2001; Eidgenössisches Departement für Umwelt Verkehr Energie und Kommunikation 2005). We will therefore analyse patterns of agglomeration transport before and after the new policy's launch in 2001. With our theoretical expectations in mind, we will, firstly, address whether and why urban transport strategies vary between agglomerations, and, secondly, assess to what extent variation enables gains in efficiency as predicted by the decentralisation theorem.

Comparative studies (Kübler 2004) as well as expert interviews conducted during our research (interviews Kübler, Schenkel, Maibach, Sager) clearly show that the planning and management of public transport differs widely between agglomerations, even though responsibilities were regionalised in most agglomerations during the late 1980s and early 1990s (Kübler 2004: 10–1). Table 7.17 illustrates, for the cases of Zurich, Lugano, Lucerne, and Lausanne, how the actors involved, the regulatory framework, and rules for deficit coverage vary significantly.

According to Kübler, the variety of governance structures is mainly caused by the territorial structure of agglomerations, the degree of political conflict over agglomeration policies, and the (historical) ownership structure of transport companies (interview Kübler). Swiss agglomerations vary, moreover, in the extent to which planning processes reflect coordination in public transport and land-use policies (Sager and Kaufmann 2006: 362; Sager et al. 1999). The differences mainly accrue from the organisational structures of the coordinating commissions.[244]

Even though the planning processes vary in ways that partly reflect subnational

---

243. *Eisenbahngesetz vom 20. Dezember 1957* (Bundesversammlung der Schweizerischen Eidgenossenschaft 1957) as well as *Verordnung über Abgeltungen, Darlehen und Finanzhilfen nach Eisenbahngesetz vom 18. Dezember 1995* (Schweizerischer Bundesrat 1995).

244. Ad hoc and centralised commissions seem to foster policy coordination more effectively than permanent commissions that mainly try to achieve intersectoral coordination. The former prevent a duplication of services, enhance a separation of negotiations from the political sphere, and prove to be more open, thereby enhancing action-oriented attitudes. Other reasons detected were the geographic context, ecological values, and the professional culture (Sager and Kaufmann 2006: 366–7).

Table 7.17: Planning and management of urban transport in Swiss agglomerations

	Zurich	Lausanne	Lucerne	Lugano
Regional bodies responsible for definition and implementation of service offers	Public Enterprise *Zürcher Verkehrsverbund*	Joint-stock company *Transports publics de la région lausannoise SA*, owned by the canton, the communes, and private shareholders	Purpose-oriented body *Zweckverband Öffentlicher Verkehr in Luzern*	Regional commission on behalf of the canton *Commissione regionale dei trasporti del luganese*
Political actors involved	Canton and all communes, main power lies with the canton	Canton and 38 communes, main power lies with the inter-communal commission	Body set up by 15 communes and the canton	87 communes
Regulatory framework	Cantonal legislation on public transport	Own statutes based on federal legislation on joint stock companies	Own statutes based on cantonal legislation on public transport and intercommunal cooperation	Cantonal legislation on public transport
Deficit coverage	Canton 50%, Communes 50%	Canton 36%, Communes 64%	Canton 20%, Communes 80%	Canton 50%, Member communes 50%
Effects as measured by service satisfaction (comparative assessment)	Relatively high	Relatively high	Medium	Relatively low

Source: Kübler 2004, modified by authors.

peculiarities and thereby also take public preferences into account (interview Maibach), it seems unwise to impute efficiency gains solely to this variety. Firstly, Kübler's study shows that differences in governance structures cause variation in service satisfaction (Kübler 2004). Public preferences thus seem to be reflected to differing extents. This interpretation was, secondly, supported by the experts interviewed who attributed considerable differences in efficiency to the varying structures of agglomeration transport (interviews Schenkel, Kübler, Maibach). In general, the strong and policy-area-specific needs for horizontal and vertical coordination seem to have been tackled ineffectively by a number of agglomerations. Efficiency losses, *inter alia* those emanating from economies of scale, are a likely result, accompanied by implementation deficits deriving from limited resources.

These inefficiencies were widely noticed by external experts (LITRA 2001) as well as policy makers, and over time the insight grew that 'there does not exist such magic as spontaneous horizontal coordination' (interview Sager).[245] The most visible effect of this recognition is the federal government's agglomeration policy[246] which supported 31 pilot projects in the period 2002–6 and 22 projects on sustainable spatial development in 2007–8. Moreover, 26 agglomeration programmes specifically devoted to transport and development are federally subsidised by up to 350 million SFR and partially financed on the basis of a newly established infrastructure fund.[247] Besides a generally positive internal evaluation of both the pilot projects (Eidgenössisches Volkswirtschaftsdepartement 2006: 17–8) and the agglomeration policy's first-generation projects (CEAT *et al*. 2010), the experts interviewed tentatively expect that the agglomeration policy will bring positive outcomes. Firstly, it will clearly lead to an improvement in output. Projects that have been long planned but not implemented due to financial constraints will be realised (interview Kübler). Secondly, it may foster a more progressive and proactive attitude in some cantons (e.g. Vaud), which will enhance intercommunal cooperation. The variation in governance structures, however, is expected to remain largely unchanged (interview Kübler). Thirdly, the programmatic

---

245. 'Was man gemerkt hat, diesen Zauber von der spontanen horizontalen Kooperation, den gibt es einfach nicht', translation by authors.

246. Even before their explicit agglomeration policy, federal authorities tried to circumvent their exclusion from urban transport policies and influence them, either on the grounds of federal responsibility for long-distance rail infrastructure (e.g. in case of the Tessin, interview Kübler) or by even more tenuous justifications for federal finance as in case of the Metro Line 1 in Lausanne that links the city centre to the federal technical university and was subsidised on these grounds (interview Kübler). However, such incidences had no systematic effect on agglomeration policies and the general view was that there further federal engagement was needed.

247. For information on the infrastructure fund which came into effect on 1.1.2008 see http://www.parlament.ch/D/dokumentation/do-archiv/Seiten/do-dopoavanti.aspx? as well as the relevant law *Bundesgesetz über den Infrastrukturfonds für den Agglomerationsverkehr, das Nationalstraßennetz sowie Hauptstraßen in Berggebieten und Randregionen* (Bundesversammlung der Schweizerischen Eidgenossenschaft 2006a). For updated information on the federal agglomeration policy, see www.agglomeration.ch.

approach may increase rationality within planning processes by structuring highly emotional and politicised transport negotiations (interview Maibach). However, the potential efficiency of the programme's implementation has been questioned. It remains to be seen whether ARE, which is responsible for the allocation of scarce resources,[248] is able to base its decisions on efficiency considerations or is significantly constrained by political lobbying (interviews Kübler, Maibach). Moreover, the agglomeration fund may only be used for financing transport infrastructure and not for follow-up costs like compensation payments to transport companies. The programme thus entails a new financial challenge for the regions (interview Maibach).

In sum, urban governance structures and transport strategies in Switzerland clearly exhibit wide variation, partly reflecting specific characteristics of the agglomerations, including political preferences. At all events the overall efficiency of strongly decentralised implementation of transport policies seems doubtful in the case of Switzerland. Many agglomerations have proven unable to effectively deal with the extensive need for vertical, horizontal, and sectoral cooperation and to provide the financial resources necessary. In this respect, the federal government's agglomeration policy might constitute a step in the right direction. Its long-term results, however, remain to be seen, particularly the potentially negative effects of high subsidies.

7.4.2 Denmark. Implementing public transport in the Copenhagen region

In Denmark, national transport policy is implemented by agencies under the control of the Ministry of Transport, such as the Road Authority and Danish National Railways (DSB). The 2007 reform split responsibility for the former county roads between the state and the municipalities, which now take care of 94 per cent (69,339 kms) of the Danish road network (Statistics Danmark). Special projects like the fixed links across Øresund and Great Belt are operated by private, state-owned companies and financed by tolls. Rail transport is provided by the state-owned DSB. Traditionally, public transport was organised at county level. The 2007 Local Government Reform concentrated public transport responsibilities at the regional level. The five regions are now responsible for public transport except for long-distance and interregional trains. In practice, all regions have outsourced public transport organisation to agencies.[249] The latter regularly put individual bus routes out to tender to private companies.[250] The system of regional planning with several competing operators is typical of Scandinavia as a whole (Costa 1996). In the following, we concentrate on public transport in the Copenhagen region.

---

248. The programmes submitted so far would need more than double the funding currently available. See http://www.are.admin.ch/dokumentation/00121/00224/index.html?lang=de&msg-id=17243.

249. These agencies are *Nordjyllands Trafikselskab* (North Jutland), *Midttrafik* (Central Jutland), *Sydtrafik* and *Fynbus* (Southern Denmark), and MOVIA for Zealand and the Capital region.

250. The largest private bus and train operator is ARRIVA with a market share of more than 50 per cent (www.arriva.dk). An exception is *Fynbus* which operates all buses on the island of Funen.

The city of Copenhagen has proven to be an area too small for effective coordination. Until 2007 the capital region was divided into fifty municipalities and five counties, meaning regional coordination was always a topic on the national agenda. In 1978, a new law required the Danish counties to strive for coordinated public transport. Most regions established a competitive model with counties setting the framework (route planning, fare system) while routes were operated by private companies (Rallis *et al.* 1984). The Copenhagen area deviated from this pattern. In 1974, the Greater Copenhagen Council (*Hovedstadsråd*) was established (Andersen and Jørgensen 1995); its main task was the coordination of regional transport, which was executed through the Greater Copenhagen Council transportation company (*Hovedstadsområdets Trafikselskab*, HT). The HT, contrary to transport companies in the rest of Denmark, took over all (public and private) bus operators in the region. Until the 1990s, transport in Copenhagen was characterised by more centralisation and less competition than in the rest of the country along with less efficient operation, as indicated by higher unit costs than in the rest of Denmark (Andersen 1992). This can be explained by higher wages and the operating conditions (Andersen 1992). The institutional arrangement of the HT, demanding unanimity of the thirty-seven participating municipalities in decision making, led to significant coordination deficits. Despite this institutional weakness, HT is considered 'a great success' (Andersen *et al.* 2002: 49) in coordinating numerous public and private bus operators. In 1988/89, the national government made another attempt to increase the efficiency of the capital's public transport, passing several bills which aimed to foster the system's market orientation. The Greater Copenhagen Council was abolished, but HT with most of its tasks persisted. The new organisational form envisaged a privatisation of 45 per cent of the bus transport by 1994, 'with the clear aims of making public transport more efficient' (Andersen 1992: 188).

In 2000, HT tasks were transferred to its successor agency HUR Trafik,[251] covering most of the capital region. During the 1990s, contracting out became more common in Copenhagen, emulating structures which had existed in the rest of Denmark for fifteen years. Rural Denmark had experienced a first round of privatisation at the end of the 1970s, when bus operation was outsourced to private companies, while the founding of HT signified a stronger public involvement in operational issues. This difference was reversed when, in 1989, the capital region was the first to introduce competitive tendering on bus routes. Following the 2007 territorial reform, HUR Trafik and the former county traffic agencies of West Zealand and Storstrøm counties formed MOVIA to cover all public transport east of the Great Belt, excluding Bornholm. At present, twenty-two companies are operating buses under the name of MOVIA. MOVIA is a milestone in the consolidation process in Copenhagen transport, but it still lacks e.g. a common fare system (www.movia.dk).

---

251. HUR Trafik is the traffic division of the Capital Development Council, covering Copenhagen, Roskilde, and Frederiksborg counties and the independent cities of Copenhagen and Frederiksberg.

A special case is the Copenhagen Metro system. In 1992, the national government and the Copenhagen municipality resolved upon the construction of the new Ørestad quarter connected to the city by a new public transport link (see Chapter 6.4.3.3). Construction of the link was the job of the Ørestad Development Corporation, which has considerable freedom of action:

> The Act on Ørestad defines the room for manoeuvre, including the limitations, but this mainly referred to institutional aspects. There was relative freedom as regards the planning goals for the area (Majoor and Jørgensen 2007: 191).

Tracks, location of stations and construction mode (underground, at-grade, elevated) were fixed by law in 1992 (Flyvbjerg 2007). Other decisions, like the type of train to be used, were left to the Development Corporation. The corporation made several questionable decisions. In 1994, the Ørestad Development Corporation decided which system was to be built: tram, light rail, or metro.[252] Its reason for choosing metro was not made public for three years. Even at the time, experts doubted this solution was the best (Hansen and Jamison 2004). With two bids for the construction of the metro system, the corporation chose the cheaper but less experienced company.[253] In 2005, with 95 per cent of the project completed, the cost overrun was 157 per cent of the original figures presented to parliament in 1991/92. While some of the fatal mistakes were caused by the actors at the decision-making stage,[254] the Corporation's management had taken several decisions that increased costs, for which it was blamed by the Danish Audit Office (Flyvbjerg 2007). The project has been criticised for its lack of transparency (Hansen and Jamison 2004). Furthermore, ministerial supervision and public accountability were poor (interview Flyvbjerg), which is to some degree attributable to the organisational form of the project as a state-owned private company, similar to other large infrastructure projects in contemporary Denmark.[255] This organisational form is empirically correlated with higher cost overruns on average (Flyvbjerg *et al.* 2004). In the Copenhagen case, cost overruns were accompanied by passenger shortfalls of around 40 per cent (Flyvbjerg

---

252. Differences between the three systems are mainly the passenger capacities and the degree to which the system is separated from other traffic. Trams are not separated at all, a metro is completely separated and light rail is somewhere in between.

253. The decision was taken despite a report predicting long delays and cost overruns caused by the company. In fact, many technical problems occurred during the construction of the metro (Hansen and Jamison 2004).

254. E.g. the financing mode or the tracking – the metro is sometimes called a 'stage coach across the prairie' (Knut Vilby, cited in Hansen and Jamison 2004) because it is situated at the boundaries of the populated area.

255. In particular the Fixed Links across the Great Belt and Øresund face the same problems as Ørestad and the Copenhagen metro: 'The [Great Belt] rail-link went bankrupt even before it opened. The Øresund link is in trouble […] the Copenhagen metro has already gone bankrupt and has been financially restructured. So the performance is very poor except for one of these projects, which is the Great Belt road-link' (interview Flyvbjerg).

2007).[256] The result is a prolonged payback period of probably seventy-six years instead of the fourteen years originally calculated.

In general, the operation of public transport works well in Denmark. The main problem for a long time was regional cooperation, largely because of the small-scale administrative structure of the capital region. The several mergers that finally led to the present single traffic company were strongly pushed by central government. As in the Swiss case, we see that horizontal cooperation often depends on incentives from high governmental levels. While public transport is not the legal responsibility of central government, and receives no financial aid from the Danish state, it is strongly influenced by its legislative framework. While central government does not interfere in operational issues, the regions' role is largely an administrative one. Moreover, the case of the Copenhagen metro shows direct interference by central government representatives in strategic as well as operational decisions.

7.4.3 Austria. Implementing public transport in the Verkehrsverbund Ostregion

Transport infrastructure in Austria is planned, constructed and maintained by the federally owned private enterprises ASFINAG (*Autobahnen-und Schnellstraßen-Finanzierungs-Aktiengesellschaft*) for roads and SCHIG (*Schieneninfrastrukturdienstleistungsgesellschaft mbH*) and ÖBB for railway tracks. Until 2005, responsibility for the construction of high-speed rail connections lay in the hands of the HL-AG (*Hochleistungsstrecken AG*); it is now incorporated in the ÖBB Holding AG.[257] Supervision of construction activities is done by the *Länder* within Indirect Federal Administration. Responsibility for public transport is divided between governmental levels. The *Bund* provides 'basic' rail services and finance, the *Länder* are responsible for planning and coordination within the regional *Verkehrsverbünde* (public transport associations) and operate regional transport, while the municipalities' transport companies provide local services.

Prior to 1999, public transport in Austria was quite centralised, and regarded as poorly organised, its financing schemes lacking clarity and transparency due to various subsidies and cross-subsidies (Wieser 2002). Federal companies ÖBB (rail), *Bahnbus* (a subdivision of ÖBB for regional bus services) and *Postbus* (a subdivision of the Austrian Postal Service for regional bus transport) dominated regional transport. Only local services were operated by municipalities. This resulted in a lack of flexibility in the peripheries and inefficient duplication of services like parallel routings of regional trains and *Postbus* lines (Lindenbaum

---

256. Flyvbjerg compares the Copenhagen metro with other cases and concludes that the Danish project performs 21 per cent poorer than the benchmark regarding cost escalations, but 6 to 11 per cent better than the benchmark in demand shortfalls (due to the fact that 91 per cent of the analysed projects showed demand shortfalls).

257. The ÖBB, the now privatised but federally owned rail company, was reorganised in 2005 so that infrastructure and operation are separate entities under the same umbrella.

2003). A new 1999 law (*Öffentlicher Personennah- und Regionalverkehrsgesetz, ÖPNRV-G, Österreichischer Nationalrat* 1999) rearranged the organisation and funding of public transport. After a first failed attempt, the *Postbus* and *Bahnbus* branches were merged into the *ÖBB-Postbus AG* in 2003.

The intention of the ÖPNRV-G was to decentralise regional transport and reduce the federal role to a purely subsidising one. However, the actual reform was of a rather incremental character. The federal government agreed to provide the basic underpinning of regional rail transport.[258] Additional rail connections as well as regional buses have to be ordered and paid for by the *Länder* and half of the *Länder*'s expenses are reimbursed by the federal government (*Bestellerförderung*). Additionally, the federal government compensates local operators for losses due to the common fare system (*Verbundtarifierung*, 59 million euros in 2005). The same holds for reduced fares for students, which amount to 360 million euros (up to 80 per cent of the associations' turnover) (Lindenbaum 2003). From the fiscal equalisation system, the *Länder* receive another 108 million euros (2005) for public transport, which they use to buy additional services from the ÖBB and pay the fee for using the federally owned rail-track infrastructure (*Infrastrukturbenützungsentgelt*, IBE; www.bmvit.gv.at).[259] Ultimately, the reform was not far-reaching in terms of redistributing competencies and fiscal responsibilities. Fiscal relations are still complex and highly interdependent, which is typical for the Austrian case. The federal level continues to pay the lion's share of regional transport costs, either through subsidies to the *Länder* and transport associations, or directly.

Apart from the complex financing system, cooperation is an issue in Austria as well. On the regional level, coordination is quite effective: Austrian territory is entirely covered by regional transport associations, the *Verkehrsverbünde*, which coordinate schedules, connections, and common fare systems. However, most of the associations cover only one *Bundesland*. A more difficult situation is to be found within the Eastern Region Transport Association (*Verkehrsverbund Ostregion*, VOR), which began operations in 1984. It was the first transport association in Austria and is still the only one covering more than one *Land* (namely Vienna, Burgenland and parts of Lower Austria). Today, the VOR includes the municipal transport companies as well as regional authorities and coordinates the municipal transport companies (the most important one is the *Wiener Linien* of Vienna), regional buses (provided by *Postbus*, the Lower Austrian *Wieselbusse*, and private bus companies like *Dr. Richard* and *Blaguss*), and the regional and local trains operated by the ÖBB and several private suppliers. Its creation and development, however, were characterised by conflicts between the participating governments and companies. From the founding of a joint transport planning venture (*Verkehrsverbundorganisationsgesellschaft*, VVO) for the capital region in 1974, it was ten years before operations started, mainly because of conflicts over

---

258. Which is defined as the level of provision as of 1999.

259. Confusingly, this federally owned infrastructure is used by federally owned trains, but as these trains run on behalf of the *Länder*, the latter have to pay the IBE.

finance and distrust between the Social Democratic governments of Burgenland and Vienna and the Conservatives of Lower Austria (Lindenbaum 2003). In 1988, the remaining areas of Lower Austria and Burgenland were brought into a cooperative (*Verkehrsverbund Niederösterreich-Burgenland*, VVNB).[260] With the ÖPNRV-G, the federal level left the transport associations to the *Länder*.[261] Simultaneously, VVNB was administratively integrated into VOR. A common tariff system is planned, but probably will not be implemented until 2013, due mainly to the Viennese authorities who are reluctant to move to further integration of VVNB into VOR structures before a complete analysis of the financial consequences (Kontrollamt Wien 2002). Thus, implementation is delayed by the complex financial situation. For the moment, VOR and VVNB continue to exist side by side and with different fare systems; VVNB is further subdivided into five semi-autonomous regions. The difficulties in establishing a cooperative arrangement between VOR and VVNB reflects the general situation in Austria. Almost everywhere, cooperation between transport associations is difficult. There is still no clear agreement on cross-border bus connections, and there are numerous examples of inefficient parallel routings. Within the VOR, too, conflicts rage. The *Wiener Linien* constantly calls for additional federal contributions to metro and suburban train investments (Goldmann 2005).

In sum, the 1999 reform produced a slight tendency towards planning decentralisation. The federal level withdrew from transport associations and left planning to the regional level. On the other hand, a federal intention to pull back to a purely subsidising role failed. A new public transport law was protracted by the *Länder* because they feared additional financial responsibilities – demonstrating their strong position in fiscal negotiations. This strength can be attributed at least partly to the softness of budget constraints (see Section 7.2.3). While cost efficiency is thus quite low, the quality of services is good, with the exception of federally provided regional rail services where cost pressure has caused deterioration in recent years (Hermann 2006). Moreover, passenger numbers have decreased despite increased resource use (Goldmann 2005). Like other policy areas, public transport is characterised by complex fiscal interrelations. This led to conflicts and delays during the establishment of the VOR. Cooperation can only be achieved by financial incentives provided by the federal level, which reimburses all costs the municipal and regional companies incur from lower income from ticket sales and seasonal tickets. Without federal transfers, regional cooperation would still not exist. It seems that while regional cooperation is aspired to by the federal government, local actors need fiscal incentives to achieve it.

---

260. Throughout the first half of the 1990s all Austrian *Länder* built up similar transport networks. VVV (Vorarlberg) was founded in 1991, VVSt (Styria) in 1994, OÖVV (Upper Austria), VVT (Tyrol), and SVV (Salzburg) in 1995.

261. Until 2002, the *Bund* owned 50 per cent of VORG (Verkehrsverbund Ostregion Gesellschaft mbH), Vienna 30, Lower Austria 15, and Burgenland 5 per cent. Now, Vienna and Lower Austria own 44, and Burgenland 12 per cent.

7.4.4   Ireland. Implementing Transport 21 and the RTI/RTP

Transport infrastructure in Ireland is traditionally provided by the public sector. The main responsibility for transport is therefore vested in the Department of Transport and the DoEHLG that funds and monitors local authorities' maintenance of non-national roads. The Department of Transport is responsible for the national roads programme, public transport provision, and the aviation sector, as well as ports and shipping. It has delegated part of its responsibility for implementation to a range of state-sponsored bodies for which it retains overall responsibility, namely the NRA, the RPA, the Dublin Transportation Office (DTO), and the state-owned company CIÉ.[262] Local authorities are responsible for non-national roads (Bannon and Russell 2001) and so they 'do prioritise, or put in place a sequence of road developments, road improvements or road maintenance' (interview Quinn). C/C, however, barely coordinate their maintenance schemes and spillovers across local authority boundaries are badly handled (Morgenroth 2000). Local authorities additionally play a major role as contractors for national road projects monitored by the NRA. However, nearly all of the grants are ring-fenced so that 'subnational discretion is extremely limited' (interview Callanan).

Any study of transport provision has to take into account its interface with planning policies. In Ireland, a major role in the planning process is played by the Irish Planning and Appeals Board *An Bord Pleanála*[263] as well as by local authorities (Bannon and Russell 2001: 75). While the latter are formally recognised as planning authorities, the former, under the Planning and Development Act 2000 (Oireachtas 2000), is responsible for determining planning appeals, referrals, compulsory purchase orders, and major infrastructure projects (including motorways, subways and protected road schemes). As such, its decisions have major impact on the implementation of infrastructure projects. This disconnect between central-level decision making in transport policies and strongly decentralised planning threatens the implementation of major infrastructural projects as the latter lacks 'the benefit of effective regional coordination' (Fitz Gerald 2002: 202). Moreover it restricts public involvement in planning applications to an advanced stage in the policy-making process (Rau and McDonagh 2007). The following case studies evaluate the implementation processes of Transport 21 and the Rural Transport Initiative/ Rural Transport Programme (RTI/RTP).

Transport 21 is a national transport infrastructure programme, with its main focus on the Greater Dublin Area. It covers investments in rail, roads, and airports as well as in trains and buses and the development of a common fare system. Since 2006, the overall responsibility for implementing Transport 21 has rested with the interdepartmental Transport 21 Monitoring Group. Its meetings are attended by the Chief Executives of those state agencies that implement the projects in

---

262. See earlier chapters for detailed information on these agencies.

263. *An Bord Pleanála* is an independent administrative body which was established in 1977 under the Local Government (Planning and Development) Act 1976. For further information see http://www.pleanala.ie

Transport 21, namely the NRA, the Irish bus company *Bus Éireann*, the Dublin bus company *Bus Átha Cliath*, Irish Railways *Iarnród Éireann*, and the RPA. These state agencies are major players in the implementation of Transport 21: they 'actually control the whole game' (interview McDonagh). In addition, with the increase in PPP projects private operators (like *Veolia Transport Ireland* in case of the light rail transit LUAS) have gained importance (Killen 2007).

The implementation of Transport 21 has been subject to criticism with regard to implementation deficits, limited regional coordination of projects, and poor accountability of agencies and departments to the public. Implementation deficits are to a great extent caused by systematic factors. Firstly, the recent downturn of the Irish economy (Barrett *et al.* 2008) has led to a cutback in infrastructure expenditure. Secondly, the deficient *ex ante* cost–benefit analysis as well as systematic underestimation of project costs contributed to significant cost overruns (Barrett 2006). Thirdly, a number of planning appeals have been made to *An Bord Pleanála*,[264] thus further decelerating implementation processes. As a consequence, project accomplishments have been systematically retarded.[265] More criticism relates to inadequate coordination of planning and transport implementation at the regional level (interview Rau). The fact that Irish cities (except Dublin) lack a Regional Transportation Office poses considerable challenges for a spatially integrated transport development. Last but not least, the high number of departments and agencies involved leads to limited accountability as it is often difficult to be sure 'who exactly had the final say and who has the responsibility' (interview McDonagh).

The Regional Transport Initiative and Programme (RTI/RTP), launched in 2006, aims to improve community-offered public transport in rural Ireland. Its implementation is managed by Pobal on behalf of the Department of Transport and carried out by 34 community transport groups.[266] Pobal selected the RTI groups in a competitive tender, manages the annual disbursement of funding, provides ongoing technical support, and monitors each group's activities (Fitzpatrick Associates 2006). It thus 'functions as intermediary between the Department of Transport and individual community groups and organisations' (Rau and Hennessy 2009: 371). RTI/RTP has effectively provided services to a target group previously completely marginalised in terms of transport accessibility. Approximately 6–9 per cent of the total rural population with unmet needs are users of the RTI (Fitzpatrick Associates 2006: 55). According to McDonagh, the RTP is 'a really good programme, [including] really excellent groups working on it that have such commitment' (interview McDonagh). Nonetheless, certain features deserve critical attention. First and foremost, the RTP places a 'considerable burden of management, administration and governance on RTI groups' (Fitzpatrick Associates 2006: 63).

264. A list of all planning appeals can be accessed under http://www.pleanala.ie/lists/.

265. E.g. a bridge over the river Corrib (Galway City) and the Western Rail Corridor (interviews McDonagh, Rau).

266. See http://www.pobal.ie/RTP for a list of the groups funded under the RTP.

Administrative costs make up 36 per cent of total expenditure. Although they should be susceptible to economies of scale, in the case of the RTP groups they have not been reduced by horizontal cooperation. The programme implementation thus features considerable inefficiencies (Fitzpatrick Associates 2006) that are fuelled by a wide variety of income levels and experience among the RTI groups.[267] Other criticisms relate to the extent as well as the type of funding provided. While the resources are only sufficient to reach a small and highly sector-specific proportion of rural dwellers with unmet transport needs, the fiscal imbalance embedded in the funding scheme has 'partly re-shaped the work of some CVS [Community and Voluntary Sector] groups by softening more critical approaches to rural transport and community development' (Rau and Hennessy 2009: 372). The RTI groups' capacity to engage in strategic planning is thus limited. The process of implementing Transport 21 is slightly different. Given the high level of investment and the strong position of government agencies, inefficiencies tend to arise from limited accountability, rent-seeking, and poor economic analysis. Moreover, the disconnect of decentralised planning and centralised transport policies contributes to implementation deficits.

7.4.5 Patterns of implementation in transport policy

Our findings in the area of transport policy suggest that efficiency gains from decentralisation directly depend on adequate coordination at the regional level. This finding supports predictions made at the outset of the qualitative part of this study and strengthens our findings regarding the area of regional development policy: coordination issues strongly influence the overall effect of decentralisation.

The countries in our sample chose different means of ensuring this cooperation. Danish central government regularly intervenes with detailed law-making, requiring a traffic company for each region and a common one for the capital region and Zealand. This means that policy discretion is reduced and the role of the regions is largely an administrative one. However, central government is not involved in the financing of regional and local public transport. In contrast, deficits in regional coordination were (in part successfully) tackled in Switzerland and Austria by federal subsidies. Swiss agglomerations show considerable variation in the provision of public transport, but this can hardly be considered as efficient. In fact, customer satisfaction varies greatly, and transport policies display deficiencies in several agglomerations due to lack of economies of scale and low investments. The federal government therefore introduced subsidies for transport infrastructure investments in an effort to foster regional cooperation. A similar approach was taken by the Austrian federal government, with the difference that pre-reform the division of labour had been overly centralised. Thus, coordination at regional level was encouraged by generous federal compensation. However,

---

267. The total income for individual RTI groups ranges from €70,000 up to €600,000, while only ten groups have a total income that is either above or near the average of €200,000 (Fitzpatrick Associates 2006: 61).

Table 7.18: Patterns of implementation in transport policy

	Switzerland	Denmark	Austria	Ireland
Policy approach	Regional and urban transport	Public transport in the capital region	Public transport in the VOR	(1) Transport 21 (2) RTI and RTP
Actors (regional actors in bold)	Cantons, communes, regional bodies	Since 2007: **Capital (Hovedstaden) and Zealand (Sjaelland) regions**, MOVIA transport company (Before 2007: three transport agencies, **two cities, five counties**)	BMVIT, ÖBB, ***Länder* governments of Vienna, Lower Austria, and Burgenland, municipal transport companies**	(1) Transport 21 Monitoring Group, NRA, RPA, CIÉ, DTO, private operators, **counties and cities as contractors** (2) Pobal, **34 community transport groups**
Financial and personnel resources	**Variance** between agglomerations	**Adequate**	**High**	(1) **High** but constrained by cost overruns (2) **Low**
Vertical fiscal imbalance	**Medium**	**High**: Regions financed by local and central government grants; transport companies financed by local and regional authorities	**High**: Complex system of transfers, reimbursements and federal provision of services	**High**
Policy discretion	**High**	**Medium**: Many implementing issues left to regions, but relatively detailed legal framework	**Medium**: Transport planning Länder task since 1999	(1) **High** for agencies, **low** for counties and cities (2) **Medium**
Degree of subnational variance	**High**	**Low**: Similar organisations countrywide	**Medium**: Mostly through geographic conditions	(1) **Low** (2) **High**

Contd

	Switzerland	Denmark	Austria	Ireland
Horizontal cooperation	**Medium:** incentives set by agglomeration policy	Since 2007: **High** due to detailed law making requiring cooperation (Before 2007: **Medium to low**: Conflictive relations between counties and municipalities)	**Low** between regions, **high** within regions	(1) **Low** due to top-down approach (2) **Low** due to limited resources
Efficiency of implementation	**Medium**: Variance in output partly reflects limited resources and cumbersome coordination	**Medium to high**: Cost refunds per passenger higher in Copenhagen than in rest of Denmark for political and economic reasons	**Medium to low**: Several examples of partial inefficiency, coordination slow and conflictual; overall quality of services good, but expensive	(1) **Low**: High implementation deficits, serious cost and time overruns (2) **Medium**: High commitment but underfunded, unutilized economies of scale with regard to administrative costs
Typical for country?	Yes	**Partly**: Coordination particularly difficult in capital area for political reasons	**Yes**	**Yes**
Theoretical expectation met?	**Partly**: Limited efficiency gains through decentralisation, high coordination needs	**Partly**: regional coordination necessary	**Partly**: policy area as seen by federal level as overly centralised, but regionalisation failed	(1) **Yes** (2) **Partly**: programme implementation is selective but severely underfunded

complex fiscal interrelations and high fiscal imbalance left the regional level uncommitted to inter-regional cooperation. Ireland is a special case since it lacks a powerful regional governmental tier and the national government refrains from any effective approach to change this situation. Accordingly, the RTI/RTP suffer from their insulated approach and stick to small-scale developments. At the same time, the nationally administered Transport 21 programme is quite distant from local needs and yields only limited regional coordination. To sum up, in implementing public transport, both centralised and decentralised countries show strong evidence of externalities that generate a high need for regional coordination, which apparently outweigh efficiency gains from decentralised organisation. In the federal countries, this cooperation could only be induced by federal co-funding which limits subnational policy discretion, as does the relatively detailed law making in the Danish case. Our findings regarding transport policy are outlined in Table 7.18.

7.5 Patterns of policy implementation in centralised and decentralised countries

In a final step, we draw conclusions about the general patterns of policy implementation in centralised and decentralised countries as well as area-specific differences. The empirical findings from the qualitative case studies generate important additional insights to our initial quantitative approach. Along the lines of our analysis of decision-making processes, first, we check the empirical relevance of the causal mechanisms by comparing centralised and decentralised countries. Second, we deal with intra-group differences, i.e. additional effects of federalism or unitarism on implementation processes. Third, we compare across policy areas and check inter-sectoral differences, seeking additional mechanisms that allow us to modify our theory.

As regards the first endeavour, our case studies in general corroborate the hypothesised effects of decentralisation upon subnational implementation as well as the preconditions for its impact. Decentralised countries show a higher level of subnational variation; and regional and local units have higher shares of their own revenue, are less dependent on transfers, and have more staff and more discretionary leeway in implementing national policies than their centralised counterparts. It is this encompassing discretion that enables subnational actors to implement regionally or locally adapted strategies. Regional development policies show most clearly how discretion leads to efficient variation in Switzerland and Denmark, while the absence of such leeway brings about allocational inefficiencies in Ireland and subregional Austria. The case of regional development policy in Austria, moreover, shows that high policy discretion does not suffice for efficient variation when fiscal interdependence is strong. Some findings of the Swiss case study point in the same direction. Our study thus emphasises the importance of financial discretion and fiscal balance.

Secondly, a comparison across the centralised countries detects four things. First, an advantage of federal–centralised countries over unitary–centralised ones: in the former, subnational entities may have substantial numbers of staff and reasonable administrative expertise at their disposal to develop innovative approaches which they can use once some policy leeway opens up. Second, we found subnational budget constraints in federal–centralised Austria to be relatively soft. This strengthens the position of regional governments when it comes to fiscal negotiations. Austrian *Länder* have therefore been able to trigger generous federal transfers, as can be seen most clearly in the case of transport. This could be associated with losses in cost efficiency. Third, with regard to regional coordination, unitary countries have much more flexibility in their territorial organisation, which was used efficiently by the Danish state. And fourth, unitary and federal states typically use different means to ensure coordination at the subnational level. While Denmark uses law making, both Switzerland and Austria rely on fiscal incentives for subnational entities.

Comparing, thirdly, the two policy areas, we can conclude that transport policy entails a much higher need for regional coordination than does regional development policy. While coordinated approaches in the latter policy area certainly have a number of advantages, their absence apparently does not cancel out decentralisation's positive effects, as in the case of transport policy. Here, Swiss (and Irish) cases show evidence for inefficiency through local variance, while all countries try to foster a more coordinated approach.

We thus conclude that our theory holds, but has to be modified in some regards. First, fiscal decentralisation is the most important, if not a necessary precondition for efficiency gains. Second, coordination is a highly important issue and its effect may, depending on the policy area, be more significant than the positive impact of decentralisation. Third, there are several relevant aspects in which the federal or unitary character of a country impacts its patterns of policy implementation.

chapter | conclusion
eight |

Do multilevel institutional arrangements matter for policy making and policy performance? In particular, does federalism have a systematic impact on policy outputs? Using a combination of theories of federalism and decentralisation, we have argued that intergovernmental negotiations in federal states may imply high transaction costs and therefore will affect policy performance negatively. Decentralised provision of budgetary and personnel resources together with enough implementation leeway will affect policy performance positively. Our statistical tests of these hypotheses for the OECD countries have shown that there are indeed systematic relationships between the patterns of territorial state organisation and policy performance.[268]

Given that the causal chain between institutional arrangements and macro-economic performance is long and complex, how can we be sure that it is indeed a country's federal or unitary structure of decision making and its decentralised or centralised provision for policy implementation which causes these effects? We have chosen a number of concrete policy projects in the areas of regional development policy and transport policy in order to study in detail the decision-making and policy-implementation stages in four countries representing different combinations of the two dimensions of territorial state organisation. Austria represents federal–centralised, Switzerland federal–decentralised, Denmark unitary–decentralised, and Ireland unitary–centralised political systems. All the projects studied have spatial implications. Essentially, they are about distributing or redistributing money to and within regions. However, regional policy and transport policy differ in one aspect: coordination needs. While these are generally low in regional development policy, they can become extremely high in transport policy. Nevertheless, what all the projects we have studied have in common is that we could observe in detail how national and regional actors interact.

Following the spirit of analytic narratives, we linked our empirical material to institutional logics stemming from our theoretical assumptions: (a) redistributive negotiations between actors on the national and the subnational level at the decision-making stage, focusing on the performance differences between federal and unitary countries, and (b) resource allocation at the implementation stage, contrasting decentralised and centralised systems. We deduced criteria from these logics to test whether the patterns found in the statistical analysis are actually rooted in systematic behavioural differences in policy making. Our qualitative evidence from the case studies on processes of decision making and implementation by and

---

268. Let us note in passing that as we have pursued a decidedly 'conservative' strategy by only report- ing statistical findings when they hold in a majority of differently specified models, we probably underestimate the robustness of our findings.

large corroborates the expected causal mechanisms emerging from our theoretical model and additionally yields insights with regard to policy-area-specific effects.

Given a strong movement for reform, processes of decision making entail higher transaction costs in federal than in unitary countries as subnational entities use their constitutionally guaranteed competences as well as informal political power (vertical party structures in the Austrian case) to push through individual interests. However, deadlock may be circumvented when the constitution remains silent about the exact distribution of competences or when there are incentives set by external actors, such as the European Union in the instance of funding regional policy projects (as can be observed in the case of Austria). Our analysis of transport projects yields two further area-specific findings. Slowing down processes of decision making does not necessarily entail negative effects, as it might prevent costly and economically inefficient decisions from being taken hastily (again, Austria is an illuminating example). Moreover, big and expensive projects in transport policy seem highly prone to pork-barrel politics which serve strong but uncoordinated local interests (as we observed in Ireland and Denmark).

With regard to the second dimension of territorial state organisation, our case studies support the assumption that decentralised allocation of resources contributes to a large variance in policy implementation (as seen in the case studies from Switzerland and Denmark, but also in Austria as regards regional policy), while centralised countries exhibit difficulties in deciding upon varying service delivery (Ireland and public transport in Austria). When subnational units dispose of own revenues and are less dependent on transfers, they can make use of relevant policy discretion. However, this variance does not necessarily entail efficiency gains as any made might be outweighed by strong and policy-area-specific needs for coordination. Regional coordination therefore seems vital in the case of public transport policies (as seen in the Swiss, Irish and Austrian case studies). High coordination needs, therefore, may explain the insignificant effect of decentralisation in this policy area. Coordination is less relevant with regard to regional economic policy. Accordingly, variance is much more visible and positively affects performance (especially in the Swiss case). Without opportunities for policy discretion high inefficiencies may be the consequence (as seen in the Irish case study).

Our case studies also corroborate our arguments about the existence and impact of budget constraints. In decentralised as well as in unitary-centralised countries the subnational level shows higher fiscal discipline. However, there is nothing automatic in the relationship between territorial state organisation and fiscal behaviour. The Swiss and Danish cases exemplify how subnational elections and/or direct democracy may serve as hard budget constraints. Similarly, the Danish case exhibits mechanisms of mutual self-control between subnational units. Conversely, soft budget constraints may not necessarily end up in high subnational debts as the Austrian case brings to light. Here, the anticipation of such an undesirable outcome was strategically used by the subnational level in fiscal negotiations with central government. As the Irish case illustrates the inefficiencies resulting from a lack of policy discretion, generous transfers in

Austria lead to inefficient implementation in transport policy.

Some of our findings, then, qualify the hypotheses derived from theories in political science and public economics with which we started this book. These additional insights can be generalised in the following way:

1. External factors: federalism's problems of intricate negotiations and high transaction costs can be – at least to some degree – offset when external actors or external threats[269] change the cost-benefit calculations of the actors involved. This may move the original prisoner's dilemma constellation to a positive-sum constellation, increasing the benefits from cooperation.

2. Interaction effects: the two dimensions of territorial state organisation do not only impact on policy making independently. They may also lead to interaction effects, to borrow a term from statistical language. One example of this is what might be called an 'anticipation effect'. As political actors do not behave mechanistically but act on the basis of experience from iterated negotiations, they may anticipate that at the policy-implementation stage there will be enough leeway for them to accommodate their preferences. This anticipation may lead to greater willingness to coordinate during the decision-making process and, accordingly, to reduced transaction costs. Another example is that federalism, precisely because it slows down decision-making processes, may function as a monitoring instrument and help improve policy performance, especially with regard to big and expensive projects. The third example has to do with economies of scale: efficiency gains depend on them. As our case studies on Austria and Switzerland illuminate, subnational units may simply be too small for reaping potential efficiency gains from decentralised policy making. Without denying that territorial reorganisation in unitary systems may also be costly, nevertheless they can solve their economies of scale problems by adapting their territorial boundaries, whereas in federal countries this is a highly protracted and in the end often hopeless endeavour.[270]

Hence, there is nothing deterministic in the impact of federalism or decentralisation on policy performance. What can be expected from the patterns we have found can be offset under specific circumstances. Ours is not a straightforward argument against federalism or even for abolishing such arrangements. It only points out that it cannot convincingly be defended on grounds of superior policy performance. Without denying the good arguments in favour of establishing federal structures to increase the participatory and inclusive potential of democratic political systems or to reconcile unity where necessary

269. The role of external threats in negotiations has also been discussed in the literature on consociationalism (Andeweg 2000).

270. See the Berlin–Brandenburg merger proposal by the two state governments, formally presented in 1995 after years of preparation: it ended in disaster after being rejected by a referendum in 1996 (Hauswirth 2003).

with variety where possible, a political-economy perspective on territorial state organisation shows that what really counts in terms of policy performance is the provision of decentralised resources.

Whether what we have found applies only to spatially focused policy areas or holds for policy making in more general terms is something we cannot say with certainty based on our empirical research. However, we are confident that it does. We see two reasons for that. One is that in modern, highly interdependent societies, essentially every policy decision has external effects which lead to pressures to coordinate between territorial units of a state. The other is that decentralised policy making in any institutional setting provides the opportunity to experiment with new policy ideas which, if perceived to be beneficial, can then diffuse to other territorial units. So, even if there is no need for positive coordination between actors from different territorial levels, decentralisation may in the end pay off.

| appendices

Appendix Table 1: Codebook of cross-sectional data

Indicator	n	min	max	description/source
country	30	–	–	character variable, country name
label	30	–	–	abbreviation of country name
federalism				
feddummy	30	0 (e.g. Denmark)	1 (e.g. Australia)	1 = federal; 0 = unitary (Elazar 1987)
fedtype	30	0 (else)	1 (Germany)	1 = Germany; 0 = else (own indicator)
fedlijp	23	−1.77 (New Zealand)	2.53 (Germany)	Lijphart's federalism indicator Source: Lijphart (1999)
fedkeman	18	−1.23 (France)	1.72 (Switzerland)	Keman's federalism indicator Source: Keman (2000)
fedtreis	29	0 (e.g. Denmark)	1 (e.g. Australia)	index of subnational autonomy Source: Treisman (2000)
fedgth	30	1 (e.g. Australia)	5 (e.g. Denmark)	indicator for federalism/ bicameralism Source: Gerring and Thacker (2004)
fedmadx	30	1 (e.g. Denmark)	3 (e.g. Australia)	federalism indicator based on Maddex (1998) Source: Keman (2000)
decentralisation				
dezrev2	19	0.05 (Italy)	0.47 (Canada)	own-source subnational revenue as share of total subnational revenue Source: Rodden (2004)
dezrev3	18	0.004 (Norway)	0.32 (Canada)	ditto; corrected for 'rate autonomy' Source: Rodden (2004)
dezrev4	18	0 (Norway)	0.30 (Canada)	ditto; corrected for 'rate and base autonomy' Source: Rodden (2004)

Indicator	n	min	max	description/source
snadm	26	0.25 (Netherlands)	0.87 (Germany)	subnational share of government employees
				Source: Schiavo-Campo et al. (1997)
dezrev1	27	0.01 (Greece)	0.48 (Canada)	subnational revenue as share of total revenue, 1994–2003 average
				Source: International Monetary Fund (various years)
dezexp	27	0.04 (Greece)	0.58 (Canada)	subnational expenditure as share of total expenditure, 1994–2003 average
				Source: International Monetary Fund (various years)

fiscal control variables

Indicator	n	min	max	description/source
pcsnborr	27	0.06 (Belgium)	0.32 (New Zealand)	subnational borrowing share on subnational expenditure
				Source: International Monetary Fund (various years)
hbc	19	1.45 (Denmark)	3.25 (Canada)	index of budget constraints as developed by the Inter-American Development Bank
				Source: Rodden (2002)
borrauton	19	1.50 (Denmark)	3.00 (USA)	modified index of budget constraints
				Source: Rodden (2002), modified as average of local and regional budget constraints (own calculation)
pcgrants	19	0.19 (Switzerland)	0.80 (Italy)	share of grants on subnational revenue
				Source: Rodden (2004)
grants	27	0.01 (New Zealand)	0.22 (Belgium)	share of grants on subnational expenditure, 1994–2003 average
				Source: International Monetary Fund (various years)
fimb1	27	0.27 (Iceland)	0.97 (Ireland)	share of subnational expenditure not covered by own tax revenue, 1994–2003 average
				Source: International Monetary Fund (various years)

Indicator	n	min	max	description/source
fimb2	27	0.21 (Ireland)	0.90 (New Zealand)	share of subnational expenditure not covered by grants, 1994–2003 average
				Source: International Monetary Fund (various years)

control variables

pop	30	281 (Iceland)	279,245 (USA)	population in 1000
				Source: Central Intelligence Agency (2005)
area	30	2,586 (Luxembourg)	9,984,670 (Canada)	area in sqkm
				Source: Central Intelligence Agency (2005)
popdens	30	2.54 (Australia)	473.62 (South Korea)	population density per sqkm (popdens=pop/area)
				Source: Own calculations based on Central Intelligence Agency (2005)
medage	29	22.90 (Mexico)	41.30 (Japan)	median age of population in 2000
				Source: United Nations (2004)
incineq1	29	24.40 (Hungary)	54.60 (Mexico)	Gini index of income inequality
				Source: United Nations Development Programme (2004)
incineq2	29	4.50 (Japan)	45.00 (Mexico)	average income of the richest 10% as a multiple of the average income of the poorest 10%
				Source: United Nations Development Programme (2004)
incineq3	23	4.90 (CzechRepublic)	14.3 (Australia)	share of population below poverty level (defined as 50% of median income)
				Source: United Nations Development Programme (2004)
ethnic	30	0.00 (South Korea)	0.67 (Canada)	ethnic fragmentation
				Source: Levinson (1998; data on ethnicities)
religion	30	0.00 (Turkey)	0.70 (United Kingdom)	religious fragmentation
				Source: Encyclopedia Britannica (1997; data on confessions)
urban	30	0.58 (Slovakia)	0.97 (Belgium)	percentage of urban population
				Source: United Nations (2001)

Indicator	n	min	max	description/source
hdi02	30	0.75 (Turkey)	0.96 (Norway)	Human Development Index 2002. Source: United Nations Development Programme (2004)
democ	30	6 (Mexico)	103 (USA)	number of democratic years 1900–2003. Source: Marshall & Jaggers 2002 (years with value >4 in Polity IV data set)
legeng	30	0 (Denmark)	1 (USA)	1 = English legal origin; 0 = other. Source: La Porta *et.al.* (1999)
legfren	30	0 (Denmark)	1 (France)	1 = French legal origin; 0 = other. Source: La Porta *et.al.* (1999)
legger	30	0 (Denmark)	1 (Germany)	1 = German legal origin; 0 = other. Source: La Porta *et.al.* (1999)
legscan	30	0 (France)	1 (Denmark)	1 = Scandinavian legal origin; 0 = other. Source: La Porta *et.al.* (1999)
polisys	23	−1.39 (Un. Kingdom)	1.87 (Switzerland)	majoritarian/consensus democracy. Source: Lijphart (1999)
tradebal10	30	0.71 (Greece)	1.34 (Norway)	trade balance (proportion exports/imports), 1994–2003 average. Source: OECD (various years)

macroeconomic indicators

Indicator	n	min	max	description/source
gdpppp94	25	5,115 (Turkey)	31,625 (Luxembourg)	GDP per capita in market prices, purchasing power parity, in US$, 1994. Source: OECD *Main Economic Indicators*
gdpppp03	30	6,937.05 (Turkey)	53,822.22 (Luxembourg)	GDP per capita in market prices, purchasing power parity, in US$, 2003. Source: OECD *Main Economic Indicators*
growth10	30	0.92 (Mexico)	1.07 (Ireland)	economic growth, 1994–2003 average. Source: OECD *Main Economic Indicators*

Indicator	n	min	max	description/source
unemp10	30	3.05 (Luxembourg)	18.55 (Slovakia)	unemployment, 1994–2003 average Source: OECD *Main Economic Indicators*
infl10	30	1.00 (Japan)	1.69 (Turkey)	inflation, 1994–2003 average Source: OECD *Main Economic Indicators*
govsize10	28	24.21 (South Korea)	61.83 (Sweden)	government size 1994–2003 average Source: OECD (various years)
socexp10	22	0.07 (Belgium)	0.28 (Denmark)	social expenditure, 1994–2003 average Source: OECD *Main Economic Indicators* and International Monetary Fund (various years)
budgdef10	29	-0.27 (Turkey)	0.22 (South Korea)	budget balance, 1994–2003 average Source: OECD *Main Economic Indicators*

policy area indicators

def	24	0 (e.g. Austria)	0.11 (Switzerland)	share of subnational expenditure in total expenditure (defence); average of 1997–2001 Source: International Monetary Fund (various years)
pcdef	27	0 (Iceland)	0.15 (Korea)	share of expenditure on defence in total expenditure; average of 1997–2001 Source: International Monetary Fund (various years)
pord	21	0.05 (Slovakia)	0.93 (Switzerland)	share of subnational expenditure in total expenditure (public order and safety); average of 1997–2001 Source: International Monetary Fund (various years)
pcpord	21	0.01 (Denmark)	0.05 (United Kingdom)	share of expenditure on public order in total expenditure; average of 1997–2001 Source: International Monetary Fund (various years)

Indicator	n	min	max	description/source
edu	22	0.20 (Luxembourg)	0.96 (Germany)	share of subnational expenditure in total expenditure (education); average of 1997–2001
				Source: International Monetary Fund (various years)
pcedu	22	0.08 (Germany)	0.19 (USA)	share of expenditure on education in total expenditure; average of 1997–2001
				Source: International Monetary Fund (various years)
health	21	0.01 (France)	0.95 (Denmark)	share of subnational expenditure in total expenditure (health); average of 1997–2001
				Source: International Monetary Fund (various years)
pchealth	22	0.08 (Denmark)	0.23 (Ireland)	share of expenditure on health in total expenditure; average of 1997–2001
				Source: International Monetary Fund (various years)
soc	22	0.01 (Slovakia)	0.54 (Denmark)	share of subnational expenditure in total expenditure (social security); average of 1997–2001
				Source: International Monetary Fund (various years)
pcsoc	22	0.21 (Iceland)	0.49 (Denmark)	share of expenditure on social security in total expenditure; average of 1997–2001
				Source: International Monetary Fund (various years)
hous	22	0.31 (USA)	0.99 (Belgium)	share of subnational expenditure in total expenditure (housing); average of 1997–2001
				Source: International Monetary Fund (various years)
pchous	22	0.01 (Belgium)	0.07 (Poland)	share of expenditure on housing in total expenditure; average of 1997–2001
				Source: International Monetary Fund (various years)

Indicator	n	min	max	description/source
rec	22	0.34 (Slovakia)	0.95 (Germany)	share of subnational expenditure in total expenditure (recreation and culture); average of 1997–2001
				Source: International Monetary Fund (various years)
pcrec	22	0.01 (Ireland)	0.06 (Iceland)	share of expenditure on recreation and culture in total expenditure; average of 1997–2001
				Source: International Monetary Fund (various years)
econ	20	0.11 (Slovakia)	0.72 (Canada)	share of subnational expenditure in total expenditure (economy); average of 1997–2001
				Source: International Monetary Fund (various years)
pcecon	27	0.03 (Greece)	0.25 (Korea)	share of expenditure on economy in total expenditure; average of 1997–2001
				Source: International Monetary Fund (various years)
agri	16	0 (Norway)	0.83 (Germany)	share of subnational expenditure in total expenditure (agriculture); average of 1997–2001
				Source: International Monetary Fund (various years)
pcagri	24	0.00 (United Kingdom)	0.08 (Korea)	share of expenditure on agriculture in total expenditure; average of 1997–2001
				Source: International Monetary Fund (various years)
tcom	15	0.22 (Hungary)	0.86 (Australia)	share of subnational expenditure in total expenditure (infrastructure); average of 1997–2001
				Source: International Monetary Fund (various years)
pctcom	20	0.02 (Poland)	0.08 (Iceland)	share of expenditure on infrastructure in total expenditure; average of 1997–2001
				Source: International Monetary Fund (various years)

Indicator	n	min	max	description/source
env	15	0.45 (Finland)	0.97 (Germany)	share of subnational expenditure in total expenditure (environment); average of 1997–2001
				Source: International Monetary Fund (various years)
pcenv	15	0.01 (Finland)	0.03 (Sweden)	share of expenditure on environment in total expenditure; average of 1997–2001
				Source: International Monetary Fund (various years)
police	22	1.57 (Finland)	5.56 (Italy)	number of police officers per 1000 inhabitants
				Source: United Nations (2002)
teacher	22	0.03 (Japan)	0.08 (Iceland)	teachers as percentage of working population
				Source: United Nations Educational Scientific and Cultural Organization, *World Education Indicators Programme*
pisa	27	–2.86 (Mexico)	1.37 (Japan)	mean of points reached in the PISA test 2000
				Source: OECD (2001).
librarians	23	0.01 (Turkey)	1.15 (Austria)	number of librarians per 1000 inhabitants
				Source: United Nations Educational Scientific and Cultural Organization, *World Education Indicators Programme*
econ1	29	17.31 (Slovakia)	100.00 (USA)	degree to which technical, scientific and human resources match the economic needs
				Source: International Institute for Management Development, *World Competitiveness Yearbook 2005*
envimp	27	3.94 (Mexico)	6.72 (Finland)	expert survey for compliance with international treaties on environmental protection
				Source: Porter *et al.* (2001)
roads	29	5,210 (Luxembourg)	4,180,053 (USA)	roads in km
				Source: United Nations Economic Commission for Europe (2005)

Indicator	n	min	max	description/source
gem_rtax	not publicly available			GEM index for taxes and regulation; expert survey in the course of the Global Entrepreneurship Monitor (GEM) 2002, for methodological details see Sternberg & Bergmann (2003)
gem_psupp	not publicly available			GEM index for public funding structures; expert survey in the course of the Global Entrepreneurship Monitor (GEM) 2002, for methodological details see Sternberg & Bergmann (2003)
gem_infr	not publicly available			GEM index for physical infrastructure; expert survey in the course of the Global Entrepreneurship Monitor (GEM) 2002, for methodological details see Sternberg & Bergmann (2003)

Appendix Table 2: Codebook of panel data

indicator	n	min	max	description/source
country	850	-	-	character variable, country name
i	850	1	30	numeric variable, country
t	850	1	34	numeric variable, time
year	850	1970	2003	numeric variable, year
aus, aut, bel, can, cze, den, fin, fra, ger, hun, ice, ire, ita, lux, mex, net, nze, nor, pol, por, spa, swe, swi, ukd, usa	850 each	0	1	country dummies
y1970, y1971, y1972, y1973, y1974, y1975, y1976, y1977, y1978, y1979, y1980, y1981, y1982, y1983, y1984, y1985, y1986, y1987, y1988, y1989, y1990, y1991, y1992, y1993, y1994, y1995, y1996, y1997, y1998, y1999, y2000, y2001, y2002, y2003	850 each	0	1	year dummies
federalism				
feddummy	850	0 (e.g. Denmark)	1 (e.g. Australia)	1 = federal; 0 = unitary *Source:* Elazar (1987)

indicator	n	min	max	description/source
decentralisation				
dezrev	632	0.01 (Netherlands)	0.51 (Canada)	subnational revenue as share of total revenue Source: International Monetary Fund (various years)
dezexp	620	0.05 (Portugal)	0.61 (Canada)	subnational expenditure as share of total expenditure Source: International Monetary Fund (various years)
dezborr	609	-0.16 (Portugal)	0.60 (Portugal)	subnational borrowing as share of subnational total revenue Source: International Monetary Fund (various years)
fiscal control variables				
grants	600	0.01 (New Zealand)	0.25 (Denmark)	share of grants on subnational expenditure Source: International Monetary Fund (various years)
fimb1	622	-0.01 (Iceland)	0.98 (Netherlands)	share of subnational expenditure not covered by own tax revenue Source: International Monetary Fund (various years)
control variables				
popsize	746	204.11 (Iceland)	291,085 (USA)	population size Source: OECD National Accounts Statistics
popdens	746	1.67 (Australia)	390.7 (Netherlands)	population density per sqkm (popdens=popsize/area) Source: Own calculations based on OECD National Accounts Statistics and Central Intelligence Agency (2005)
tradebal	746	0.57 (Portugal)	1.60 (Norway)	trade balance (proportion exports/imports) Source: OECD (various years)

indicator	n	min	max	description/source
macroeconomic indicators[1]				
growth	722	0.16 (Mexico)	1.12 (Mexico)	economic growth Source: OECD *Main Economic Indicators*
unemp	746	0.00 (Switzerland)	19.93 (Poland)	unemployment Source: OECD *Main Economic Indicators*
infl	739	0.99 (Netherlands)	1.84 (Iceland)	inflation Source: OECD *Main Economic Indicators*
govsize	376	30.05 (Switzerland)	72.93 (Sweden)	government size Source: OECD (various years)
socexp	237	0 (Australia)	0.31 (Denmark)	social expenditure Source: OECD *Main Economic Indicators* and International Monetary Fund (various years)
budgdef	618	-0.28 (Italy)	0.29 (Norway)	budget balance Source: OECD *Main Economic Indicators*

1. For all macroeconomic indicators we have taken the logarithmic form for the panel analysis. The transformed variables are also included in the panel data set and begin with "ln" (e.g. 'lngovsize').

| references

Bibliography

Adamovich, I. B. and Hosp, G. (2003) 'Fiscal federalism for emerging economies: lessons from Switzerland?', *Publius: Journal of Federalism,* 33: 1–21.

Adelsberger, H. (2003) 'Wieder im Herzen Europas – die Raumwirksamkeit des österreichischen Generalverkehrsplans', in Österreichische Raumordnungskonferenz (ed.) *Raumordnung im Umbruch – Herausforderungen, Konflikte, Veränderungen. Festschrift für Eduard Kunze,* Wien: ÖROK, 138–46.

Adshead, M. (2003) 'Policy networks and sub-national government in Ireland', in M. Adshead and M. Millar (eds) *Public Administration and Public Policy in Ireland: Theory and methods,* New York: Routledge, pp. 108–28.

—— (2005) 'Europeanization and changing patterns of governance in Ireland', *Public Administration,* 83: 159–78.

Adshead, M. and Quinn, B. (1998) 'The Move from Government to Governance – Irish development policy's paradigm shift', *Policy & Politics,* 26: 209–225.

Ahedo Santisteban, M. (2006) *Industrial Clusters in Spain and Denmark: Contextualized institutional strategies for endogeneous development,* European Urban and Regional Studies Conference, Roskilde.

Aigner, D., Fallend, F., Mühlböck, A. and Wolfgruber, E. (2001) '"Europäisierung" der lokalen Politik in Österreich?', DVPW, ÖGPW and SVPW Conference, Berlin.

Akaike, H. (1973) 'Information Theory and an extension of the maximum likelihood principle', in B. N. Petrov and F. Csaki (eds) *Second Symposium on Information Theory,* Budapest: Akademiai Kiado, pp. 267–81.

Allen, K. (2000) *The Celtic Tiger: The myth of social partnership in Ireland,* Manchester/New York: Manchester University Press.

Almy, T. A. (1980) 'The development and evolution of city-county management in Ireland: an illustration of central-local administrative relationships', *International Journal of Public Administration,* 2: 477–500.

Amin, A. and Thomas, D. (1996) 'The negotiated economy: state and civic institutions in Denmark', *Economy and Society,* 25: 255–81.

An Bord Pleanála, http://www.pleanala.ie (Accessed January 8, 2009) – *Weekly lists,* http://www.pleanala.ie/lists/ (Accessed January 8, 2009).

Andersen, B. (1992) 'Factors affecting European privatization and deregulation policies in local public transport: the evidence from Scandinavia', *Transportation Research Part A,* 26: 179–91.

Andersen, H. T., Hansen, F. and Jørgensen, J. (2002) 'The fall and rise of metropolitan government in Copenhagen', *GeoJournal,* 58: 43–52.

Andersen, H. T. and Jørgensen, J. (1995) 'City profile Copenhagen', *Cities,* 12: 13–22.

Andersen, J. (2003) 'Gambling Politics or Successful Entrepreneurialism? The Orestad project in Copenhagen', in F. Moulaert, A. Rodriguez and E. Swyngedouw (eds) *The Globalized City: Economic Restructuring and Social Polarization in European Cities,* Oxford: Oxford University Press, pp. 91–106.

Andeweg, R. B. (2000) 'Consociational Democracy', *Annual Review of Political Science,* 3: 509–36.

APA (2007a) 'Gusenbauer pocht auf Koralm- und Semmeringtunnel', 9 February 2007.

— (2007b) 'Koralmbahn: Haider will gegen Regierung und ÖBB klagen', 5 February 2007.

— (2007c) 'Voves sieht Bahntunnel als Jahrhundertprojekt', 7 February 2007.

Armingeon, K. (2000) 'Swiss Federalism in Comparative Perspective', in U. Wachendorfer-Schmidt (ed.) *Federalism and Political Performance,* London: Routledge, pp. 112–29.

Association of County and City Councils, http://www.councillors.ie/Publications.html (Accessed January 8, 2009).

Bachtler, J. and Yuill, D. (2001) 'Policies and Strategies for Regional Development: A shift in paradigm', 'Regional and Industrial Policy Paper 46', European Policies Research Centre, University of Strathclyde.

BADAC, http://www.badac.ch (Accessed January 8, 2009).

Baldi, B. (1999) 'Beyond the Federal-Unitary Dichotomy', working paper, Institute of Governmental Studies, University of Berkeley.

Bannon, M. J. and Russell, P. (2001) 'Structures for Policy-Making and the Implementation of Planning in the Republic of Ireland', in R. Alterman (ed.) *National-Level Planning in Democratic Countries,* Liverpool: Liverpool University Press, pp. 65–84.

Banting, K. G. (1987) *The Welfare State and Canadian Federalism,* 2nd ed, Kingston: McGill-Queen's University Press.

Barrett, A., Kearney, I. and O'Brien, M. (2008) 'Quarterly economic commentary: Summer 2008', *ESRI Macroeconomic Forecasting Series. Quarterly Economic Commentary,* http://www.esri.ie/UserFiles/publications/20080623114553/QEC2008Sum.pdf (Accessed December 4, 2008).

Barrett, S. D. (2001) 'Bus deregulation in Ireland', *Trinity Economics Papers,* http://www.tcd.ie/Economics/research/tep/2001/TEPNo8SB21.pdf (Accessed November 27, 2008).

— (2006) 'Evaluating Transport 21 – some economic aspects', *Quarterly Economic Commentary,* 36–58.

Barrington, T. J. (1991) 'The Crisis of Irish Local Government', in J. J. Hesse (ed.) *Local Government and Urban Affairs in International Perspective,* Baden-Baden: Nomos, pp. 141–66.

— Barry, F. (2003) 'Irish Economy Development over Three Decades of

EU Membership', http://www.ucd.ie/economic/staff/barry/papers/Finance%20a%20Uver.pdf (Accessed December 2, 2008).

— (2005) *European Union Regional Aid and Irish Economic Development*, Washington: World Bank.

Bauer, H. (1991) 'Reviving Local Government in Austria', in J. J. Hesse (ed.) *Local Government and Urban Affairs in International Perspective: Analyses of twenty Western industrialised countries*, Baden-Baden: Nomos, pp. 387–408.

Beck, N. (2001) 'Time-series cross-section data: what have we learned in the past few years?', *Annual Review of Political Science*, 4: 271–93.

Beck, N. and Katz, J. N. (1995) 'What to do (and not to do) with time-series cross-section data', *American Political Science Review*, 89: 634–47.

Bednar, J., Eskridge, W. N. and Ferejohn, J. (1999) 'A Political Theory of Federalism', in J. Ferejohn, J. N. Rakove and J. Riley (eds) *Constitutional Culture and Democratic Rule*, New York: Cambridge University Press, pp. 223–67.

Beer, S. H. (1977) 'A Political Scientist's View of Fiscal Federalism', in W. E. Oates (ed.) *The Political Economy of Fiscal Federalism*, Lexington: D.C. Heath and Company, pp. 21–46.

Benz, A. (1998) 'Dezentralisierung und Demokratie: Anmerkungen zur Aufgabenverteilung im Bundesstaat', in U. Männle (ed.) *Föderalismus zwischen Konsens und Konkurrenz*, Baden-Baden: Nomos, pp. 21–9.

— (2001) 'Themen, Probleme und Perspektiven der vergleichenden Föderalismusforschung', in A. Benz and G. Lehmbruch (eds) *Föderalismus. Analysen in entwicklungsgeschichtlicher und vergleichender Perspektive*, PVS Sonderheft 32, Opladen: Westdeutscher Verlag, pp. 9–50.

Berchtold, K. (1988) *Die Verhandlungen zum Forderungsprogramm der Bundesländer seit 1956*, Wien: Braumüller.

Biaggini, G. (2006) 'Der neue Finanzausgleich in der Schweiz', in P. Bußjäger (ed.) *Finanzausgleich und Finanzverfassung auf dem Prüfstand*, Wien: Braumüller, pp. 55–75.

Bieger, T., Rey, M., Scherer, R., Schnell, K.-D., Sfar, D., Strebel, N. and Reinhard, M. (2004) *Evaluation der Investitionshilfe für Berggebiete (IHG)*, Institut für Öffentliche Dienstleistungen und Tourismus der Universität St. Gallen, St. Gallen/Lausanne.

Bird, R. M. and Tarasov, A. V. (2004) 'Closing the gap: fiscal imbalances and intergovernmental transfers in developed federations', *Environment and Planning C: Government and Policy*, 22: 77–102.

Bjorna, H. and Jenssen, S. (2006) 'Prefectoral systems and central-local government relations in Scandinavia', *Scandinavian Political Studies*, 29: 308–32.

Blom-Hansen, J. (1999a) 'Avoiding the "joint-decision trap": lessons from intergovernmental relations in Scandinavia', *European Journal of Political Research*, 35: 35–67.

— (1999b) 'Policy-making in central-local government relations: balancing local autonomy, macroeconomic control, and sectoral policy goals',

Journal of Public Policy, 19: 237–64.

—— (2002) 'Budget procedures and the size of the budget: evidence from Danish local government', *Scandinavian Political Studies,* 25: 85–106.

Blom-Hansen, J. and Pallesen, T. (2001) 'The fiscal manipulation of a decentralized public sector: macroeconomic policy in Denmark', *Environment and Planning C: Government and Policy,* 19: 607–23.

Bochsler, D., Koller, C., Sciarini, P., Traimond, S. and Trippolini, I. (2004) *Die Schweizer Kantone unter der Lupe. Behörden, Personal, Finanzen,* Bern/ Stuttgart/Wien: Haupt Verlag.

Boekholt, P. and Thuriaux, B. (1999) 'Public Policies to Facilitate Clusters: Background, Rationale, and Policy Practices in International Perspective', in OECD (ed.) *Boosting Innovation: The Cluster Approach,* Paris: OECD, pp. 381–412.

Bogason, P. (1982) 'Denmark: the Regional Development Council', in D. Yuill (ed.) *Regional Development Agencies in Europe,* Aldershot: Gower, pp. 107–28.

—— (1987) 'Denmark', in E. C. Page and M. J. Goldsmith (eds) *Central and Local Government Relations. A comparative analysis of West European unitary states,* London: Sage, pp. 46–67.

—— (1991) 'Danish Local Government: Towards an Effective and Efficient Welfare State', in J. J. Hesse (ed.) *Local Government and Urban Affairs in International Perspective: Analyses of twenty Western industrialised countries,* Baden-Baden: Nomos, 261–90.

Bolleyer, N. (2006a) 'Consociationalism and intergovernmental relations – linking internal and external power-sharing in the Swiss federal polity', *Swiss Political Science Review,* 12: 1–34.

—— (2006b) 'Federal dynamics in Canada, the United States, and Switzerland: how substates' internal organization affects intergovernmental relations', *Publius: Journal of Federalism,* 36: 471–502.

—— (2006c) 'Intergovernmental arrangements in Spanish and Swiss federalism: the impact of power-concentrating and power-sharing executives on intergovernmental institutionalization', *Regional and Federal Studies,* 16: 385–408.

Boylan, T. A. (2002) 'From Stabilisation to Economic Growth: The contribution of macroeconomic policy', in G. Taylor (ed.) *Issues in Irish Public Policy,* Dublin/Portland: Irish Academic Press, pp. 9–27.

Boyle, G. E., McCarthy, T. G. and Walsh, J. (1999) 'Regional income differentials and the issue of regional equalisation in Ireland', *Journal of the Statistical and Social Inquiry Society of Ireland,* XXVIII: 155–210.

Boyle, M. (2000) 'Euro-regionalism and struggles over scales of governance: the politics of Ireland's regionalisation approach to Structural Fund allocations 2000–2006', *Political Geography,* 19: 737–69.

Brandner, P., Frisch, H., Grossmann, B. and Hauth, E. (2005) *Eine Schuldenbremse für Österreich – Studie im Auftrag des Staatsschuldenausschusses,* Wien: Bundesministerium für Finanzen.

Braun, D. (ed.) (2000a) *Public Policy and Federalism*, Aldershot: Ashgate.
—   (2000b) 'Territorial Division of Power and Public Policy-Making: An assessment', in D. Braun (ed.) *Public Policy and Federalism*, Aldershot: Ashgate, pp. 27–56.
—   (2000c) 'Territorial Division of Power and Public Policy-Making: An overview', in D. Braun (ed.) *Public Policy and Federalism*, Aldershot: Ashgate, pp. 1–26.
—   (2003) 'Dezentraler und unitarischer Föderalismus. Die Schweiz und Deutschland im Vergleich', *Swiss Political Science Review*, 9: 57–89.
—   (2007) 'How to make German fiscal federalism self-enforcing: a comparative analysis', *Zeitschrift für Staats- und Europawissenschaften*, 5: 235–62.
—   (2010) 'Making Fiscal Federalism Self-Enforcing: Germany, Australia, and Switzerland compared', in W. Swenden and J. Erk (eds) *Exploring new avenues of comparative federalism research*, London: Routledge, pp. 172–87.
Braune, F. (2000) 'Seanad Éireann: Die Zweite Kammer Irlands', in G. Riescher, S. Ruß and C. M. Haas (eds) *Zweite Kammern*, München/Wien: Oldenbourg, pp. 288–97.
Breton, A. (1987) 'Towards a theory of competitive federalism', *European Journal of Political Economy*, 3: 269–329.
Bröthaler, J., Bauer, H. and Schönbäck, W. (2006) *Österreichs Gemeinden im Netz der finanziellen Transfers: Steuerung, Förderung, Belastung*, Wien: Springer.
Bröthaler, J., Sieber, L., Schönbäck, W., Maimer, A. and Bauer, H. (2002) *Aufgabenorientierte Gemeindefinanzierung in Österreich*, Wien: Springer.
Buhr, W. (2009) 'Infrastructure of the Market Economy', http://www.uni-siegen. de/fb5/vwl/repec/sie/papers/132–09.pdf (Accessed February 10, 2010).
Bund, Länder und Gemeinden Österreichs (2006) *Vereinbarung zwischen dem Bund, den Ländern und den Gemeinden über eine Weiterführung der stabilitätsorientierten Budgetpolitik* (Österreichischer Stabilitätspakt 2005)', *BGBl. I Nr. 19/2006*.
Bundes-Verfassungsgesetz der Republik Österreich (B-VG) vom 1. Jänner 2009.
Bundesamt für Raumentwicklung, *Agglomerationspolitik*, www.agglomeration.ch (Accessed January 8, 2009).
—   *Medienmitteilung vom 12.02.2008: 30 Agglomerationsprogramme eingereicht*, http://www.are.admin.ch/dokumentation/00121/00224/index. html?lang=de&msg-id=17243 (Accessed January 8, 2009).
Bundesamt für Statistik, *Amtliches Gemeindeverzeichnis der Schweiz*, http:// www.bfs.admin.ch/bfs/portal/de/index/infothek/nomenklaturen/blank/ blank/gem_liste/03.html (Accessed January 8, 2009).
—   *Comparator*, http://www.bfs.admin.ch/bfs/portal/de/index/regionen/ regionalportraets/comparator.html (Accessed January 8, 2009).
—   *Karte. Die wirtschaftlichen Erneuerungsgebiete (WEG 01) der Schweiz*, http://www.bfs.admin.ch/bfs/portal/de/index/regionen/11/geo/regional-

politische_gliederungen/04.html (Accessed January 8, 2009).

— *Kosten und Finanzierung des Verkehrs – Daten, Indikatoren, Externe Kosten,* http://www.bfs.admin.ch/bfs/portal/de/index/themen/11/02/blank/key/externe_kosten.html (Accessed January 8, 2009).

— *Themen – Mobilität und Verkehr,* http://www.bfs.admin.ch/bfs/portal/de/index/themen/11.html (Accessed January 8, 2009).

Bundeskanzleramt Österreich, www.bka.gv.at (Accessed January 8, 2009).

Bundesministerium für Finanzen der Republik Österreich (2005) *Finanzausgleichsgesetz 2005, Übersicht über die Änderungen; Korrektur des Volkszählungsergebnisses 2001,* Wien: Bundesministerium für Finanzen.

Bundesministerium für Verkehr Innovation und Technologie der Republik Österreich, www.bmvit.gv.at (Accessed January 8, 2009).

— *Generalverkehrsplan Österreich 2002,* http://www.bmvit.gv.at/verkehr/gesamtverkehr/generalverkehrsplanung/downloads/gvk.pdf (Accessed December 2, 2008).

— *Verkehr in Zahlen,* http://www.bmvit.gv.at/verkehr/gesamtverkehr/statistik/downloads/viz07gesamt.pdf (Accessed December 2, 2008).

Bundesverfassung der Schweizerischen Eidgenossenschaft vom 18. April 1999 *SR 101.*

Bundesversammlung der Schweizerischen Eidgenossenschaft, *Dokumentation. Dossiers A – Z,* http://www.parlament.ch/D/dokumentation (Accessed January 8, 2009).

— *Dossier. Bahn 2000,* http://www.parlament.ch/d/dokumentation/do-archiv/Seiten/do-bahn-2000.aspx (Accessed January 8, 2009).

— *Dossier. Infrastrukturfonds für Agglomerationen und Nationalstrassennetz,* http://www.parlament.ch/D/dokumentation/do-archiv/Seiten/do-dopoavanti.aspx? (Accessed January 8, 2009).

— (1957) 'Eisenbahngesetz vom 20. Dezember 1957 (EBG)', *SR 742.101.*

— (1967) 'Bundesgesetz über die Förderung des Hotel- und Kurortkredits (HKG)', *SR 935.12.*

— (1976) 'Bundesgesetz über die Gewährung von Bürgschaften und Zinskostenbeiträgen in Berggebieten (BGB)', *SR 901.2.*

— (1978) 'Bundesbeschluss zugunsten wirtschaftlich bedrohter Regionen', *SR 951.93.*

— (1997a) 'Bundesbeschluss über die Unterstützung des Strukturwandels im ländlichen Raum', *SR 901.03.*

— (1997b) 'Bundesgesetz über die Förderung von Innovation und Zusammenarbeit im Tourismus', *SR 935.22.*

— (1997c) 'Bundesgesetz über Investitionshilfe im Berggebiet (IHG)', *SR 901.1.*

— (2006a) 'Bundesgesetz über den Infrastrukturfonds für den Agglomerationsverkehr, das Nationalstraßennetz sowie Hauptstraßen in Berggebieten und Randregionen', *SR 725.13.*

— (2006b) 'Bundesgesetz über Regionalpolitik (NRPG)', *SR 901.0.*

Bundgaard, U. and Vrangbaek, K. (2007) 'Reform by coincidence? Explaining the policy process of structural reform in Denmark', *Scandinavian Political Studies,* 30: 491–520.

Busch, A. (1995) *Preisstabilitätspolitik: Politik und Inflationsraten im internationalen Vergleich,* Opladen: Leske + Budrich.

Buser, B. (2005) *Regionale Wirtschaftskreisläufe und regionale Wachstumspolitik. Regionalpolitische Prioritäten für unterschiedliche Regionen im Schweizer Alpenraum auf der Basis regionaler Input-Output Tabellen,* unpublished thesis, ETH Zürich.

Bußjäger, P. (2002) 'Der sklerotische Bundesstaat: Modernisierungsprobleme im österreichischen föderalen System', *Zeitschrift für Politik,* 49: 149–70.

— (2006) 'Der Schein der Normalität – Österreich ein Jahr nach dem Konvent', in Europäisches Zentrum für Föderalismus-Forschung Tübingen (ed.) *Jahrbuch des Föderalismus 2006,* Baden-Baden: Nomos, pp. 370–84.

— (2007) 'Föderalismus durch Macht im Schatten? – Österreich und die Landeshauptmännerkonferenz', in Europäisches Zentrum für Föderalismus-Forschung Tübingen (ed.) *Jahrbuch des Föderalismus 2007,* Baden-Baden: Nomos, pp. 79–99.

Bußjäger, P., Bär, S. and Willi, U. (2005) *Kooperativer Föderalismus im Kontext der Europäischen Integration,* Innsbruck: Institut für Föderalismus.

Callanan, M. (2003) 'Where Stands Local Government?', in M. Callanan and J. F. Keogan (eds) *Local Government in Ireland: Inside out,* Dublin: Institute of Public Administration, pp. 475–501.

— (2005) 'Institutionalizing participation and governance? New participative structures in local government in Ireland', *Public Administration,* 83: 909–29.

Cameron, D. R. (1978) 'The expansion of the public economy: a comparative analysis', *American Political Science Review,* 72: 1243–61.

Carroll, W. G. and Byrne, T. (1999) 'Regional Policy and Ireland', in J. Dooge and R. Barrington (eds) *A Vital National Interest – Ireland in Europe 1973–1998,* Dublin: Institute of Public Administration, pp. 172–85.

Castles, F. (2000) 'Federalism, Fiscal Decentralization and Economic Performance', in U. Wachendorfer-Schmidt (ed.) *Federalism and Political Performance,* London: Routledge, pp. 177–95.

Castles, F. and McKinlay, R. D. (1979) 'Does politics matter: an analysis of the public welfare commitment in advanced democratic states', *European Journal of Political Research,* 7: 169–86.

CEAT, Basler, E, Partner, E. B. and Infras (2010) *Evaluation der Agglomerationspolitik des Bundes 2002–2009.* Schlussbericht, www.are.admin.ch/themen/agglomeration (Accessed September 27, 2012).

Central Intelligence Agency (2005) 'CIA World Factbook 2005', http://www.cia.gov/cia/publications/factbook/index.html (Accessed January 8, 2009).

Christensen, J. G. (2000) 'The dynamics of decentralization and recentralization', *Public Administration,* 78: 389–408.

Christensen, J. G. and Pallesen, T. (2001) 'Institutions, distributional concerns, and public sector reform', *European Journal of Political Research,* 39: 179–202.

Christiansen, P. M. and Rommetvedt, H. (1999) 'From corporatism to lobbyism? parliaments, executives, and organized interests in Denmark and Norway', *Scandinavian Political Studies,* 22: 195–220.

Christoffersen, H. (2005) *Local Government Structural Reform and the Efficiency Potential in Larger Organisational Units,* Copenhagen: AKF Institute of Local Government Studies.

Christoffersen, H. and Larsen, K. B. (2007) 'Economies of scale in Danish municipalities: expenditure effects versus quality effects', *Local Government Studies,* 33: 77–95.

Chubb, B. (1992a) 'The Central Administration and the Civil Service', in B. Chubb (ed.) *The Government and Politics of Ireland,* 3rd edn, London: Longman, pp. 227–44.

— (1992b) *The Government and Politics of Ireland,* 3rd edn, London: Longman.

Collins, N. (1985) 'Councillor/Officer relations in Irish local government: alternative models', *Public Administration,* 63: 327–44.

Collins, N. and Butler, P. (2001) 'Cute Hoors as local heroes: politicians and public service delivery', *Irish Journal of Management,* 22: 113–26.

Collins, N. and Quinlivan, A. (2005) 'Multi-Level Governance', in J. Coakley and M. Gallagher (eds) *Politics in the Republic of Ireland,* 4th edn, London: Routledge, pp. 384–403.

Commission on Fiscal Imbalance (2001) *Intergovernmental Fiscal Arrangements – Germany, Australia, Belgium, Spain, United States, Switzerland,* Québec: Commission on Fiscal Imbalance.

Connolly, E. (2005) 'The Government and the Governmental System', in J. Coakley and M. Gallagher (eds) *Politics in the Republic of Ireland,* 4th edn, London: Routledge, pp. 328–51.

Constitution of Ireland – Bunreacht na hÉireann (1937).

Constitutional Act of Denmark (1953).

Cornett, A. P. (1997) 'Decentralisation of Business Development Policy: Challenge or New Opportunity', *European Regional Science Association – 38th European Congress,* Rome.

Costa, Á. (1996) 'The organisation of urban public transport systems in Western European metropolitan areas', *Transportation Research Part A,* 30: 349–59.

Council of Europe (1998) *Structure and Operation of Local and Regional Democracy: Denmark,* Strasbourg: Council of Europe.

Crepaz, M. M. L. (1996) 'Consensus versus majoritarian democracy: political institutions and their impact on macroeconomic performance and industrial dispute', *Comparative Political Studies,* 29: 4–26.

— (2002) 'Global, constitutional, and partisan determinants of redistribution in fifteen OECD countries', *Comparative Politics,* 34: 169–88.

Cullen T.D., M. (2005) 'Speech at the Launch of Transport 21', http://www.

transport21.ie/MEDIA/Launch_Material/Speech_by_Martin_Cullen_TD.html (Accessed January 8, 2009).

Dachs, H. (1996) 'The Politics of Regional Subdivisions', in V. Lauber (ed.) *Contemporary Austrian Politics,* Boulder: Westview Press, pp. 235–51.

— (2002) 'Struktur und aktuelle Fragen des Föderalismus in Österreich', in U. Margedant (ed.) *Föderalismusreform: Föderalismus in Europa I,* Sankt Augustin: Konrad-Adenauer-Stiftung, pp. 32–47.

— (2003) 'Politische Parteien in Österreichs Bundesländern – zwischen regionalen Kalkülen und bundespolitischen Loyalitäten', in H. Dachs (ed.) *Der Bund und die Länder: Über Dominanz, Kooperation und Konflikte im österreichischen Bundesstaat,* Wien/Köln/Weimar: Böhlau Verlag, pp. 69–138.

Dafflon, B. (1996) 'The Requirement of a Balanced Local Budget: Theory and evidence from the Swiss experience', in G. Pola, G. France and R. Levaggi (eds) *Developments in Local Government Finance – Theory and Policy,* Cheltenham: Edward Elgar, pp. 228–49.

— (1999) 'Fiscal Federalism in Switzerland: A survey of constitutional issues, budget responsibility and equalisation', in A. Fossati and G. Panella (eds) *Fiscal Federalism in the European Union,* London/New York: Routledge, pp. 255–94.

— (2002) 'Capital Expenditures and Financing in the Communes in Switzerland', in B. Dafflon (ed.) *Local Public Finance in Europe,* Cheltenham: Edward Elgar, pp. 209–29.

Dafflon, B. and Pujol, F. (2001) 'Fiscal preferences and fiscal performance: Swiss cantonal evidence', *International Public Management Review,* 2: 54–76.

Damborg, C. and Halkier, H. (1998) *Development Bodies, Networking and Business Promotion in North Jutland*, European Studies Series of Occasional Papers, Aalborg: European Studies Unit, Aalborg University.

Danish Ministry of Finance, http://www.skm.dk (Accessed January 8, 2009).

Danske Regioner, http://www.regioner.dk (Accessed January 8, 2009).

Daugaard, S. (2002) 'Enhancing Expenditure Control With A Decentralised Public Sector in Denmark', *OECD Economics Department Working Papers No. 320,* Paris: OECD.

Davis, T. (2003) 'Local Government Finance: The financial process', in M. Callanan and J. F. Keogan (eds) *Local Government in Ireland: Inside out,* Dublin: Institute of Public Administration, pp. 341–51.

Davoudi, S. and Wishardt, M. (2005) 'The polycentric turn in the Irish spatial strategy', *Built Environment,* 31: 122–32.

Department of the Environment Heritage and Local Government, 'Local Authority Budgets 2007', http://www.environ.ie/en/LocalGovernment/LocalGovernmentAdministration/LocalGovernmentFinance/PublicationsDocuments/FileDownLoad,17421,en.pdf (Accessed January 7, 2009).

— 'Local Authority Key Financial Data', http://www.environ.ie/en/LocalGovernment/LocalGovernmentAdministration/LocalGovernmentFinance/ (Accessed January 7, 2009).

— (1986) 'Transport (Re-organisation of Córas Iompair Éireann) Act', *No. 31/1986.*

— (1996) 'Better Local Government'. Dublin.

— (2008) 'Stronger Local Democracy – Options for Change'. Dublin.

Dirninger, C. (2003) '"Wer zahlt und wer schafft an?" Traditionen – Positionen – Konfliktzonen im finanz- und wirtschaftspolitischen Föderalismus Österreichs seit 1945', in H. Dachs (ed.) *Der Bund und die Länder. Über Dominanz, Kooperation und Konflikte im österreichischen Bundesstaat,* Wien/Köln/Weimar: Böhlau Verlag, pp. 229–308.

Dollard, G. (2003) 'Local Government and Finance: The policy context', in M. Callanan and J. F. Keogan (eds) *Local Government in Ireland: Inside out,* Dublin: Institute of Public Administration, pp. 325–40.

Dosenrode, S. and Halkier, H. (eds) (2004) *The Nordic Regions and the European Union,* Aldershot: Ashgate.

Downes, R. (2000) 'EU and National Regional Policies in Austria', in M. Danson, H. Halkier and G. Cameron (eds) *Governance, Institutional Change and Regional Development,* Aldershot: Ashgate, pp. 246–65.

Draxl, P., Schneidewind, P., Downes, R. and Bucek, M. (2004) *Systematische Evaluierung des Regionalmanagements in Österreich. Endbericht an das Bundeskanzleramt. Abteilung IV/4,* Wien: Bundeskanzleramt.

Drejer, I., Kristensen, F. S. and Laursen, K. (1997) *Studies of Clusters as a Basis for Industrial and Technology Policy in the Danish Economy,* DRUID Working Paper, Aalborg.

Dublin Transportation Office (2001) *A Platform for Change – Final Report,* Dublin, http://www.dto.ie/ (Accessed January 8, 2009).

Eidgenössisches Departement für Umwelt Verkehr Energie und Kommunikation, http://www.uvek.admin.ch/ (Accessed January 8, 2009).

— *Faktenblatt: Infrastrukturfonds für den Agglomerationsverkehr und das Nationalstraßennetz,* https://www.news-service.admin.ch/NSBSubscriber/messages/message/de/attachments/1135/2662/698/Faktenblatt%20de.pdf (Accessed December 10, 2008).

Eidgenössisches Departement für Umwelt Verkehr Energie und Kommunikation. Bundesamt für Verkehr (2007) *Gesamtschau FinöV – Bericht über die Ergebnisse der Vernehmlassung,* Berne.

Eidgenössisches Finanzdepartment 'Datenbank der Bundessubventionen', http://www.efv.admin.ch/d/themen/bundesfinanzen/subventionen/subventionsdb8.php (Accessed January 8, 2009).

— 'Geltender Finanzausgleich – NFA (seit 1. Januar 2008 in Kraft)', http://www.efv.admin.ch/d/themen/finanzausgleich/ (Accessed January 8, 2009).

— (2004) 'NFA Faktenblatt 11. Interkantonale Zusammenarbeit mit Lastenausgleich', http://www.efv.admin.ch/d/dokumentation/downloads/themen/finanzausgleich/faktenblaetter/11-NFA_Faktenblatt_11_IKZ_d.pdf (Accessed January 8, 2009).

Eidgenössisches Volkswirtschaftsdepartement (2004a) *Bundesgesetz über Regio-*

nalpolitik (NRPG) – Ergebnisse des Vernehmlassungsverfahrens, Berne.
— (2004b) *Neue Regionalpolitik (NRP) – 1. Bundesgesetz über Regionalpolitik – 2. Erläuternder Bericht*, Berne.
— (2006) *Agglomerationspolitik des Bundes: Zwischenbericht 2006*, Berne.
Elazar, D. J. (1987) *Exploring Federalism*, Tuscaloosa: University of Alabama Press.
Elklit, J. (2005) 'Denmark: Simplicity Embedded in Complexity (or is it the Other Way Round)?', in M. Gallagher and P. Mitchell (eds) *The Politics of Electoral Systems*, Oxford: Oxford University Press, pp. 452–71.
Encyclopedia Britannica (1997) *Britannica Book of the Year*, Chicago: Encyclopedia Britannica Inc.
Enemark, S. and Jorgensen, I. (2001) 'National-Level Planning in the Danish System', in R. Alterman (ed.) *National-Level Planning*, Liverpool: Liverpool University Press, pp. 148–67.
Erk, J. (2004) 'Austria: a federation without federalism', *Publius: Journal of Federalism*, 34: 1–20.
European Round Table of Industrialists (1984) 'Missing Links', http://www.ert.eu/ERT/Docs/0062.pdf (Accessed December 12, 2011).
Eustace, J. G. (1982) 'Ireland: The Industrial Development Authority', in D. Yuill (ed.) *Regional Development Agencies in Europe*, Aldershot: Gower, pp. 235–96.
Fallend, F. (1997) 'Regierungsproporz in der Krise', *Österreichische Zeitschrift für Politikwissenschaft*, 26: 23–40.
— (2000) 'Der Bundesrat in Österreich', in G. Riescher, S. Ruß and C. M. Haas (eds) *Zweite Kammern*, München/Wien: Oldenbourg, pp. 97–113.
— (2001) 'Zwischen politischer Dynamisierung und finanziellen Beschränkungen: Veränderungen im föderalen Gefüge Österreichs 1999/2000', in Europäisches Zentrum für Föderalismus-Forschung Tübingen (ed.) *Jahrbuch des Föderalismus 2001*, Baden-Baden: Nomos, pp. 250–64.
— (2003) 'Föderalismus – eine Domäne der Exekutiven? Die Bund-Länder-Verhandlungen über die Länderforderungsprogramme und die Bundesstaatsreform in Österreich seit 1945', in H. Dachs (ed.) *Der Bund und die Länder. Über Dominanz, Kooperation und Konflikte im österreichischen Bundesstaat*, Wien/Köln/Weimar: Böhlau, pp. 17–68.
— (2005) 'Bund-Länder-Beziehungen', in H. Dachs, P. Gerlich, H. Gottweis, H. Kramer, V. Lauber, W. C. Müller and E. Tálos (eds) *Politik in Österreich*, Wien: Manz, pp. 1025–40.
— (2007) *Does Federalism Matter? Comparing regional economic policies in Austria, Belgium, the Netherlands and Sweden'*, ECPR 35th Joint Sessions of Workshops, Helsinki.
Feiock, R. C. and Scholz, J. T. (2010) *Self-Organizing Federalism: Collaborative mechanisms to mitigate institutional collective action dilemmas*, New York: Cambridge University Press.
Feld, L. P. (1997) 'Exit, voice and income taxes: the loyalty of voters', *European Journal of Political Economy*, 13: 455–78.

Feld, L. P. and Kirchgässner, G. (2006) 'On the Effectiveness of Debt Brakes: The Swiss experience', CREMA Working Paper No. 2006 – 21, http://www.crema-research.ch/papers/2006–21.pdf (Accessed December 8, 2008).

Feld, L. P., Kirchgässner, G. and Schaltegger, C. A. (2005) 'Fiskalischer Föderalismus und wirtschaftliche Entwicklung; Evidenz für die Schweizer Kantone', *Jahrbuch für Regionalwissenschaft*, 25: 3–25.

Feld, L. P. and Schaltegger, C. A. (2005) 'Voters as a hard budget constraint: on the determination of intergovernmental grants', *Public Choice*, 123: 147–69.

Figueroa, M. J. (2005) *Democracy and Environmental Integration in Decision-Making: An evaluation of decisions for large infrastructure projects*, unpublished thesis, Roskilde University.

Fischer, A. (2006) 'Das Kantonsreferendum: Wirkungsweise und Reformansätze', in A. Vatter (ed.) *Föderalismusreform: Wirkungsweise und Reformansätze föderativer Institutionen in der Schweiz*, Zürich: NZZ Verlag, pp. 132–51.

Fischer, R., Beljan, T. and Fivaz, J. (2003) 'Mehr Chancengleichheit und Eigenverantwortung: Der neue Schweizer Finanzausgleich zwischen Bund und Kantonen', *Vierteljahreshefte zur Wirtschaftsforschung*, 72: 407–22.

Fitz Gerald, J. (2002) 'Has Ireland Outgrown Its Clothes? Infrastructural and environmental constraints in Ireland', in V. G. Munley, R. J. Thornton and J. R. Aronson (eds) *The Irish Economy in Transition: Successes, Problems and Prospects*, Amsterdam: JAI Press, pp. 179–203.

Fitzpatrick Associates (2006) *Progressing Rural Public Transport in Ireland – A Discussion Paper*, Dublin.

Fleiner, T. (2002) 'Recent developments of Swiss federalism', *Publius: Journal of Federalism*, 32: 97–123.

Flyvbjerg, B. (2007) 'Cost overruns and demand shortfalls in urban rail and other infrastructure', *Transportation Planning and Technology*, 30: 9–30.

Flyvbjerg, B., Bruzelius, N. and Rothengatter, W. (2003) *Megaprojects and Risk: An anatomy of ambition*, Cambridge: Cambridge University Press.

Flyvbjerg, B., Skamris Holm, M. K. and Buhl, S. (2004) 'What causes cost overrun in transport infrastructure Projects?', *Transport Reviews*, 24: 3–18.

Folketing 'Parliamentary Elections and Election Administration in Denmark', www.folketinget.dk/BAGGRUND/00000048/00232623.htm (Accessed January 8, 2009).

—— (1992) 'Lov om Ørestaden m.v.', *477/24 af 24–06–1992*.

Forde, C. (2004) 'Local government reform in Ireland 1996–2004: a critical analysis', *Administration*, 52: 57–72.

—— (2005) 'Participatory democracy or pseudo-participation? Local government reform in Ireland', *Local Government Studies*, 31: 137–48.

Freiburghaus, D. and Vital, Z. (2003) *Horizontale Kooperation zwischen den Kantonen der Zentralschweiz*, Working Paper de l' IDHEAP, http://www.idheap.ch/idheap.nsf/view/903A578A3B5659CEC1256CE50062AD46/$File/wp%204–2003%20df.pdf (Accessed December, 8 2008).

Freitag, M. and Vatter, A. (2004) 'Föderalismus und staatliche Verschuldung. Ein makro-quantitativer Vergleich', *Österreichische Zeitschrift für Politik-wissenschaft*, 33: 175–90.

— (2008) 'Decentralization and fiscal discipline in sub-national govern-ments: evidence from the Swiss federal system', *Publius: The Journal of Federalism*, 38: 272–94.

Frenkel, A., Shefer, D. and Roper, S. (2003) 'Public policy, locational choice and the innovation capability of high-tech firms: a comparison between Israel and Ireland', *Papers in Regional Science*, 82: 203–21.

Frey, R. L. (1985) *Regionalpolitik: Eine Evaluation*, Bern/Stuttgart: Haupt.

Gallagher, M. and Komito, L. (2005) 'The Constituency Role of Dáil deputies', in J. Coakley and M. Gallagher (eds) *Politics in the Republic of Ireland*, 4th edn, London: Routledge, pp. 242–71.

Gamper, A. (2000) 'Österreich – Das Paradoxon des zentralistischen Bundesstaa-tes', in Europäisches Zentrum für Föderalismus-Forschung Tübingen (ed.) *Jahrbuch des Föderalismus 2000*, Baden-Baden: Nomos, pp. 251–65.

Gerring, J. (2004) 'What is a case study and what is it good for?', *American Politi-cal Science Review*, 98: 341–54.

Gerring, J. and Thacker, S. C. (2004) 'Political institutions and corruption: the role of unitarism and parliamentarism', *British Journal of Political Science*, 34: 295–330.

Glassmann, U. (2007) *Staatliche Ordnung und räumliche Wirtschaftspolitik: Eine Analyse lokaler Produktionssysteme in Italien und Deutschland*, Wiesba-den: VS Verlag für Sozialwissenschaften.

Gleeson, L. (2003) 'Water Services', in M. Callanan and J. F. Keogan (eds) *Local Government in Ireland: Inside out*, Dublin: Institute of Public Admini-stration, pp. 209–20.

Goldmann, W. (2005) 'Der öffentliche Personennah- und Regionalverkehr in Österreich', *Österreichische Gemeindezeitung*, 71: 18–22.

Goodspeed, T. J. (2002) 'Bailouts in a Federation', *International Tax and Public Finance*, 9: 409–21.

Government of Ireland (1993) *Local Government Act 1991 (Regional Authorities Establishment Order 1993)*, Dublin.

— (1999) *National Development Plan 2000 – 2006*, Dublin.

— (2002) *National Spatial Strategy for Ireland – 2002–2020 – People, Places and Potential*, Dublin.

— (2007) *National Development Plan 2007–2013. Transforming Ireland – A Better Quality of Life for All*, Dublin.

Gray, G. (1991) *Federalism and Health Policy: The development of health systems in Canada and Australia*, Toronto: University of Toronto Press.

Greve, C. and Ejersbo, N. (2002) *When Public-Private Partnerships Fail: The ex-treme case of the NPM-inspired local government of Farum in Denmark*, Nordisk Kommunalforskningskonference, Odense.

Grist, B. (2003) 'Planning', in M. Callanan and J. F. Keogan (eds) *Local Govern-ment in Ireland. Inside out*, Dublin: Institute of Public Administration, pp. 221–52.

Grossmann, B. and Hauth, E. (2004) *Entwicklung der öffentlichen Beschäftigung in Österreich – Projektbericht im Auftrag des Staatsschuldenausschusses*, Vienna.

Halkier, H. (2000) 'The Regionalisation of Danish Regional Policy: Governance and resource dependencies in transition', in M. Danson, H. Halkier and G. Cameron (eds) *Governance, Institutional Change and Regional Development*, Aldershot: Ashgate, pp. 221–45.

—— (2001) 'Regional policy in transition: a multi-level governance perspective on the case of Denmark', *European Planning Studies*, 9: 323–38.

—— (2006) *Denmark: An Overview of Recent Regional Policy Change*, Vaarst: KatPlan.

Hansen, F. and Jensen-Butler, C. (1996) 'Economic crisis and the regional and local economic effects of the welfare state: the case of Denmark', *Regional Studies*, 30: 167–87.

Hansen, K. (1997) 'The municipality between central state and local self-government: towards a new municipality', *Local Government Studies*, 23: 44–69.

Hansen, K. B. and Jamison, A. (2004) *Regional/Local Transport Policy: the Ørestad/Metro project*, Science and technology policy. Research Report 3/2004, Department of Development and Planning, Aalborg University.

Hardiman, N. (1992) 'The State and Economic Interests: Ireland in comparative perspective', in J. H. Goldthorpe and C. T. Whelan (eds) *The Development of Industrial Society in Ireland*, Oxford: Oxford University Press, pp. 329–58.

—— (2002) 'From conflict to co-ordination: economic governance and political innovation in Ireland', *West European Politics*, 25: 1–24.

Haslam, R. (2003) 'The Origins of Irish Local Government', in M. Callanan and J. F. Keogan (eds) *Local Government in Ireland: Inside out*, Dublin: Institute of Public Administration, pp. 14–40.

Hauswirth, I., Herrschel, T. and Newman, P. (2003) 'Incentives and disincentives to city-regional cooperation in the Berlin-Brandenburg conurbation', *European Urban and Regional Studies*, 10: 119–34.

Heintel, M. (2004) 'Regionalpolitik in Österreich. Retrospektive und Perspektive', *Österreichische Zeitschrift für Politikwissenschaft*, 33: 191–208.

—— (2005) 'Regionalmanagements in Österreich. Ergänzendes Instrument der Raumordnungs- und Regionalpolitik in einem politischen Mehrebenensystem', *Österreich in Geschichte und Literatur*, 49: 373–86.

Hermann, C. (2006) 'Liberalisation, privatisation and regulation in the Austrian local public transport sector: Austrian Country Report', Vienna: Forschungs- und Beratungsstelle Arbeitswelt.

Hirschi, C., Schenkel, W. and Widmer, T. (2002) 'Designing sustainable transportation policy for acceptance: a comparison of Germany, the Netherlands and Switzerland', *German Policy Studies / Politikfeldanalyse*, 2(4): 1–40.

Höschen, M. (2007) *Nationaler Starrsinn oder ökologisches Umdenken? Politische Konflikte um den Schweizer Alpentransit im ausgehenden 20.Jahrhundert*, München: M-Press.

House, J. D. and McGrath, K. (2004) 'Innovative governance and development in the new Ireland: social partnership and the integrated approach', *Governance,* 17: 29–58.

Howell, P. J. (2003) 'Roads and Road Traffic', in M. Callanan and J. F. Keogan (eds) *Local Government in Ireland: Inside out,* Dublin: Institute of Public Administration, pp. 189–208.

Huber, S. (2002) *Regionale Wirtschaftspolitik im Bundesland Salzburg. Eine Analyse der 90er Jahre unter besonderer Berücksichtigung der wirtschaftspolitischen Rahmenbedingungen,* unpublished thesis, Universität Salzburg.

Huber, W. (1999) 'Fünf Jahre EU-Regionalförderung in Österreich', *Die Union. Vierteljahreszeitschrift für Integrationsfragen,* 3/4: 13–22.

Immergut, E. M. (1992) *Health Politics: Interests and institutions in Western Europe,* Cambridge: Cambridge University Press.

Indecon International Economic Consultants RPS and Savills HOK (2008) *Cork Area Strategic Plan 2001 – 2020,* Dublin.

Indenrigs- og Sundhedsministeriet Danmark (2002) *Municipalities and Counties in Denmark – Tasks and Finance,* Copenhagen.

—   (2004) *Agreement on a Structural Reform,* Copenhagen.

Indenrigs- og Sundhedsministeriet Danmark. The Commission on Administrative Structure (2004) *Recommendation of the Commission on Administrative Structure – Summary,* Recommendation no. 1434, Copenhagen.

Inman, R. P. (2003) 'Transfers and Bailouts: Enforcing local fiscal discipline with lessons from U.S. federalism', in J. A. Rodden, G. S. Eskeland and J. I. Litvack (eds) *Fiscal Federalism and the Challenge of Hard Budget Constraints,* Cambridge/London: MIT Press, pp. 35–83.

Institut für Föderalismus (2005) *30. Bericht über den Föderalismus in Österreich (2005),* Innsbruck: Institut für Föderalismus.

Institut für Verkehrsplanung und Verkehrstechnik (TUW-IVV) (2007) *Stellungnahme zu den Entscheidungsgrundlagen der Koralmbahn,* Vienna: Technical University of Vienna.

Inter-American Development Bank (1997) 'Fiscal Decision Making in Decentralized Democracies', in Inter-American Development Bank (ed.) *Latin America after a Decade of Reforms,* Washington, DC, pp. 151–84.

International Institute for Management Development, *World Competitiveness Yearbook 2005,* http://www.imd.ch/wcc (Accessed January 08, 2009).

International Monetary Fund (2008) *Government Finance Statistics Yearbook 2007,* Washington.

—   (various years) *Government Finance Statistics,* Washington.

Jacobsen, D. and Kirby, P. (2000) 'Globalisation and Ireland', in D. Jacobsen, P. Kirby and D. Ó Broin (eds) *Taming the Tiger: Social exclusion in a globalised Ireland,* Dublin: New Island, pp. 1–22.

Jensen-Butler, C. (1992) 'Rural industrialisation in Denmark and the role of public policy', *Urban Studies,* 29: 881–904.

Jochimsen, R. (1966) *Theorie der Infrastruktur, Grundlagen der marktwirtschaftli-*

chen Entwicklung, Tübingen: J. C. B. Mohr (Paul Siebeck).

John, G. and Weissensteiner, N. (2002) 'Hohe Stirn, flaches Land', *Falter*, 28 August 2002.

Jorgensen, H. (2002) *Consensus, Cooperation and Conflict: The policy making process in Denmark*, Cheltenham: Edward Elgar.

Kaiser, A. (1997) 'Types of democracy: from classical to New Institutionalism', *Journal of Theoretical Politics*, 9: 419–44.

—— (1998) 'Vetopunkte der Demokratie. Eine Kritik neuerer Ansätze der Demokratietypologie und ein Alternativvorschlag', *Zeitschrift für Parlamentsfragen*, 29: 525–41.

—— (2004) 'Föderalismus. Renaissance eines politischen Ordnungsprinzips?', *Neue Politische Literatur*, 49: 85–113.

Kanonier, A. (2003) 'Jüngere Entwicklungen im österreichischen Raumordnungsrecht', in Österreichische Raumordnungskonferenz (ÖROK) (ed.) *Raumordnung im Umbruch – Herausforderungen, Konflikte, Veränderungen. Festschrift für Eduard Kunze*, Wien: ÖROK, pp. 52–9.

Karpf, P. and Adamovich, L. (eds) (2006) *Die Ortstafelfrage aus Expertensicht. Eine kritische Beleuchtung*, Klagenfurt: Verlag Land Kärnten.

Katzenstein, P. J. (1985) *Small States in World Markets: Industrial policy in Europe*, Ithaca: Cornell University Press.

Keane, M. (2002) 'Ireland in the 1990s: The problem of unbalanced regional development', in V. G. Munley, R. J. Thornton and J. R. Aronson (eds) *The Irish Economy: Successes, Problems, and Prospects*, Amsterdam: JAI Press, pp. 205–23.

Keller, M., Frick, R. and Sager, F. (2008) 'Rail 2000: infrastructure modernization in the light of the National Transport Policy', *Flux: Cahiers scientifiques internationaux réseaux et territoires*, 72/73: 65–77.

Keman, H. (2000) 'Federalism and Policy Performance: A conceptual and empirical inquiry', in U. Wachendorfer-Schmidt (ed.) *Federalism and Political Performance*, London: Routledge, pp. 196–227.

Kenny, L. (2003) 'Local Government and Politics', in M. Callanan and J. F. Keogan (eds) *Local Government in Ireland: Inside out*, Dublin: Institute of Public Administration, pp. 103–22.

Killen, J. E. (2007) 'Transport', in B. Bartley and R. Kitchin (eds) *Understanding Contemporary Ireland*, London/Ann Arbor: Pluto Press, pp. 100–11.

Killen, L. and Ruane, F. (1998) *The Regional Dimension of Industrial Policy and Performance in the Republic of Ireland*, Trinity Economic Paper Series 98/3, Dublin.

Kirby, P. (2007) 'Foreword', in D. O'Broin and E. Waters (eds) *Governing Below the Centre: Local governance in Ireland*, Dublin: New Island Books, pp. 13–6.

Kirchgässner, G. (2004) *Die langfristige Entwicklung der Bundesfinanzen, 1960–2002*, Schweizerisches Institut für Aussenwirtschaft und Angewandte Wirtschaftsforschung, St. Gallen.

—— (2005) 'Sustainable fiscal policy in a federal state: the Swiss example', *Swiss Political Science Review*, 11: 19–46.

Kirchgässner, G. and Pommerehne, W. W. (1996) 'Tax harmonization and tax competition in the European Union: lessons from Switzerland', *Journal of Public Economics*, 60: 351–71.

Kittel, B. and Winner, H. (2005) 'How reliable is pooled analysis in political economy? The globalization-welfare state nexus revisited', *European Journal of Political Research*, 44: 269–93.

Kjaer, P. and Pedersen, O. K. (2001) 'Translating Liberalization: Neoliberalism in the Danish negotiated economy', in J. L. Campbell and O. K. Pedersen (eds) *The Rise of Neoliberalism and Institutional Analysis*, Princeton/ Woodstock: Princeton University Press, pp. 219–48.

Kjellberg, F. (1988) 'Local Government and the Welfare State: Reorganization in Scandinavia', in B. Dente and F. Kjellberg (eds) *The Dynamics of Institutional Change: Local Government reorganization in Western Democracies*, London: Sage, pp. 39–69.

Kluth, M. F. and Andersen, J. B. (1994) *Societal Transformation and New Modes of Governance: Danish industrial policy instruments of the nineties*, Paper Presented at the Supreme Rada's Conference on the Social and Economic Problems of Ukraine as a Transitional Society at the Break of the Millennium, Kiev.

Kommunernes Landsforening, http://www.kl.dk (Accessed January 8, 2009).

Konferenz der kantonalen Direktoren des öffentlichen Verkehrs (2007) *Gesamtschau FinöV: Vernehmlassungsantwort der KÖV zu ZEB*, Zürich.

Kontrollamt Wien (2002) *Prüfung des Gesellschafterwechsels bei der VOR Ges.m.b.H.*, Vienna.

Kriesi, H. (1994) *Les démocraties occidentals: Une approche comparée*, Paris: Economica.

Kristensen, P. H. (1990) 'Industrial Districts in West Jutland, Denmark', in F. Pyke and W. Sengenberger (eds) *Industrial Districts and Local Economic Regeneration*, Geneva: International Institute for Labour Studies, pp. 122–74.

Kristinsson, G. H. (1996) 'Parties, States and Patronage', *West European Politics*, 19: 433–57.

Krogstrup, S. and Wälti, S. (2008) 'Do fiscal rules cause budgetary outcomes?', *Public Choice*, 136: 123–38.

Kübler, D. (2004) *Impacts of New Regionalism on the Relationship between the Citizens and the State: Evidence from Switzerland*, ECPR Joint Sessions of Workshops, Uppsala.

Kübler, D. and Scheuss, U. (2005) 'Metropolitanization and Political Change in Switzerland', in V. Hoffmann-Martinot and J. Sellers (eds) *Metropolitanization and Political Change*, Wiesbaden: VS Verlag für Sozialwissenschaften, pp. 211–29.

La Porta, R., Lopez-de-Silanes, F., Shleifer, A. and Vishny, R. (1999) 'The quality of government', *Journal of Law, Economics, and Organization*, 15: 222–79.

Laakso, M. and Taagepera, R. (1979) 'Effective number of parties: a measure with application to West Europe', *Comparative Political Studies,* 12: 3–27.

Laffan, B. (1996) 'Ireland: A Region without Regions – The odd man out?', in L. Hooghe (ed.) *Cohesion Policy and European Integration: Building multi-level governance,* Oxford: Oxford University Press, pp. 320–41.

Lancaster, T. D. and Hicks, A. M. (2000) 'The Impact of Federalism and Neo-Corporatism on Economic Performance: An analysis of eighteen OECD Countries', in U. Wachendorfer-Schmidt (ed.) *Federalism and Political Performance,* London: Routledge, pp. 228–42.

Lane, J.-E. and Ersson, S. (1997) 'Is Federalism Superior?', in B. Steunenberg and F. A. van Vught (eds) *Political Institutions and Public Policy,* Dordrecht: Kluwer, pp. 85–113.

Larsen, C. A. (2002) 'Municipal size and democracy: a critical analysis of the argument of proximity based on the case of Denmark', *Scandinavian Political Studies,* 25: 317–32.

Larsen, S. K., Lassen, C. and Seibæk, A. I. (1999) *Ørestad – fup & fakta, om hvordan nationale visioner har betydning for offentlighedens indsigt og inddragelse I planlægningen,* Aalborg: Aalborg University.

Lehner, G. (2002) *Finanzielle Beziehungen zwischen Bundesländern und Gemeinden,* Wien: Österreichisches Institut für Wirtschaftsforschung.

— (2006) 'Der Finanzausgleich 2005 – 2008', in P. Bußjäger (ed.) *Finanzausgleich und Finanzverfassung auf dem Prüfstand,* Wien: Braumüller, pp. 33–54.

Levin, J. (1991) 'Measuring the Role of Subnational Governments', in R. Prud'homme (ed.) *Public Finance with Several Levels of Government, Proceedings of the 46th Congress of the IIPF Brussels 1990,* The Hague: Foundation Journal Public Finance, pp. 21–36.

Levinson, D. (1998) *Ethnic Groups Worldwide: A ready reference handbook,* Phoenix: Oryx Press.

Lidström, A. (2001) 'Denmark: Between Scandinavian Democracy and Neo-liberalism', in J. Loughlin (ed.) *Subnational Democracy in the European Union,* Oxford: Oxford University Press, pp. 343–63.

Lieberman, E. S. (2005) 'Nested analysis as a mixed-method strategy for comparative research', *American Political Science Review,* 99: 435–52.

Lijphart, A. (1999) *Patterns of Democracy: Government forms and performance in thirty-six countries,* New Haven: Yale University Press.

Lindenbaum, H. (2003) 'Eine Republik auf Rädern. Infrastruktur- und Verkehrspolitik als Spannungsfeld zwischen Bund und Ländern seit 1945. 1980–2003: Schiene statt Verkehrslawine? Umgekehrt!', in H. Dachs (ed.) *Der Bund und die Länder. Über Dominanz, Kooperation und Konflikte im österreichischen Bundesstaat,* Wien/Köln/Weimar: Böhlau Verlag, pp. 359–420.

Linder, W. and Vatter, A. (2001) 'Institutions and outcomes of Swiss federalism: the role of the cantons in Swiss politics', *West European Politics,* 24: 95–122.

LITRA (2000) *Bahnreform in der Schweiz – Die Erfahrungen nach dem Jahre 1*, Berne: LITRA.
— (2001) *Finanzierung des Agglomerationsverkehrs – Berichte, Erläuterungen und Empfehlungen*, Berne: LITRA.
Lotz, J. (2005) 'Accountability and control in the financing of local government in Denmark', *OECD Journal on Budgeting*, 5: 55–67.
Loughlin, J. (2001) 'Ireland: From colonized nation to "Celtic Tiger"', in J. Loughlin (ed.) *Subnational Democracy in the European Union. Challenges and Opportunities*, Oxford: Oxford University Press, pp. 61–80.
Lundquist, K. -J., and Winther, L. (2006) 'The Interspace between Denmark and Sweden: The Industrial Dynamics of the Öresund Cross-Border Region', *Danish Journal of Geography*, 106(1): 115–129.
Lundvall, B. A., Johnson, B., Andersen, E. S. and Dalum, B. (2002) 'National systems of production, innovation and competence building', *Research Policy*, 31: 213–31.
McDonagh, J. (2001) *Renegotiating Rural Development in Ireland*, Aldershot: Ashgate.
McDonald, F. and Nix, J. (2005) *Chaos at the Crossroads*, Oysterhaven: Gandon Books.
MacGrath, J. (2003) 'Recreation and Amenity Services', in M. Callanan and J. F. Keogan (eds) *Local Government in Ireland. Inside out*, Dublin: Institute of Public Administration, pp. 268–78.
Maddex, R. L. (1998) *Constitutions of the World*, Washington, D.C.: CQ Press.
Maier, G., Tödtling, F. and Trippl, M. (2006) *Regional- und Stadtökonomik 2. Regionalentwicklung und Regionalpolitik*, Wien/New York: Springer.
Majoor, S. and Jørgensen, J. (2007) 'Copenhagen Ørestad: Public partnership in search of the market', in W. Salet and E. Gualini (eds) *Framing Strategic Urban Projects – Learning from the current experiences in European urban regions*, London: Routledge, pp. 172–98.
Markovitz, A. S. (1996) 'Austrian Corporatism in Comparative Perspective', in G. Bischof and A. Pelinka (eds) *Austro-Corporatism: Past, present, future*, New Brunswick: Transaction Publishers, pp. 5–20.
Marshall, M. G. and Jaggers, K., *Polity IV Dataset*, Computer file, Version p4v2002.
Meyler, A. and Strobl, E. (2000) 'Job Generation and regional industrial policy in Ireland', *The Economic and Social Review*, 31: 111–28.
Mitchell, P. (2006) '"Ireland: O What a Tangled Web...": Delegation, accountability, and executive power', in K. Strøm, W. C. Müller and T. Bergman (eds) *Delegation and Accountability in Parliamentary Democracies*, Oxford: Oxford University Press, pp. 418–44.
Morgenroth, E. (2000) 'Regionalisation and the Functions of Regional and Local Government', in A. Barrett, R. Barrett and D. J. Duffy (eds) *Budget Perspectives: Proceedings of a conference held on 19 September 2000*, Dublin: ESRI, pp. 1–19.
— (2006) *Economic Integration and Structural Change: The case of Irish Regions*, ESRI Working Paper, Dublin: ESRI.

—   (2010) 'Regional dimension of taxes and public expenditure in Ireland',
          Regional Studies, 44(6): 777–89.
Moseley, M. J., Cherrett, T. and Cawley, M. (2001) 'Local partnerships for rural
          development: Ireland's experience in context', *Irish Geography,* 34:
          176–93.
Movia, http://www.movia.dk (Accessed January 8, 2009).
Müller, W. C. (2005) 'Austria: A complex electoral system with subtle effects',
          in M. Gallagher and P. Mitchell (eds) *The Politics of Electoral Systems,*
          Oxford: Oxford University Press, pp. 397–416.
Murphy, A. E. (2000) *The 'Celtic Tiger': An analysis of Ireland's economic growth
          performance*, EU Working Papers, Robert Schuman Centre for Advanced
          Studies, European University Institute.
Murphy, G. (2005) 'Interest Groups in the Policy-Making Process', in J. Coakley
          and M. Gallagher (eds) *Politics in the Republic of Ireland,* London: Rout-
          ledge, pp. 352–83.
Musgrave, R. A. (1959) *The Theory of Public Finance*, New York: McGraw-Hill.
Nannestad, P. (2008) 'Gesetzgebung im politischen System Dänemarks', in W.
          Ismayr (ed.) *Gesetzgebung in Westeuropa. EU-Staaten und Europäische
          Union,* Wiesbaden: VS Verlag für Sozialwissenschaften, pp. 133–58.
National Roads Authority, http://www.nra.ie/ (Accessed January 8, 2009).
—   *Road Traffic Forecasts,* http://www.nra.ie/Publications/RoadTraffic/
          (Accessed January 08, 2009).
Neubauer, J., Dubois, A., Hanell, T., Lähteenmäki-Smith, K., Pettersson, K., Roto,
          J. and Steineke, J. M. (2007) *Regional Development in the Nordic Coun-
          tries 2007*, Nordregio Report 2007:1, Stockholm: Nordregio.
Norregaard, J. (1997) 'Tax Assignment', in T. Ter-Minassian (ed.) *Fiscal Federal-
          ism in Theory and Practice,* Washington: International Monetary Fund,
          pp. 49–72.
Norris, M. (2003) 'Housing', in M. Callanan and J. F. Keogan (eds) *Local Govern-
          ment in Ireland: Inside out,* Dublin: Institute of Public Administration,
          pp. 165–88.
North, D. C. (1990a) *Institutions, Institutional Change, and Economic Perfor-
          mance*, Cambridge: Cambridge University Press.
—   (1990b) 'A Transaction Cost Theory of Politics', *Journal of Theoretical
          Politics*, 2: 355–67.
O'Broin, D. and Waters, E. (2007) *Governing Below the Centre: Local governance
          in Ireland*, Dublin: TASC at New Island.
O'Donnell, R. (1998) *Ireland's Economic Transformation: Industrial policy, Eu-
          ropean Integration and social partnership*, Working Paper, Pittsburgh,
          PA: European Union Center, University Center for International Studies,
          University of Pittsburgh.
O'Halpin, E. and Connolly, E. (1999) 'Parliaments and Pressure Groups: The
          Irish experience of change', in P. Norton (ed.) *Parliaments and Pressure
          Groups in Western Europe,* London: Cass, pp. 124–44.
O'Leary, E. (2003a) 'A Critical Evaluation of Irish Regional Policy', in E. O'Leary

(ed.) *Irish Regional Development: A New Agenda,* Dublin: Liffey Press, pp. 15–37.

— (2003b) 'Introduction', in E. O'Leary (ed.) *Irish Regional Development: A new agenda,* Dublin: Liffey Press, pp. 1–12.

O'Riordain, S. (2003) 'The Environment: Protection and Services', in M. Callanan and J. F. Keogan (eds) *Local Government in Ireland: Inside out,* Dublin: Institute of Public Administration, pp. 253–268.

O'Sullivan, T. (2003) 'Local Areas and Structures', in M. Callanan and J. F. Keogan (eds) *Local Government in Ireland: Inside out,* Dublin: Institute of Public Administration, pp. 41–81.

Oates, W. E. (1972) *Fiscal Federalism,* London: Harcourt Brace Jovanovich.

— (2002) 'A Reconsideration of Environmental Federalism', in J. List and A. D. Zeeuw (eds) *Recent Advances in Environmental Economics,* Cheltenham: Edward Elgar, pp. 1–32.

— (2005) 'Toward a second-generation theory of fiscal federalism', *International Tax and Public Finance,* 12: 349–73.

Obinger, H. (2002) 'Föderalismus und wohlfahrtsstaatliche Entwicklung. Österreich und die Schweiz im Vergleich', *Politische Vierteljahresschrift,* 43: 235–71.

OECD (1997) *Managing Across Levels of Government,* Paris: OECD.

— (2001) *Lernen für das Leben: Erste Ergebnisse von PISA 2000,* Paris: OECD.

— (2006) *Economic Survey of Ireland 2006,* Paris: OECD.

— (2008) *OECD Public Management Reviews: Ireland. Towards an integrated public service,* http://www.bettergov.ie/attached_files/upload/IRELAND-Towards%20An%20Integrated%20Public%20Service.pdf (Accessed October 8, 2008).

— (various years) *Economic Outlook,* Paris: OECD.

— *Main Economic Indicators,* http://www.sourceoecd.org (Accessed January 8, 2009).

— National Accounts Statistics, doi:10.1787/data-00369-en (Accessed December 14, 2011).

Office of the Attorney General, *Irish Statute Book. Acts of the Oireachtas by decade,* http://www.Irishstatutebook.ie/acts.html (Accessed January 8, 2009).

Oireachtas (1991) *Local Government Act 1991,* Number 11 of 1991, Dublin.

— (1997) *Public Service Management Act 1997,* Number 27 of 1997, Dublin.

— (2000) *Planning and Development Act 2000,* Number 30 of 2000, Dublin.

— (2001) *Local Government Act 2001,* Number 37 of 2001, Dublin.

— (2003) *Local Government (No. 2) Act 2003,* Number 17 of 2003, Dublin.

— (2006) *Local Government (Business Improvement Districts) Act 2006,* Number 42 of 2006, Dublin.

Økonomi- og Erhvervsministeriet (1993) *Business Environment in Denmark,* Copenhagen.

— (2003) *The Danish Regional Growth Strategy,* Copenhagen.

Olson, M. (1969) 'The principle of "Fiscal Equivalence": the division of responsibilities among different levels of government', *American Economic Review,* 59: 479–87.

Österreichische Forschungsförderungsgesellschaft (FFG), www.ffg.at (Accessed November 21, 2008).

Österreichische Raumordnungskonferenz (ÖROK), www.oerok.gv.at (Accessed January 8, 2009).

Österreichische Raumordnungskonferenz (ÖROK), *ÖROK-Atlas,* www.oerok-atlas.at (Accessed January 7, 2009).

—   (2002) *Österreichisches Raumentwicklungskonzept 2001,* Vienna.

—   (2006) *STRAT.AT 2007|2013: Nationaler Strategischer Rahmenplan Österreich 2007–2013,* Vienna.

Österreichischer Nationalrat (1999) *Bundesgesetz über die Ordnung des öffentlichen Personennah- und Regionalverkehrs (Öffentlicher Personennah- und Regionalverkehrsgesetz 1999 – ÖPNRV-G 1999),* BGBl, I 204/99.

—   (2001) *Vereinbarung zwischen dem Bund, den Ländern und den Gemeinden über eine Verstärkung der stabilitätsorientierten Budgetpolitik (Österreichischer Stabilitätspakt 2001),* BGBl. I Nr. 39/2002.

—   (2006) *Vereinbarung zwischen dem Bund, den Ländern und den Gemeinden über eine Weiterführung der stabilitätsorientierten Budgetpolitik (Österreichischer Stabilitätspakt 2005),* BGBl. I Nr. 19/2006.

Österreichischer Städtebund (2008) *Österreichs Städte in Zahlen,* Vienna: Österreichischer Städtebund/Statistik Austria.

Österreichisches Bundeskanzleramt, http://www.bka.gv.at/ (Accessed December 14, 2011).

Ostrom, E. (1990) *Governing the Commons: The evolution of institutions for collective action,* Cambridge: Cambridge University Press.

Ostrom, V. (1973) 'Can federalism make a difference?', *Publius: The Journal of Federalism,* 3: 197–238.

Owens, J. and Panella, G. (eds) (1991) *Local Government: An international perspective,* Amsterdam: North Holland.

Page, E. C. (1991) *Localism and Centralism in Europe: The political and legal bases of local self-government,* Oxford: Oxford University Press.

Painter, M. (1998) *Collaborative Federalism: Economic reform in Australia in the 1990s,* Cambridge: Cambridge University Press.

Pallaver, G. (2008) 'Ein Jahr im Tiefflug – Föderalismus in Österreich: Ein Rückblick auf das Jahr 2006', in Europäisches Zentrum für Föderalismus-Forschung Tübingen (ed.) *Jahrbuch des Föderalismus 2007,* Baden-Baden: Nomos, pp. 355–72.

Paulick, S. (2006) 'Grosse Lücken und wenig Geld zum Stopfen', *Wirtschaftsblatt,* 30 May 2006.

Pedersen, N. J. M. (2002a) 'Challenges of the Danish Equalization Scheme: Redistribution and incentives', in G. Färber and N. Otter (eds) *Reform of Local Fiscal Equalization in Europe,* Speyer: Forschungsinstitut für öffentliche Verwaltung, pp. 131–62.

—   (2002b) 'Local Government and Debt Financing in Denmark', in B. Dafflon (ed.) *Local Public Finance in Europe: Balancing the budget and controlling debt,* Cheltenham: Edward Elgar, pp. 93–114.

Pedersen, O. K. (2006) 'Corporatism and Beyond: The negotiated economy', in J. L. Campbell, J. A. Hall and O. K. Pedersen (eds) *National Identity and the Varieties of Capitalism: The Danish experience,* Montreal/Kingston: McGill-Queen's University Press, pp. 245–70.

Pelinka, A. (1997) 'Das politische System Österreichs', in W. Ismayr (ed.) *Die politischen Systeme Westeuropas,* Opladen: Leske + Budrich, pp. 479–508.

—   (2008) 'Gesetzgebung im politischen System Österreichs', in W. Ismayr (ed.) *Gesetzgebung in Westeuropa. EU-Staaten und Europäische Union,* Wiesbaden: VS Verlag für Sozialwissenschaften, pp. 431–61.

Peneder, M. (1999) 'Creating a Coherent Design for Cluster Analysis and Related Policies: The Austrian "tip" experience', in OECD (ed.) *Boosting Innovation: The cluster approach,* Paris: OECD, pp. 339–59.

Pernthaler, P. and Wegschneider, E. (2000) *Der Konsultationsmechanismus in der österreichischen Finanzverfassung,* Innsbruck: Institut für Föderalismus.

Peterson, P. E. (1995) *The Price of Federalism,* Washington: Brookings.

Petersson, O. (1994) *The Government and Politics of the Nordic Countries,* Stockholm: Fritze.

Picard, L. A. (1983) 'Decentralization, "Recentralization" and "Steering Mechanisms": paradoxes of local government in Denmark', *Polity,* 15: 536–54.

Pierson, P. (1995) 'Fragmented welfare states: federal institutions and the development of social policy', *Governance,* 8: 449–78.

—   (1998) 'Irresistible forces, immovable objects: post-industrial welfare states confront permanent austerity', *Journal of European Public Policy,* 5: 539–60.

Planungsgemeinschaft Ost, www.pgo.wien.at (Accessed August 5, 2008).

Plümper, T., Tröger, V. and Manow, P. (2005) 'Panel data analysis in comparative politics: linking method to theory', *European Journal of Political Research,* 44: 327–54.

Pobal, *Rural Transport Programme,* http://www.pobal.ie/RTP (Accessed January 8, 2009).

Pommerehne, W. W., Kirchgässner, G. and Feld, L. P. (1996) 'Tax Harmonization and Tax Competition at State-Local Levels: Lessons from Switzerland', in G. Pola, G. France and R. Levaggi (eds) *Developments in Local Government Finance: Theory and policy,* Cheltenham: Edward Elgar, pp. 251–330.

Porter, M. E. (1990) *The Competitive Advantage of Nations,* New York: The Free Press.

Porter, M. E., Cornelius, P. K., McArthur, J., Sachs, J. D. and Warner, A. (2001) *The Global Competitiveness Report 2001,* New York: Oxford University Press.

Pujol, F. and Weber, L. (2003) 'Are preferences for fiscal discipline endogenous?', *Public Choice*, 114: 421–44.

Railway Procurement Agency, http://www.rpa.ie/ (Accessed January 8, 2009).

Rallis, T., Meulengracht, K. and Vilhof, P. (1984) 'The organization of public transport in Denmark', *Transportation Research Part A*, 18: 163–75.

Rau, H. and Hennessy, C. (2009) 'The Road to Sustainable Transport? Rural transport programmes and policies in Ireland', in J. McDonagh, A. Varley and S. Shortall (eds) *A Living Countryside? The Politics of Sustainable Development in Rural Ireland*, Aldershot: Ashgate, pp. 361–80.

Rau, H. and McDonagh, J. (2007) 'Transport Policy in Ireland', NUIG working paper, Galway.

Reeves, E. (2003) 'Public-private partnerships in Ireland: policy and practice', *Public Money & Management*, 23: 163–70.

Reynolds-Feighan, A. (2003) 'Accessibility, Transportation, Infrastructure Planning and Irish Regional Policy: Issues and dilemmas', in E. O'Leary (ed.) *Irish Regional Development: A new agenda*, Dublin: Liffey Press, pp. 163–79.

Ridge, M. (1992) 'Local government finance and equalisation: the case of Ireland', *Fiscal Studies*, 13: 54–73.

Riker, W. H. (1969) 'Six books in search of a subject or does federalism exist and does it matter?', *Comparative Politics*, 2: 135–46.

Rodden, J. A. (2002) 'The dilemma of fiscal federalism: grants and fiscal performance around the world', *American Journal of Political Science*, 46: 670–87.

— (2004) 'Comparative federalism and decentralization: on meaning and measurement', *Comparative Politics*, 36: 481–99.

Rodden, J. A., Eskeland, G. S. and Litvack, J. (eds) (2003) *Fiscal Decentralization and the Challenge of Hard Budget Constraints*, Cambridge/London: MIT Press.

Rohlfing, I. (2008) 'What you see and what you get: pitfalls and principles of nested analysis in comparative research', *Comparative Political Studies*, 41: 1492–1514.

Rohlfing, I. (2012) *Case Studies and Causal Inference: An integrative framework*, Basingstoke: Palgrave Macmillan.

Rosner, A. (2000) *Koordinationsinstrumente der österreichischen Länder*, Innsbruck: Institut für Föderalismus.

Ross, J. F. L. (1995) 'When co-operation divides: Öresund, the channel tunnel and new politics of European transport', *Journal of European Public Policy*, 2: 115–46.

Saalfeld, T. (2008) 'Gesetzgebung im politischen System der Irischen Republik', in W. Ismayr (ed.) *Gesetzgebung in Westeuropa. EU-Staaten und Europäische Union*, Wiesbaden: VS Verlag für Sozialwissenschaften, pp. 201–28.

Sabel, C. (1996) *Ireland: Local Partnerships and Social Innovations*, Paris: OECD.

Sager, F. (2003) 'Kompensationsmöglichkeiten föderaler Vollzugsdefizite. Das Beispiel der kantonalen Alkoholpräventionspolitiken', *Swiss Political Science Review*, 9: 309–33.

— (2006) 'Infrastrukturpolitik: Verkehr, Energie und Telekommunikation', in U. Klöti, P. Knoepfel, H. Kriesi, W. Linder, Y. Papadopoulos and P. Sciarini (eds) *Handbuch der Schweizer Politik*, 4th edn, Zürich: NZZ Verlag, pp. 709–36.

Sager, F. and Kaufmann, V. (2006) 'The coordination of local policies for urban development and public transportation in four Swiss cities', *Journal of Urban Affairs*, 28: 353–74.

Sager, F., Kaufmann, V. and Joye, D. (1999) 'Die Koordination von Raumplanung und Verkehrspolitik in urbanen Räumen der Schweiz: Determinanten der politischen Geographie, der politischen Kultur oder der institutionellen Struktur', *Swiss Political Science Review*, 5: 25–55.

Sager, F. and Rüefli, C. (2005) 'Die Evaluation öffentlicher Politiken mit föderalistischen Vollzugsarrangements. Eine konzeptionelle Erweiterung des Stufenmodells und eine praktische Anwendung', *Swiss Political Science Review*, 11: 101–29.

Sager, F. and Steffen, I. (2006) 'Die Kantone im Vernehmlassungsverfahren des Bundes: Wirkungsweise und Reformansätze', in A. Vatter (ed.) *Föderalismusreform: Wirkungsweise und Reformansätze föderativer Institutionen in der Schweiz*, Zürich: NZZ Verlag, pp. 152–73.

Sawer, G. (1969) *Modern Federalism*, Carleton: Pitman Australia.

Schaltegger, C. A. (2001) 'Ist der Schweizer Föderalismus zu kleinräumig?', *Swiss Political Science Review*, 7: 1–18.

Schaltegger, C. A. and Frey, R. L. (2003) 'Finanzausgleich und Föderalismus: Zur Neugestaltung der föderalen Finanzbeziehungen am Beispiel der Schweiz', *Perspektiven der Wirtschaftspolitik*, 4: 239–58.

— (2004) 'Fiskalische Budgetbeschränkungen zur Stabilisierung öffentlicher Haushalte', *Die Volkswirtschaft – Das Magazin für Wirtschaftspolitik*, 1 April 2004, 16–19.

Scharpf, F. W. (1987) *Sozialdemokratische Krisenpolitik in Europa*, Frankfurt am Main: Campus.

— (1992) 'Koordination durch Verhandlungssysteme. Analytische Konzepte und institutionelle Lösungen', in A. Benz, F. W. Scharpf and R. Zintl (eds) *Horizontale Politikverflechtung: Zur Theorie von Verhandlungssystemen*, Frankfurt a. M.: Campus, pp. 51–96.

— (1993) 'Positive und negative Koordination in Verhandlungssystemen', in A. Héritier (ed.) *Policy Analyse. Kritik und Neuorientierung*, Politische Vierteljahresschrift, Sonderheft 24, Opladen: Westdeutscher Verlag, pp. 57–83.

— (1997) *Games Real Actors Play: Actor-centered institutionalism in policy research*, Boulder: Westview Press.

Scharpf, F. W., Reissert, B. and Schnabel, F. (1976) *Politikverflechtung: Theorie und Empirie des kooperativen Föderalismus in der Bundesrepublik*, Kronberg: Scriptor Verlag.

Schenkel, W. (2001) 'Die Agglomeration im schweizerischen Föderalismus', *Swiss Political Science Review*, 7: 141–46.

Scherer, R. and Schnell, K.-D. (2008) 'Die ‚Neue‘ Regionalpolitik in der Schweiz: Von und für Europa lernen?', in Europäisches Zentrum für Föderalismus-Forschung Tübingen (ed.) *Jahrbuch des Föderalismus 2007 – Föderalismus, Subsidiarität und Regionen in Europa*, Baden-Baden: Nomos, pp. 620–34.

Schiavo-Campo, S., de Tommaso, G. and Mukherjee, A. (1997) *An International Statistical Survey of Government Employment and Wages*, World Bank Policy Research Working Paper 1806, Washington: World Bank.

Schindegger, F. (1999) *Raum. Ordnung. Politik.*, Wien: Böhlau.

Schmidt, M. G. (1996) 'When parties matter: A review of the possibilties and limits of partisan influence on public policy', *European Journal of Political Research*, 30: 155–83.

Schneider, F. (2002) 'Local fiscal equalisation based on fiscal capacity: the case of Austria', *Fiscal Studies*, 23: 105–33.

Schönbäck, W. and Bröthaler, J. (2005) 'Zur horizontalen Verteilungsgerechtigkeit im kommunalen Finanzausgleich Österreichs', *Rechts- und Finanzierungspraxis der Gemeinden*, 1: 4–13.

Schremmer, C. and Tödtling, F. (1996) *Regionale Industriepolitik für Österreich*, Wien: Österreichisches Institut für Raumplanung.

Schwab, B. and Kübler, D. (2001) *Metropolitan governance and the "democratic deficit". Theoretical issues and empirical findings*, http://www.sbi.dk/eura/workshops/papers/workshop2/schwab.pdf (Accessed December 11, 2008).

Schwarz, W. (2003) 'Regionalpolitik im Wandel: Von zentralistischer Planung zu partnerschaftlichen Netzwerken – das Modell Niederösterreich', in Österreichische Raumordnungskonferenz (ÖROK) (ed.) *Raumordnung im Umbruch: Herausforderungen, Konflikte, Veränderungen. Festschrift für Eduard Kunze*, Wien: ÖROK, pp. 74–89.

Schweizerischer Bundesrat (1994) *Bericht über die erste Etappe von Bahn 2000 vom 11.Mai 1994*, Berne.

— (1995) *Verordnung vom 18. Dezember 1995 über Abgeltungen, Darlehen und Finanzhilfen nach Eisenbahngesetz (Abgeltungsverordnung, ADFV)*, SR 742.101.1, Berne.

— (2006) *Bericht des Bundesrates über die Schuldenentwicklung der öffentlichen Haushalte vom 23. August 2006*, Berne.

— (2007a) *Botschaft zur Gesamtschau FinöV. Bau und Finanzierung von Infrastrukturvorhaben des öffentlichen Verkehrs*, Berne.

— (2007b) *Subventionsbericht 2008 des Bundesrats*, Berne.

Scocozza, B. and Jensen, G. (2005) *Politikens Etbinds Danmarkshistorie*, 3rd edn, Copenhagen: Politikens Forlag.

Scruggs, L. (2003) *Sustaining Abundance: Environmental performance in industrial democracies*, Cambridge: Cambridge University Press.

Searing, D. D. (1994) *Westminster's World: Understanding political roles*, Cambridge/London: Harvard University Press.

Sekretariat für Wirtschaft. Seco, *Auswahl an guten Beispielen der aktuellen Regionalpolitik,* http://www.seco.admin.ch/themen/00476/00496/00498/00503/index.html?lang=de (Accessed January 8, 2009).

— *Pilotprojekte zur neuen Regionalpolitik,* http://www.seco.admin.ch/themen/00476/00496/00498/00504/index.html?lang=de (Accessed January 8, 2009).

— *Neue Regionalpolitik,* http://www.seco.admin.ch/themen/00476/00496/00498/index.html?lang=de (Accessed January 8, 2009).

Sheehy, E. (2003) 'City and County Management', in M. Callanan and J. F. Keogan (eds) *Local Government in Ireland. Inside out,* Dublin: Institute of Public Administration, pp. 123–42.

Smith, N. J.-A. (2004) 'Deconstructing "globalisation" in Ireland', *Policy & Politics,* 32: 503–19.

Smith, R. L. and Young, K. D. S. (2001) *Linear Regression.* Draft version for lectures in statistics at the University of North Carolina, Chapel Hill, USA, and the University of Surrey, Guildford, UK.

Spahn, P. B. (1997a) 'Intergovernmental Transfers in Switzerland and Germany', in E. Ahmad (ed.) *Financing Decentralized Expenditures: An international comparison of grants,* Cheltenham: Edward Elgar, pp. 103–33.

— (1997b) 'Switzerland', in T. Ter-Minassian (ed.) *Fiscal Federalism in Theory and Practice,* Washington: International Monetary Fund, pp. 324–41.

Statistics Danmark, http://www.dst.dk (Accessed January 8, 2009).

Statistik Austria, www.statistik.at (Accessed January 25, 2009).

Statsforvaltningerne, http://www.statsforvaltning.dk (Accessed January 8, 2009).

Stauffer, T. (2001) *Instrumente des Haushaltsausgleichs: Ökonomische Analyse und rechtliche Umsetzung,* Basel: Helbing & Lichtenhahn.

Steiner, M. and Jud, T. (1998) 'Regional Development Institutions in Austria: Trends in organisation, policies and implementation', in H. Halkier, M. Danson and C. Damborg (eds) *Regional Development Agencies in Europe,* London/Philadelphia: Jessica Kingsley, pp. 48–65.

Sternberg, R. and Bergmann, H. (2003) *Global Entrepreneurship Monitor – Länderbericht Deutschland 2002,* Köln: Universität zu Köln, Wirtschafts- und Sozialgeographisches Institut.

Storey, D. (1999) 'Issues of integration, participation and empowerment in rural development: the case of LEADER in the Republic of Ireland', *Journal of Rural Studies,* 15: 307–15.

Taylor, G. (2005) *Negotiated Governance and Public Policy in Ireland,* Manchester: Manchester University Press.

Ter-Minassian, T. (ed.) (1997) *Fiscal Federalism in Theory and Practice,* Washington: International Monetary Fund.

The Copenhagen Post Online (2002) 'Mayor flees fraud scandal', 14 February 2002.

Thierstein, A. and Behrendt, H. (2001) *Überprüfung der Zielerreichung der Schweizer Regionalpolitik – im Auftrag des Staatssekretariats für Wirtschaft (seco)*, Zürich: Institut für Orts-, Regional- und Landesplanung ORL – Fachbereich Raumordnung der ETH Zürich.

Thöni, E., Garbislander, S. and Haas, D.-J. (2002) 'Local Budgeting and Local Borrowing in Austria', in B. Dafflon (ed.) *Local Public Finance in Europe*, Cheltenham: Edward Elgar, pp. 45–73.

Thorlakson, L. (2003) 'Comparing federal institutions: power and representation in six federations', *West European Politics*, 26: 1–22.

Tiebout, C. M. (1956) 'A pure theory of local expenditures', *Journal of Political Economy*, 64: 416–24.

— (1961) 'An Economic Theory of Fiscal Decentralization', in National Bureau of Economic Research (ed.) *Public Finances: Needs, Sources, Utilization*, Princeton: Princeton University Press, pp. 79–96.

Tonboe, J. (1991) 'Centralized Economic Control in a Decentralized Welfare State: Danish central-local government relations 1970–86', in C. Pickvance and E. Preteceille (eds) *State Restructuring and Local Power: A comparative perspective*, London/New York: Pinter Publishers, pp. 18–47.

Transport 21 Division – Department of Transport (2008) *Transport 21 – Second Annual Progress Report to the Government – 2007*, Dublin, http://www.transport21.ie/ (Accessed January 8, 2009).

Treisman, D., *Decentralization and the Quality of Government*, http://www.sscnet.ucla.edu/polisci/faculty/treisman/DecandGovt.pdf (Accessed December 5, 2008).

Tsebelis, G. (2002) *Veto Players: How political institutions work*, Princeton: Russell Sage Foundation.

Tsebelis, G. and Money, J. (1997) *Bicameralism*, Cambridge: Cambridge University Press.

Turok, I. (2000) *Local Partnerships in Ireland. Report for the OECD*, Glasgow: Glasgow University.

United Nations (2001) *World Urbanization Prospects: The 2001 revision*, New York: Population Division of the United Nations Secretariat.

— (2002) *Seventh United Nations Survey of Crime Trends and Operations of Criminal Justice Systems, covering the period 1998–2000*, New York: United Nations Office on Drugs and Crime, Centre for International Crime Prevention.

— (2004) *World Population Prospects: The 2004 revision*, New York: Population Division of the United Nations Secretariat.

United Nations Development Programme (2004) *Human Development Report 2004*, New York: UNDP.

United Nations Economic Commission for Europe (2005) *Annual Bulletin of Transport Statistics for Europe and North America*, Geneva: UNECE.

United Nations Educational Scientific and Cultural Organization, *World Education Indicators Programme*, http://www.uis.unesco.org (Accessed December 5, 2008).

van der Kamp, H. W. (2001) 'Transport in Ireland: development of a sustainable infrastructure', *International Journal of Environmental Technology and Management,* 1: pp. 283–86.

Varley, T. and Curtin, C. (2002) 'Community Empowerment *via* Partnership? The "local community" in rural Ireland's area based development regime', in G. Taylor (ed.) *Issues in Irish Public Policy,* Dublin: Irish Academic Press, pp. 127–150.

Vatter, A. (2002) *Kantonale Demokratien im Vergleich: Entstehungsgründe, Interaktionen und Wirkungen politischer Institutionen in den Schweizer Kantonen,* Opladen: Leske + Budrich.

—   (2005) 'The transformation of access and veto points in Swiss federalism', *Regional and Federal Studies,* 15: 1–17.

—   (2008) 'Swiss consensus democracy in transition: a re-analysis of Lijphart's concept of democracy for Switzerland from 1997 to 2007', *World Political Science Review,* 4: 1–40.

Veraguth, T. (2003) 'Der Wirtschaftsförderungsindex – eine Analyse der einge-setzten Ressourcen zur Promotion kantonaler Standorte', http://emaga-zine.credit-suisse.com/app/_customtags/download_tracker.cfm?dom =emagazine.credit-suisse.ch&doc=/data/_product_documents/_arti-cles/32252/Wirtschaftsf%25c3%25b6rderung.pdf&ts=20081124123222 (Accessed January 8, 2009).

Verheijen, T. and Millar, M. (1998) 'Reforming public policy processes and secur-ing accountability: Ireland in a comparative perspective', *International Review of Administrative Sciences,* 64: 97–118.

Villadsen, C. (2002) 'Clusters crossing borders: Aalborg University and regional development in Northern Jutland, Denmark', *Industry and Higher Edu-cation,* 16: 117–21.

von Maravic, P. (2007) *Verwaltungsmodernisierung und dezentrale Korruption,* Bern/Stuttgart/Wien: Haupt.

von Stokar, T., Vettori, A., Steinemann, M., Schmidt, N., Schoenenberger, A. and Bohr, N. (2004) *Evaluation des Bundesbeschlusses zugunsten wirtschaft-licher Erneuerungsgebiete – Schlussbericht,* Zürich: SECO.

Wachendorfer-Schmidt, U. (1999) 'Der Preis des Föderalismus in Deutschland', *Politische Vierteljahresschrift,* 40: 3–39.

—   (2000) 'Introduction', in U. Wachendorfer-Schmidt (ed.) *Federalism and Political Performance,* London: Routledge, pp. 1–17.

Walsh, J. (1998) 'Local development and local government in the Republic of Ireland', *Local Economy,* 12: 329–41.

—   (2000) 'Dynamic Regional Development in the EU Periphery: Ireland in the 1990s', in P. Roberts, D. Shaw and J. Walsh (eds) *Regional Planning and Development in Europe,* London: Ashgate, pp. 117–37.

—   (2002) 'The National Spatial Strategy as a Framework for Achieving Bal-anced Regional Development', in J. McDonagh (ed.) *Economy, Society and Peripherality: Experiences from the West of Ireland,* Galway: Arlen House, pp. 55–79.

Wälti, S. (1996) 'Institutional reform of federalism: changing the players rather than the rules of the game', *Swiss Political Science Review,* 2: 1–29.

— (2004) 'How multilevel structures affect environmental policy in industrialized countries', *European Journal of Political Research,* 43: 599–634.

Wälti, S. and Bullinger, A.-B. (2000) 'Regional Policy and Energy Policy in the Light of Swiss Federalism', in D. Braun (ed.) *Public Policy and Federalism,* Aldershot: Ashgate, pp. 78–107.

Waterford City Council (2002) *Waterford Planning Land Use and Transportation Study (PLUTS),* Waterford.

Watts, R. L. (1999) *Comparing Federal Systems,* Kingston: McGill Queens University Press.

Weber, K. (1992) 'Macht im Schatten?', *Österreichische Zeitschrift für Politikwissenschaft,* 21: 405–18.

Weingast, B. R. (1995) 'The economic role of political institutions: market-preserving federalism and economic development', *Journal of Law, Economics, and Organization,* 11: 1–31.

— (2006) 'Second Generation Fiscal Federalism: Implications for Decentralized Democratic Governance and Economic Development', http://papers.ssrn.com/sol3/papers.cfm?abstract_id=1153440 (Accessed December 12, 2008).

Weingast, B. R. and Qian, Y. (1997) 'Federalism as a commitment to preserving market incentives', *Journal of Economic Perspectives,* 11: 83–92.

Whitelegg, K. (2004) *Patchwork policy making – linking innovation and transport policy in Austria: Austrian transport case study for the OECD NIS MONIT Network,* Wien: Österreichisches Institut für Wirtschaftsforschung.

Wibbels, E. (2000) 'Federalism and the politics of macroeconomic policy and performance', *American Journal of Political Science,* 44: 687–702.

Wieser, R. (2002) 'Wettbewerb im öffentlichen Personennah- und -regionalverkehr', *Wifo-Monatsberichte,* 03/2002, pp. 167–178.

Wilensky, H. L. (1975) *The Welfare State and Equality,* Berkeley: University of California Press.

Williamson, O. E. (1985) *The Economic Institutions of Capitalism: Firms, markets, relational contracting,* New York/London: Free Press, Collier Macmillan.

— (1991) 'Comparative economic organization: the analysis of discrete structural alternatives', *Administrative Science Quarterly,* 36: 269–96.

Wirtschaftsblatt (2002) 'Interview mit Matthias Reichhold', 26 February 2002.

Wolfgruber, E. (1997) 'Das Tätigkeitsprofil der Abgeordneten in ausgewählten österreichischen Bundesländern', *Österreichische Zeitschrift für Politikwissenschaft,* 26: 7–22.

Wyss, K. and Lorenz, N. (2000) 'Decentralization and central and regional coordination of health services: the case of Switzerland', *International Journal of Health Planning and Management,* 15: 103–14.

Yuill, D., Ferry, M. and Gross, T. (2007) *Review, Revision, Reform: Recent regional policy developments in the EU and Norway,* EoRPA Paper 07/1, Glasgow: University of Strathclyde.

Zank, W. (1991) 'Brückenschlag für Volvo', *Die ZEIT,* 5 April 1991.

Expert Interviews

Switzerland

Boesch, Martin, Professor of Theoretical and Applied Economic and Social Geography, University of St Gallen, 14.5.2008

Braun, Dietmar, Professor at and Director of the Institut d'études politiques et internationales (IEPI), University of Lausanne, 7.7.2007

Dafflon, Bernard, Professor of Public Finance, University of Fribourg, 5.7.2007

Kirchgässner, Gebhard, Professor of Economics and Econometrics, University of St Gallen, 4.7.2007

Kübler, Daniel, Assistant Professor of Political Science, University of Zurich, 15.5.2008

Ladner, Andreas, Professor of Institutional Policies, Swiss Graduate School of Public Administration (IDHEAP), Lausanne, 7.7.2007

Maibach, Markus, Economist, Project Manager in the Area of Transport, Infras, Zurich, 13.5.2008

Papadopoulos, Ioannis, Professor at the Institut d'études politiques et internationales (IEPI), University of Lausanne, 6.7.2007

Sager, Fritz, Assistant Professor of Policy Analysis and Evaluation, University of Berne, 5.7.2007

Schenkel, Walter, Political Scientist, Head of the Work Areas Environment and Energy, Urban and Regional Policies, Political Processes and Institutions, Synergo, Zurich, 15.5.2008

Vatter, Adrian, Professor of Political Science, University of Zurich, 8.7.2007

Widmer, Thomas, Lecturer and Head of the research unit 'Policy Analysis and Evaluation', University of Zurich, 14.5.2008

Austria

Bröthaler, Johann, Assistant Professor of Public Finance and Infrastructure Policy, Vienna University of Technology, 3.9.2008

Fallend, Franz, Assistant Professor of Political Science, University of Salzburg, 27.9.2007

Grossmann, Bernhard and Eva Hauth, Central Bank of the Republic of Austria (OeNB), Vienna, 26.9.2007

Heintel, Martin, Associate Professor of Geography and Regional Studies, University of Vienna, 2.9.2008

Macoun, Thomas, Associate Professor of Traffic Planning and Traffic Engineering, Vienna University of Technology, 3.9.2008

Mayerhofer, Peter, Austrian Institute for Economic Research (WIFO), Vienna, 2.9.2008

Müller, Wolfgang C., Professor of Political Science, University of Mannheim, 20.9.2007

Obermann, Gabriel, Professor of Public Finance, Vienna University of Economics and Business Administration, 25.9.2007

Pitlik, Hans, Austrian Institute for Economic Research (WIFO), Vienna, 24.9.2007
Seidl, Markus, Austrian Conference on Spatial Planning (ÖROK), Vienna, 1.9.2008
Tödtling, Franz, Associate Professor of Regional Development and Environment, Vienna University of Economics and Business Administration, 1.9.2008

Denmark

Andersen, Torben M., Professor of Economics, University of Aarhus, 19.6.2007
Blom-Hansen, Jens, Professor of Political Science, University of Aarhus, 21.6.2007
Christensen, Jorgen Grønnegard, Professor of Public Administration, University of Aarhus, 21.6.2007
Christoffersen, Henrik, *Anvendt KommunalForskning* (AKF) [Danish Institute of Governmental Research], Copenhagen, 18.06.2007
Dahlin, Ulrik, Journalist, *Information*, Copenhagen, 26.6.2008
Flyvbjerg, Bent, Professor of Infrastructure Policy and Planning, University of Aalborg, 31.3.2008
Halkier, Henrik, Professor of Tourism and Regional Studies, University of Aalborg, 20.6.2007
Mouritzen, Poul Erik, Professor of Political Science, University of South Denmark, Odense, 20.6.2007
Pallesen, Thomas, Assistant Professor of Political Science, University of Aarhus, 22.6.2007

Ireland

Bartley, Brendan, Deputy Director, National Institute for Regional and Spatial Analysis, NUI Maynooth, 25.9.2007
Breathnach, Proinnsias, Senior Lecturer, National Institute for Regional and Spatial Analysis, NUI Maynooth, 25.9.2007
Quinn, Bríd, Lecturer, Department of Politics and Public Administration, University of Limerick, 26.9.2007
Adshead, Maura, Senior Lecturer, Department of Politics and Public Administration, University of Limerick; and Chris McInerney, Doctoral Student, University of Limerick, 26.9.2007
Callanan, Mark, Public Policy Specialist, Institute for Public Administration, Dublin, 27.9.2007
Ó Broin, Deiric, Chief Executive, NorDubCo, Dublin, 9.9.2008
Rau, Henrike, Lecturer, Department of Political Science and Sociology, NUI Galway, 11.9.2008
McDonagh, John, Lecturer, Department of Geography, NUI Galway, 12.9.2008

| index

www.ingramcontent.com/pod-product-compliance
Lightning Source LLC
Chambersburg PA
CBHW072103020426
42334CB00017B/1617